FAITH AND LOGIC

FAITH AND LOGIC

OXFORD ESSAYS IN PHILOSOPHICAL THEOLOGY

EDITED BY

BASIL MITCHELL

RUSKIN HOUSE

GEORGE ALLEN & UNWIN LTD

MUSEUM STREET LONDON

FIRST PUBLISHED IN 1957
SECOND IMPRESSION 1958

PRINTED IN GREAT BRITAIN
BY NOVELLO & COMPANY LTD
LONDON W.1

CONTENTS

INTRODUCTION

SHORTLY after the war a small group of philosophers and theologians in Oxford began to meet regularly in one another's rooms to discuss whatever questions each felt like raising. There was no set programme and no thought whatever of writing a book. The nearest thing to a manifesto was the choice of a name, 'The Metaphysicals'. This title voiced a common dissatisfaction with the restrictions which tacitly governed philosophical discussion at a time when 'metaphysical' was the rudest word in the philosopher's vocabulary. In an atmosphere thick with inhibitions, we wanted to be free to ask what questions we liked, even if some of them turned out to be 'ultimate questions' of an allegedly unanswerable and, indeed, unaskable sort.

Our desultory and unorganized discussions tended, as time went on, to centre upon the nature and justification of Christian belief. This was natural enough, since for Christian believers, as we all were,* it is at this point that the philosophical dispute about the possibility of metaphysics assumes decisive importance. For Christian belief presupposes the existence of God and here, if anywhere, is a metaphysical problem. If this has the air of a defiant and wholesale protest (salutary or reactionary, as you will) against what has become known, with some injustice to Cambridge, as 'Oxford Philosophy', we must seek to correct the impression. A protest it no doubt was, but one which sprang in the first instance from a lively appreciation of the virtues of contemporary empiricism.

It is generally recognized that a change has come over British philosophy in the last fifty years. The extent of the change has sometimes been exaggerated. It represents less a radically new departure than the reassertion of characteristic emphases in our philosophical tradition. Nevertheless it has been drastic enough to alter considerably the relationship between philosophers and

* The contributors to this volume are, as it happens, all Anglicans.

I

theologians. Theologians – and with them the educated public at large – have been used to think of philosophers as being concerned primarily with certain very general questions about the nature of things. The philosopher, like the theologian, had his pulpit; and the two of them were, if not always allies, at least rivals. If the philosopher were an ally, he might undertake to demonstrate, for example, the existence of God, leaving the theologian to fill in His properties. If he were a rival, he might deny on metaphysical grounds the Christian doctrine of creation and posit instead the dependence of the world on an impersonal Absolute. Idealist philosophers were fond of constructing hierarchies, in which philosophy, art, religion, science would be allotted their proper place. There might be arguments as to whether philosophy or theology should occupy the apex, but this was almost a domestic dispute.

The contemporary philosopher makes it plain that he does not claim for his philosophy a place in such a hierarchy. He regards it as no part of his business to discover truths about God and the universe. His concern is with meaning rather than with truth. He is, therefore, neither ally nor rival of the theologian. He is, if anything, his critic. 'If anything'. In point of fact there has been relatively little philosophical criticism of theology in recent years, partly no doubt through lack of interest, but chiefly because philosophers have been pre-occupied with technical advances in logic and epistemology. The philosopher has descended from his pulpit and gone into the market place or the laboratory, leaving the theologian to preach alone.

This development, in so far as he has noticed it, has been disconcerting to the theologian, who finds the familiar relationships of alliance, rivalry, or straightforward antagonism exchanged for indifference tinged with hostility. For on the relatively few occasions that the philosopher has turned in his direction from his new pursuits his voice has tended to assume a somewhat provocative tone. 'In our half century,' says Professor Gilbert Ryle, 'philosophy and theology have not been on speaking terms.'

Across the widening gulf it is not surprising if only the more strident voices have been heard, so that misunderstanding has still further increased. Philosophers have often been accused of a frivolous and irresponsible abdication from their traditional function, and theology dismissed as so much meaningless metaphysics. It would be surprising if either of these charges turned out to be wholly true, and we shall do well to stand back from the confusing scene and try to trace briefly the recent development of the empiricist critique of theology.

This assumed its most striking and aggressive form in the work of the 'Logical Positivists' and was first formulated explicitly in this country by Professor A. J. Ayer in his *Language, Truth and Logic*. In this work Ayer proposed the elimination of metaphysics and sought to achieve it by laying down a criterion of meaning which metaphysical statements could not satisfy. A statement to have meaning must either be analytic (true by definition) or empirical (verifiable in sense experience). The first class included the propositions of logic and mathematics, together with definitions, the second class included scientific hypotheses and commonsense statements, which were regarded as rudimentarily scientific. The former said nothing about the world, but merely recorded our determination to use symbols in a certain way; the latter alone imparted information. Most of the propositions of metaphysics, ethics and theology fell into neither class and were, accordingly, dismissed by Ayer as nonsensical pseudo-propositions; strictly speaking they had no meaning.

This constituted a far more radical attack upon theology than any conducted by earlier empiricists. Hume's attack, which in some ways prefigured it, bore almost entirely on 'natural' or 'rational' theology, on attempts at theological proof, and so left it open to Christians to base their beliefs, not upon proof, but upon faith. Indeed this was the course which Hume himself recommended. 'The truths of our religion,' he said, 'find their best and most solid foundation in Faith and Divine Revelation.' But it was no defence against the positivist assault, because what was now being challenged was not the *truth* of the beliefs, but their *significance*.

It is helpful to an understanding of Logical Positivism to realize that its exponents were primarily philosophers of science. They sought to discover a formula which would distinguish clearly between scientific statements and all other statements. They thought they had found this in the verification principle. The only accredited methods for finding out about the nature of things were scientific. The traditional notion that philosophers could – just by thinking and without experiment – discover facts about the world was in their opinion, as in Hume's, a mistake. So a division of labour was proposed between philosophy and science. It was the function of science to distinguish between what was true and what was false; it was the function of philosophy to discriminate between the meaningful and the meaningless. Logical Positivism was thus a very simple doctrine, but its simplicity was achieved at the cost of a certain air of paradox. For it led one to class as 'nonsense' all sorts of things that people were constantly saying – not only philosophers and theologians, but plain ordinary people. To this the reply was made that 'nonsense' was being used in a very strict sense that was not necessarily pejorative. Some kinds of nonsense might be very useful, even necessary. Some religious talk, for example, might be remarkably *profound* nonsense, and ethical talk was nonsense of high pragmatic value.

Through the raising and answering objections of this kind Logical Positivism began to alter its character, and the empiricist attack on religion entered its present phase, in which it ceases largely, perhaps altogether, to be an attack. It is convenient to restrict the term 'Logical Positivist' to those who regard the verification principle as the sole criterion of meaning. In this sense of the word there are few Logical Positivists in the field to-day. It began to be apparent that, instead of looking for a clear-cut criterion for distinguishing between the meaningful and the meaningless, it might be more profitable to recognize different sorts of meaning. Thus, rather than embrace the paradox that moral judgments are meaningless, philosophers began to suggest that they were indeed meaningful, but that the sort of meaning they possessed differed from that of straightforward factual statements. It might be called 'emotive meaning'; so that although people who differed on a moral matter could not be said to disagree in *belief*, they could be said to disagree in *attitude*. An alternative suggestion was that moral principles were best understood neither as statements of fact nor as expressions of emotion, but as rules; and as such resembled generalized commands or imperatives.

Thus the positivist rejection of ethics served to concentrate attention on the ways in which moral judgments differed from statements of fact, and this development (greatly stimulated by the influence of Wittgenstein), contributed to a fresh approach to the question of meaning. Philosophers who adopt this approach (they are sometimes called 'Linguistic Analysts'), differ from the Logical Positivists in this characteristic way: in place of the dogmatic *assertion* that those statements alone have meaning which are empirically verifiable, they ask the *question* – of any class of statements – 'what is the logic of statements of this kind?' that is to say, 'how are they to be verified, or tested or justified? What is their use and function, what jobs do they do?'

How will philosophers of this persuasion tend to approach theology? Three things are, I think, clear.

(1) They will not, as did the Idealists, put forward (at least explicitly) a world-view or philosophy of life, which might conflict with Christianity; because they regard the development of such world-views as no part of a philosopher's business.

(2) They will not (at least they should not) rule out theological statements from the start on the ground that they are meaningless, as the Logical Positivists did.

(3) They will ask the same sort of questions about theological statements as they do about statements of other kinds, viz. 'How are they verified? What sort of arguments or observations tend to confirm or refute them?' In short, 'What is their logic?'

From this it will be apparent why I hesitated to call this phase of the empiricist critique an *attack* on theology at all. The asking of such questions is, or purports to be, an entirely neutral undertaking; an attempt to understand, not to refute. He would be a very unempirical empiricist who presumed to pronounce, in advance of careful investigation, that the claims of theology were unfounded, and a very complacent theologian who expected to learn nothing from a philosophical movement which has brought needed clarification into other disciplines. Yet there is not at present much mutual confidence or understanding. The philosopher is apt to deal brusquely with the complex pattern of theological language, which he feels must harbour mystifications and confusions; the theologian may see himself as the guardian of mysteries which the philosopher's equipment is too clumsy or too limited to penetrate.

There is, then, a need for careful and sensitive examination of the bearing of contemporary philosophy upon Christian faith. The general topic has been ventilated for some time in philosophical periodicals* and in broadcast talks and discussions, but is only now beginning to reach a wider public in a more permanent form. We felt that there was a place for a book written jointly by philosophers and theologians who through long discussion have reached a certain unity of approach. We might, at least, hope to avoid one obvious danger in this sort of discussion, the naiveté of philosophers about theology and of theologians about philosophy. These essays are offered as a contribution to a continuing debate, which is, perhaps, reaching the end of one of its phases. The nature of this debate can very easily be made to appear as a straightforward encounter between readily identifiable opponents, but anyone who reflects seriously upon the complex and difficult issues involved knows that this is not so. I have said that the contributors to this book share a certain unity of approach, but the reader will notice nevertheless some striking differences of opinion, as for example between Mr Hare and Mr Crombie. These differences remain after long discussion, and it seemed fairer and more illuminating to let them appear than to exclude any point of view that had persistently been represented in our

* For a valuable selection of essays and discussions on this topic, see *New Essays in Philosophical Theology*, edited by Antony Flew and Alasdair MacIntyre.

discussions. Moreover, in most of these essays there appears a character termed now 'the objector', now 'the critic', now 'the empiricist philosopher'. I have tried to give a brief life history of this character, which will help to show that he is no man of straw. He is indeed, in most cases, the author himself, who feels the objections in his own person before projecting them upon this imaginary opponent. We do not feel that his objections can be lightly dismissed, although Mr Foster* has suggested that he may have his limitations.

'All right,' the reader may now want to say, 'you are offering us a set of studies in philosophical theology which have been shaped under the pressure of current developments in philosophy. But this sort of philosophy is, at best, a highly specialized affair, and, at worst, a merely parochial preoccupation of academic philosophers in parts of the Anglo-Saxon world. Does it merit this solemn treatment, and, even if it does, what has it to do with the ordinary man's perplexities – be he believer or enquirer, or both?'

The answer, I suggest, is that, when certain differences of approach have been allowed for, the questions which the contemporary empiricist asks of Christian faith are fundamental questions which, in different formulations, have a recognizable ancestry in previous theological discussion. And the differences of approach, where they are found, are the consequences for philosopher and layman alike of the age in which we live. The central question: 'How is it possible for man to think about God?' which is sharply posed by contemporary empiricism, is one which many traditional theologians have been concerned to answer. If this is a legitimate question for a Christian to ask, we may properly be grateful to any philosophers who help us to get it clear. It is, indeed, an 'academic' question; and ours is an 'academic' enquiry, but one which cannot for that reason be safely neglected. We often hear that the old beliefs have 'lost their meaning' and that people to-day no longer find them relevant to the rest of their thought and practice. Christians are accused of a kind of 'double-

* In Chapter VIII of this volume.

think' by which they contrive to talk two entirely independent languages with no way of relating what is said in one to what is said in the other. The more massive the development of the sciences and their attendant technologies, the more acute the problem of communication seems to become. The philosophical critic with his careful attention to the way in which expressions are used, and his tendency to distrust any but scientific explanations is here representative of a generation which dumbly shares his own perplexities. It may be possible, though it is increasingly difficult, for simple and devout believers to live out their lives untroubled by these perplexities, but this innocent way is not open to the Christian philosopher who is committed to a certain agnosticism both by the demands of his profession and by his Christian vocation.

It will be evident that the type of enquiry we have in mind is not best pursued by way of a systematic philosophical treatment of the principal topics of theology. What it needs – and what we have tried to provide – is a set of essays loosely organized round a central theme, to which they are all in different ways relevant. The book is designed to be read consecutively, but each chapter is self-contained enough to be intelligible to the reader who prefers to pick his own way. Two of its chapters have been communicated to the Oxford University Socratic Club, Ch. V in its finished form, Ch. VIII at an early stage of its development.

The contributors wish to acknowledge their indebtedness to one another and also to Dr E. L. Mascall, who convened the group in the first instance and whose unobtrusive care has kept it in being for over ten years; and to other past or present members who have taken part in its discussions or helped with their criticism, especially to Miss Iris Murdoch, Professor I. T. Ramsey, and Mr O. P. Wood.

CHAPTER I

A STARTING-POINT
FOR THE PHILOSOPHICAL EXAMINATION
OF THEOLOGICAL BELIEF
by Austin Farrer

I

THE old method of philosophizing about theology was the endeavour to prove. This meant, to prove theological conclusions from non-theological premises; otherwise the argument would have seemed circular. Admittedly there were topics of doctrine which did not allow of philosophical proof, but only of historical evidence; divine revelation, for example. To reveal Himself or not was a free choice lying in God's will; that He had revealed Himself was a certainty resting on testimony alone. Yet even in this field there was something for the philosopher to attempt. He could hope to establish *a priori* and from non-theological premises the possibility, even the naturalness, of revelation; could hope to show that God was such, and man was such, that it was more credible God would reveal Himself to man, than that he would not.

Such a method of proceeding is now out of fashion, not so much because theology cannot be philosophically demonstrated as because nothing can; not, that is, in the implied sense of 'demonstrated'. Every science, art, or manner of speaking is now supposed to find its own justification in its own use. Philosophical analysis tries to show how any sort of talk goes, and what it does. This does not mean that no accustomed province of discourse has anything to fear from philosophical examination. Its pretensions may, on the contrary, be severely curtailed; if, for example, it emerges that theology is an art of talking oneself out of anxiety by the entertainment of unreal supposition.

In such a philosophical climate the difference of status noted above between the demonstrable and the indemonstrable parts of theology, between 'rational' and 'revealed' doctrines, largely disappears. The God about whom, and to whom, believers speak is the self-revealing God. The 'God of pure reason' is scarcely encountered outside philosophical argument and it is harder to see what function, if any, talk about him performs. Let us, then, take typical sentences about the self-revealing God, or about the dealings we have with Him in consequence of His having revealed Himself. Here, if anywhere, is religious language in real use. Let philosophy proceed to see what the use is and how the language works.

No proposal, you might think, could be more straightforward. But there is an unlucky complication. How does the philosopher proceed? He takes specimen sentences from the language he investigates, he isolates them, he subjects them to analysis. If his procedure is to be fruitful, two conditions must be fulfilled. First, the sentences selected must be understood at the ordinary, pre-philosophical level before they are analysed; and second, they must be analysed adequately. What philosophers like to do is to make sure that no difficulty will arise over the fulfilment of the first condition by picking specimen sentences which everyone understands at first sight. Then they can proceed without more ado to the analysis which is, after all, their proper philosophical task. But it is the peculiar difficulty of philosophizing about theology that it contains no sentences about which such immediate and agreed understanding is forthcoming.

Because the primary subject of theological statements is, according to unbelievers, preposterous and according to believers 'transcendent', the statements about Him cannot be anything but parables borrowed from the world of our more direct acquaintance. And since He is by supposition very different from those things or persons from which the parabolic material is borrowed, no parable of itself expresses Him truly, and every parable needs to be balanced by a different parable with a contrasting bias. The art of balancing parables is acquired in use by believers, without their being conscious of it. That they use such an art becomes evident as soon as we attempt to fix upon them all the apparent logical consequences from any single parable. They will then begin to pick and choose, admitting some consequences and refusing others: and if we ask them why, they will draw in further parables supporting what they allow, and hostile to what they reject. 'God became "flesh" ' – 'He is, then, subject to change?' – 'By no means: He did not change Himself, it was the "flesh" He changed, by acting uniquely in it' – 'You would wish, then, to withdraw the statement that He became flesh?' – 'No, I would not: it expresses as nothing else can His complete self-identification with His incarnate action'. And so forth.

It is plain, then, that we cannot take a single sentence in this area of speech and proceed forthwith to its logical analysis. For the sentence will be a parable, and to establish its mere religious sense is to recover the context of very strangely contrasted parables in which it stands, together with the art of balancing parables. This is a long and complicated task. And it is a task for believers. It is impossible to study the art except from within the serious personal use of it; for the believer has the art, and to him one use of parable is truth and another nonsense or heresy; to the unbeliever it is all nonsense, he lacks the criterion of use. It is possible for the unbeliever to acquire a sympathy which enables him to see himself believing; but there are specially strong and notorious obstacles in the way of his doing so. It is difficult for him to study the supposed apprehension of an activity most vigorous and present (that of God) in terms which to him are empty and absurd. And even if he has the intellectual sympathy, will he have the patience? It seems that the tendency of the unbelieving philosopher is to seek a short way with the believer. And it is only reasonable that a man should either let alone what he is inwardly convinced is rubbish, or else look for a quick means to rid the world of it.

But some philosophers, anyhow, are believers; so why should they not go quietly on with the work? Why should we always have our heads turned over our shoulders, watching to see how our unbelieving colleagues are taking it? Well, certainly believers can philosophize to themselves about their own belief. But philosophy is a debate, or a complex of debates, actually proceeding in the world; and no one who contracts out seems quite to be philosophizing. Besides, the believing philosopher who remains within the world at all cannot escape from intellectual sympathy with unbelief. Unbelief may write belief off, but belief feels the force of unbelief and wrestles with it.

If, then, we are to keep in the ring, what ground shall we take? There is another side to theological talking, beside the nice art of balancing parables; there is the referring of the parables to that to which they apply. Here lies the hope of a more promising start. The parables themselves appear to unbelievers to be all up in the air; but that to which they are applied may be, by common consent, solid ground. 'That to which the parables are applied' is, indeed, an ambiguous phrase. In one sense the parables are applied to God, and to His action. But in another sense the whole parabolic discourse about God and His action is applied to 'life'; in 'life' divine action finds an effect which it concerns us to acknowledge or to deny. And life, anyhow, is lived. No one disputes that.

We cannot, obviously, set out to discuss anything so vague as 'life', but only some aspect of it to which religious language applies. But is there any one such aspect? Belief defines God as universal cause and will not allow His action to be excluded from anything. No; but belief is speaking here with a somewhat theoretical voice. If challenged, the believer must be prepared conscientiously to read the parables of belief into almost anything that comes before his attention. His doing so is no mere apologetic dodge; it is part of the exercise of his faith, that it should set itself to embrace all things. Nevertheless there remains a difference between those things *into* which we have to read divine activity, and those things *off* which we simply do read it. We could scarcely claim the status of believers if we had to read divine activity *into* everything and read it *off* nothing; if, for example, duty sounded in our ears no echo of the voice of God.

From a strictly formal point of view there may be no ultimate difference between 'reading into' and 'reading off'. To interpret without conscious effort is still to interpret; the intellectual form does not change its logical nature because it is used without fuss. Yet practically the difference is real enough. While we are reading the interpretation into the thing, the thing merely admits of the interpretation. But when the interpretation is read off the thing, it is for us part and parcel of the thing, not to be stripped away without maiming or falsifying the object. Now some sorts of interpretation do not begin to have their full characteristic use or effect until they are 'read off'. For whereas the value of scientific hypotheses is independent of our actually seeing things as concrete instances of our theorems, the value of personal interpretations (for example) is not. We interpret people so as to react to them appropriately, and the reaction is scarcely forthcoming until we see them in terms of the interpretation. Psychological theory is the test case. We think it will help us to understand our friends, but we find that the more we psychologize them the less we can live with them; for we cannot see our neighbours as embodied psychological theorems, or not without falling into a sort of notional lunacy.*

It is scarcely necessary to draw out the theological application. Religious belief has its use in evoking our responses, and this it does when it is 'read off', not when it is 'read into', our life. What we have to consider, then, is some aspect of our life, or some class of situations, *off* which ordinary believers read the action of God. We have already thrown out the suggestion that our moral life, with its characteristic situations, carries such a significance. But we do not propose to content ourselves with so jejune an observation. Moral activity or experience is a complex and many-sided thing, and we will endeavour to show in which of its aspects its religious meaning is found to lie.

* This is not to deny that psychological theory assists us to form personal interpretations. What is so corrosive is the application of the theory 'neat'.

II

The philosopher who approaches religion through moral thinking finds his feet on the beaten track to a mare's nest. For philosophy likes to concern itself with the logical analysis of formulated discourse in common use, and especially of argument. Now men talk and argue a great deal about morality, but scarcely about that aspect of it on which religion comes principally to bear.

The foundations of morality are platitudinous valuations; the subjects of moral discussion are contested priorities. People who discuss the platitudes are intolerable – who try, for example, to make an issue of the question, whether it is good that we should care for other men or for ourselves alone; or whether instinctive appetite should ever be controlled. But we can fairly discuss the priority to be given to the objects of this and that appetite or interest; we can discuss the priority of the claim made upon us by humanity in general or by particular loyalty; and within the area of loyalty, the claim of this person or group, and of that. Moral rules, like moral discussions, aim at the settlement of priorities; and the difference between one civilized 'way of life' and another, so far as it is a moral difference, lies in the priorities it assigns.

Moral thinking, then, is taken to be the discussion, assertion, or working out of moral priorities; and religion is taken to be the assertion and veneration of some absolute authority. Bring the two into direct relation, and it is obvious what conclusion results. God's will must be the ultimate authority for priorities. In the end, we hear it said, there is no earthly appeal in moral argument, and no earthly authority for moral rules, beyond the whole mental attitude and way of life proper to the culture we accept. Since (hitherto at least) the several cultures of mankind have taken a tinge from the religion prevalent in each, it may be true in some measure that the moral differences between cultures are differences of religion. And the fact that religion is ultimately belief – that its evidence is somehow intrinsic – seems to square with the fact that the moral 'options' of a culture are in the last resort simply those which the men of that culture cannot help thinking it right to uphold. Is not this ultimate option religious belief? Or is not religious belief a special way of feeling, backing, or formulating this ultimate option?

Following such a line of thought we come to see religion as that whereby men's attitudes to life differ. But such a way of regarding religion is at best extrinsic and casts no light on the nature of religion, still less of its object. It would be like describing the aesthetic sense as that in virtue of which Englishmen, Indians and Chinese differ in their attitude to volcanoes and fruit blossom. The aesthetic sense is not primarily a cause of division and mutual incomprehension; it is a common way of reacting to things, having a specific character which distinguishes it from other, non-aesthetic, ways of reacting. When we first become aware of differences in the standard of taste from nation to nation our feeling is one of surprise. We do not dream of saying 'Of course; for isn't "aesthetic sensibility" just a class of attitudinal oppositions?' It takes us time and thought to see how a common thing, good taste, can admit the varieties it exhibits without forfeiting its whole virtue.

It is true, no doubt, that several religious cultures appeal each to their God (or to God as each conceives Him) in support of their way of life. But none of them would dream of saying that the purpose of divine direction is to create interesting moral differences between cultures; or (alternatively) to save nations the perplexity of choosing between open options, by laying down local and arbitrary by-laws. Cultures differ not through understanding the will of God but through taking partial views of it. The priorities, so far as they differ, are all too human, and result from divergent appreciations of the fundamental values between which priorities are assigned. The 'authority' is in the values themselves, which 'demand' to be graded one way rather than another. The direct impact of the divine will is to be found, if anywhere, in the platitudinous region of basic valuation.

Valuation is of two sorts, if both of them ought to be called valuation: (1) We value human beings, and any other beings we

can regard in the same way – angels if we can know them, dogs
if we can love them. But for the purposes of the present discussion
we will leave the dogs and angels out. (2) Because we value
human beings, we value what we take to be desirable features in
human life, or things contributory to the realization of such
features.

The second sort of valuation differs from the first in being
disputable. We try to have a 'correct' valuation of the several
features or constituents of human life, and we disagree. Valuation
of this sort requires good judgment. But in the valuation of persons there is no 'correct' and no 'incorrect', nor any exercise of
judgment: only sensitiveness, depth, sincerity, or the reverse of
these. And since valuation suggests the valuer, going round and
sticking his labels of comparative price on one thing after another,
the very phrase 'valuation of persons' is detestable. We respond
to, care about, love, or, in the ancient sense, worship our neighbour. Unless, of course, we ignore, neglect, hate, dishonour him;
but these are not alternative expressions of moral judgment; they
are crimes. It is not an error of moral judgment to care about a
blackguardly cousin, but only to mistake what spoils him for
what it spoils in him. We may, indeed, commend him to the hang-
man. But that is not the effect of valuation (1). It is due to the
intervention of valuation (2). We are viewing him not in himself
as a person, but as a feature in the moral landscape of others. A
violent clash between the two sorts of valuation results: we must
love him as a cousin, and hang him as a nuisance. But we cannot
do both. Hence the moral agony of destructive punishment – not
to mention military slaughter.

Even though in such instances the two sorts of valuation may
compete for the guidance of our action, they are on different
logical levels and any direct comparison between them is, in the
logical sense, nonsensical. 'Which is healthier, beer or cider?'
But not 'Which is healthier, beer or Henry?' 'Which is more
valuable, Bulganin's plan or Malenkov's?' But not 'Which is more
valuable, Bulganin's plan or Comrade Ivanovich?' unless we are
regarding Ivanovich's personal qualities (for which Bulganin's

plan affords no scope) as being of service to the Russians; and similarly Henry might be more healthy than beer, as a means of keeping Mary in good spirits.

It would be convenient if we could find a single word for the value we place on the human being. The difficulty is that all our words are used antithetically. Take 'regard' for example. 'I have a regard for Henry, but none for John'. It is true that my uncle may retort, 'Then you ought to be ashamed of yourself', but in that case I shall feel that he has unfairly changed the meaning of the word 'regard', in order to preach at me. I did not mean that I have a policy of disregarding John; I meant that, in the sense in which no one can help having personal preferences, my regard goes to Henry. There is a sense, no doubt, in which it is a crime not to regard John, or any other person with whom I have to do; and the force of my uncle's sophistry lies in the closeness to one another of the two senses of 'regard'. My first line of defence will be to distinguish them sharply: 'I ought to regard John' means 'I ought to allow him his rights'; 'I have a regard for Henry' means 'I pay him friendly attention'. But as soon as I have said this, I see that it will not do. It is a good quarrelling position, the masculine pose. It throws on my disputant the ridicule of being soft; but it does not convince my heart. The regard I ought to pay to John is hard to distinguish from the regard I do pay to Henry. I ought to open myself to John, to appreciate him, to consider him, to put myself in the way of feeling the pull of his humanity, and to be willing to act in accordance with my resulting sense of the man. Maybe I do not have to go so far with John as with Henry; and certainly it comes more natural with Henry than with John. But something of the same sort is called for in both cases. My regarding of Henry is itself not effortless; if I do not take trouble about it when Henry is provoking, I shall lose his friendship.

There is, then, a sense of regard in which regard is universally due, and such regard is the heart of virtue. Ethical men regard their friends and are fair to their neighbours; good men regard their neighbours and love their friends. For want of a better word, we will call the first sort of valuation which we distinguished above 'regard', reserving 'valuation' itself for the second sort. We will say that persons are regarded, while everything else is valued in relation to them.

If all men are to be regarded, it should be possible to say something about men in general, in virtue of which they are all the proper objects of regard. If we say 'Because they are men', we may seem to make regard coterminous with the race-consciousness of a species. But in that case we should feel it tautological to say 'Man is a proper object of our regard', and absurd to suggest that we could even establish communication with creatures of another species who would be fit objects of our regard. And we do not find either the second idea absurd, or the first tautological.

We might agree about certain limits to the range of our regard – we cannot *regard* anything that is not sentient, and does not develop some degree of rational activity: always understanding that 'activity' may be talking or thinking as well as doing, and that 'rational' is a conventional term distinguishing the characteristically human level of action from the brutish.

'Rational agent' may be a true description of the proper object of regard, but it is not a complete description. I may say that it is with the insurance agent that I do business; it is irrelevant that he is Mr Jones and that he loves his children or plays the piano. It is not similarly the rational agent that I regard, but Tom, Dick, or Harry; and in regarding any one of them I abstract from nothing that makes the man. Beauty cannot move my senses, this lovely picture may. Rational agency cannot waken my regard, Henry may.

Henry may, and what is more, he *should*, move my regard, in the sense that I *ought* so to consider him and respond to him, as to give him every chance of moving it, and that there is something amiss if he fails to move it. And by what is he to move it? By all that he is. And what is he? Whatever is expressed in the action of his life, good, bad, or indifferent is Henry, and Henry is the object of my regard. It appears, then, that forms of action which considered abstractly are disvalued, become when considered in the agent of them the object of positive regard; and this appears psychologically impossible. For if something is disvalued, we are against it; and if it is regarded, we are for it. Can we be for, and against, the same thing at the same time? Well – to complete the cliché – not, anyhow, 'in the same respect'. When we are valuing or disvaluing forms of action, we are holding them away from the agent, we are considering them as alternative suits of clothes his conduct might put on, to his credit or his discredit. But once he has clothed himself in one of them, if it is a bad one, we may say, 'Poor Henry! He's done it again!' To regret a man's error or even his crime for his own sake is a way of being for him, not against him. We do not at once both disvalue, and regard, the form of the unhappy act. We simply disvalue it; but we *regard* the man expressing himself in it, because he expresses himself in other ways at other times; he is a luminary of whom we regret the present eclipse.

But the more unfortunate choices Henry makes, the harder it is to be all for his 'normal' self, to let ourselves go in the simple warmth of regard for him. Sympathy is the magic word; and yet if we sympathize with a man for failing to pursue a good which he does not value in the least, it is difficult to see what we are sympathizing with: not with the man who is, but with some shadow of a man who should be. And realities, not desirabilities, are the objects of regard. I am to love my neighbour, and not my idea of my neighbour.

The misfit between the absolute regardableness of men, and the relative disvalue of their lives, gives rise to all sorts of strains and impurities in our regard for them. We abdicate all judgment and worship what we should condemn, or we let detached censure freeze regard; or, the most gross and common fault of all, we do not sufficiently see men for what they are in themselves, to regard them, because their lines of action make no easy or harmonious contact with our own.

We are talking now in a somewhat pedantic and general way about what everyone knows to be the chief difficulties of personal life. Every sort of practical 'philosophy', or what does duty for one, grapples with these troubles, and in so doing shows its serious practicality. It is obvious that Christianity claims moral efficacy in claiming to do the same job uniquely well. It commands us to carry regard for our neighbours to the point of loving them as we love ourselves; and it teaches us how to do this by directing us first so to worship God that we love Him with all our mind.

The worship of God is most directly brought to support the regarding of man through prayer. Speaking psychologically, and leaving aside all religious mysteries, we can say that prayer places the neighbour we pray for in relation with the action of God, and that it views this action in two lights. On the one hand the action of God is creation; through all the processes of events contributory to the formation of our neighbour, God has shaped and is shaping an unique creature, and is to be reverenced in His handiwork, in the very man as he is. On the other hand, God's action is redemption. Patient of the man's imperfections, God forgives but does not tolerate. For, by a costly and incessant action bearing on the man's free will, He persuades him towards his everlasting good.

Our sole present concern with these sentences of doctrine is to observe their effect on regard for our fellow man. The regard we owe him is unqualified, because it is owed to God through him. And yet he is no mere channel through which regard is paid to God, for God is regarded by regard for what He regards, and what He regards is the man. The worth of the man is determined by his place in God's purposes; and it is not a worth which in any way hides or palliates his imperfections. For it is measured by the infinite cost at which God is willing to redeem him from them. His worth lies, however, in nothing else than in what he actually is, for this is the subject of divine redemption, this very man whom I know: not, indeed, as God knows him; but in so far as I have any capacity for knowing my fellow-creatures at all, what I know is what God redeems.

This is the man whom, with God, I am bound to regard, and prayer itself is an exercise of such regard, which, Christians claim, does not terminate in itself. For though no one lives as he prays, no one who genuinely prays lives as though he did not.

Our business is not with religious commonplace but with its philosophical criticism, and we have in mind a criticism which finds a clue to the meaning of discourse in the uses of it. Now if the whole use of the discourse we have been illustrating, that is to say, of prayer, is denied, then there will be nothing to discuss. But if, for the sake of argument, it is acknowledged, what is the first question to arise? The philosopher wishes to restrict the meaning of language within the bounds of its real use. He will ask, there-fore, whether the sober and human task of talking ourselves into due regard for our neighbours can require the use of statements which seriously mean that God, a spirit dwarfing us and them and all our world into insignificance, is the actual maker, producer, and redeemer of men? The terms of the task are, to see how we may so describe men as to regard them worthily; and the means arrived at are, that we place them in an admittedly parabolical frame of description, calling them the objects of divine making and redemption. Surely, then, the real objects of our contempla-tion are the same at the completion of the task as they were in the first statement of it. All that has been added is a parabolic conven-tion in which to describe them. We have no business with meta-physical assertion; we have all that we require if we set ourselves to feel for our neighbours *as though* they were the creatures, etc., of an infinite living goodness.

Nothing can be more instructive than an examination of this suggestion, and we will take it up in the terms in which it is stated, even though it is necessary, before we do so, to enter a protest. The suggestion makes all theology ridiculous by the implied assumption that religion is *essentially* the discharge of finite obligations by invoking an infinite metaphysical credit. But no one who believes any religion will agree to this for a moment. The inadequacies of our finite equipment for our finite tasks are some slight signs and tokens of our relation to God, but that relation is far more important for its own sake than for its supple-mentation of human defects. The evidence of God is not essen-tially that in Him we can see our neighbours straight, but that in so seeing our neighbours, we are drawn into relation with Him.

The detached critic of belief wields a Morton's fork, and we can do little in our own defence while we leave this instrument in his hands. 'Either,' he says, 'your evidence of God is His special impact on you, or else it is the way things are. If it is His special impact on you, it is something you may acknowledge, but no one else can. If it is the way things are, we should all be able to acknowledge it. But the way things are is the subject of empirical description, or the field of particular action; and though there are many mysterious factors in the natural scene, it is scarcely worth considering whether any one of them can be shown to be infinite, supernatural, and absolute.' Like most sophistical dilemmas, this one is sufficiently exposed by being openly stated. There is no need to choose between an evidence by impact and an evidence lying in the way things are. The impact is through the way things are. The unbelieving mind acknowledges the way things are, but not the divine impact. We try to explain how our view of the way things are is illuminated by our acknowledgment of the divine impact. Our present argument is a case in point.

So much for the protest. We return to the question whether the function of religious language in establishing a proper regard for our neighbour involves a serious intention to assert God's existence. The first point to consider is the relation in general between existential assertion and an attitude of regard. And about this we must say that the paying of regard involves an existential assertion of a special kind. Students of philosophy are most familiar with existential assertions about physical objects, and have, perhaps, learnt to abandon as meaningless or at least unfruitful the question what any physical thing or process 'essentially is'. It is enough to assert that the constituents of our physical environment make themselves felt in the way they environ us. Whatever we have to reckon with on the level of physical action is physically real. But if we are going to *regard* anything we must be convinced not only that it is there, but that it really possesses in itself, and not merely in our sense of it, those characteristics in virtue of which we regard it. The test case is that in which we risk our lives out of regard for another; we certainly should not do so for the most exalted of notions, or for the most useful and enjoyable feature of our environment. The first step to regarding our neighbour as ourself is to see that he is as real as ourself, and that his reality has the same sort of actual structure and quality as our own.

To turn, now, to the theological question. What was the praying mind seen to do? It steadied and reinforced regard for man by relating it to regard for God; or, to put it another way, acknowledged that what makes the unqualified claim on our regard is not simply our neighbour, but our neighbour and God in a special sort of relation with one another. If God is not an object of our regard, or, to speak less artificially, of our worship, the whole action of our prayer is paralysed. But if God is regarded, then He is taken as real, just as seriously as our neighbour is. You may hold that prayer is the highest wisdom or the flimsiest folly, but in any case the assertion of God's existence is integral to it.

Yet even though God's existence is accepted by the praying mind as something beside the existence of the friend for whom prayer is being made, it is not in some fabulous world beside the human that God is recognized or honoured, but in the friend. We distinguish the action of God from the mere conduct and character of our friend, but that does not mean that God's action is expressed to us in terms of something different from the man or his ways. God the creator of the man is seen and regarded in the man, even if the man has rebelled against his creator. Creation is, of course, creation, an unique and uniquely divine act about the nature of which we might philosophize a great deal. But creation is met and acknowledged in its only effect and only possible phenomenon, the creature. Similarly, redemptive love: it is itself, and real in God, but not to be encountered by us except in the case of the man whom it forgives, whom it persuades, and whom it calls. The forgiveness, the persuasion and the calling are acknowledged in the man's actual defects and graces, and in the paths of possible good which open from his actual character or situation.

III

We began this chapter with a distinction between the parables of religious belief, and those fields of common experience *off* which (and not merely *into* which) the parables are read. It seemed that the proper business of a philosophical critique was to examine the parables, and see how they were used; but it appeared that, if we plunged straight into such a critique we might find ourselves all up in the air. And so we decided to start with a description of a commonly acknowledged province of thinking, and show how it receives that immediate religious interpretation which we call 'reading off'. And this we have attempted to do. Even if we have succeeded, we have not reached any end, but only a beginning. We have come round to the parables, though by a more circuitous route; and the parables have still to stand their philosophical trial. For the divinity which we find as it were embedded in the believer's account of his neighbour is already parabolic. What is 'creation'? What is 'redemption'? My neighbour may be the case, but of what is he the case? Creation is a parable from human invention or manufacture; redemption is a tissue of figures from various types of deliverance and restoration met with in human life. Even the divine love which animates both redemption and creation is a parable from human kindness.

Philosophers tend to be less interested in arguments than in the form and force of arguments. We have sketched out an argument: let us now consider what sort of an argument it is. It seems tempting to compare the procedure we have suggested with a classic example. In the *Critique of Pure Reason* Kant raised the ghosts of theological parable; in his moral writings he let them drink the blood of life. First, that is to say, he showed how and out of what materials the parable of creative providence arises, and how purely parabolic, that is to say, how dubious, its logic is. Only afterwards he set out to show that, whatever its logic may be, it is treated as real in our personal or moral life, because the action of moral persons is so directed as to count God in as a real power. As part of a total picture of the world, held away from us and contemplated, the Kantian theological ideas are utterly unconvincing, they are the veriest ghosts of thought. They receive reality when they condition our moral action. Kant's 'world' is the merest diagram; whereas moral action is for him the exercise of real existence and concerns itself with real existences. Kant takes the cosmological diagram first, with its ghostly theological extensions. We propose the opposite order, and begin with the moral life; we give the ghosts the blood first, surmising that, until they have drunk it, they will not speak to us.

But, however tempting the Kantian analogy is, we must not allow it to mislead us. We are not ourselves talking Kantianism; not even Kantianism in reverse. We could not accept as it stands any part of Kant's doctrine, either where it concerns the logic of theological parable or where it concerns the way in which God enters into moral life. Nor can we argue with Kant's assurance. He claimed to give an account of moral principle in which all honest men capable of philosophy must recognize the very form of their consciences. And on the basis of this account he claimed to show them that a duty was incumbent upon them which they could not undertake with any intelligent hope of fulfilling it unless they counted on the action of God. He regarded his argument as a demonstration at both stages, not as a persuasion. He did not persuade us in favour of certain moral principles; he proved that these principles were morality and that morality was these. Nor did he persuade us to see the obligation to justice in the setting of Providential Government; he proved that the very intention to discharge the obligation implied a belief in the Providence.

So at least Kant claimed. We do not claim for our argument any such rigour. It is a persuasion, though, of course, a persuasion of a very special kind. We persuade men of the importance of so contemplating their fellows that they may regard them. We persuade them that regard should acknowledge no limits but those set by the conditions of our life. We persuade them that this regard should be at once so pure and so entire as to find its frustration in the imperfections of men. We persuade them that the frustration is due to an incomplete definition of the object of regard – that what claims our regard is not simply our neighbour, but God in our neighbour and our neighbour in God. Here are four stages of persuasion, and at any stage the persuasion can fail. We shall probably have to be content, like Gideon, to reduce our following step by step as we advance. Most of our fellow-tribesmen will take the first step with us; they will go with us in admitting a duty to cultivate regard for their neighbours. It's a persuasion of which they are already persuaded. But the next step may well halve our following, the third halve it again, and the fourth yet again.

Those who draw their swords for the Lord are aware that they must face the Gideon predicament. If the canon is laid down that nothing is to be accepted for philosophical consideration but what is at least virtually contained in the flattest common sense and that the *homme moyen sensuel* is to be the measure of all things, the Christian argument has nothing to say. We know, surely, that the acknowledgement of God involves a sharpening and stirring of the conscience, an acceptance of unqualified claims. This acceptance may be forced upon us in more ways than one: through our being thrown into situations which bring the weight of such claims to bear on us; through the example of others; through verbal persuasion.

Acquiescence in the Gideon predicament may suggest an ultimate reliance on the exquisite discernment of a spiritual élite, who have cultivated their sentiments to a pitch of unreal refinement. Such a suggestion insinuates artificiality and saps the force of the persuasive argument. No doubt people can make a cult of moral refinement and reflect curiously on the purity of their personal attitudes, especially if they have no more pressing business on hand. But their doing so may appear an odd basis for serious metaphysical belief.

We have several things to say about this suspicion, and here is the first. Although our persuasive argument, as it advances, may lose adherents, it begins not from any point of special exquisiteness but from the broad platitudes of the moral mind. Nor, in advancing, does it leave the main road for any finicking bypaths;

it merely takes a platitudinous persuasion in deadly earnest and follows it as far as it leads. The principle of utter devotion or unlimited regard is acceptable to the most work-a-day people. When Gideon's army has become small enough to reach its objective, he finds himself still surrounded by common faces, indistinguishable from those which turned away.

Now to the second point. The sort of enthusiasm which leads the three hundred to follow Gideon is not anything induced by his militant demagogy, nor is it anything peculiar to the emotional constitution of the three hundred. On every side we see men for whom it is a necessity to acknowledge an absolute claim and to spend themselves in answering it. If they are not shouting for the Lord and Gideon, they will be crying 'One race, one realm, one leader' or whatever is the enthusiasm of the time. Gideon has no need to create devotion, he need only capture and direct it. It is not, of course, evident without examination that the capacity for devotion to an object of limitless regard belongs to the moral perceptiveness of man. It might be an endemic psychological disease; and if it is not a disease itself, it is unquestionably liable to dangerous diseases. Maybe it could be wholly eliminated by conditioning or psychological manipulation; and so, perhaps, could many of what we take to be features of the human spirit. Surgical interference with the brain might ensure an even more effective riddance. But whether such a modification of the human being would ennoble or debase him is what we should have to judge, and could not evade judging; let everyone consider what he thinks.

Devotion, though constantly deceived, and bestowing its worship on preposterous objects, must suppose them to call for what it bestows on them; for otherwise it loses the nature of devotion. And this consideration brings us to the third point we have to make about the seriousness of our persuasive argument. It is not a persuasion towards adopting a policy or taking up an attitude, although it involves doing both. No, primarily it is the persuasion to acknowledge a claim. Now it may be that there is something pedantic and gratuitous about refining too much upon moral self-culture whether individual or corporate; and that persuasions about this, pushed beyond a point, become fantastic and impertinent. But if what our neighbours are, whether in themselves or as the objects of divine care, claims our devotion, then it seems we can scarcely go too far in advancing a persuasion which has the effect of bringing us to acknowledge both the claim and the reality which makes the claim. We are in no danger of being over-nice in clearing our eyes so that they may see.

The metaphor of sight, though a very violent figure in this connexion, is useful by way of corrective to a far more disastrous linguistic violence. Logic establishes that no 'is' implies an 'ought', no factual assertion allows the inference of an imperative. There is nothing of which the claim upon our attention or action can be deduced from the descriptions we give ourselves of what it is like. The only sort of sentence from which such a claim could be deduced would be a precept commanding us to bestow attention or action of a certain sort upon a class of objects inclusive of the thing before us. But such a precept appears itself to rest on something more fundamental: the decision that such behaviour is the appropriate reaction to such an object. And so we are led on to say that our duties to our neighbour are what *we decide* to be due. The 'we' is editorial; it stands for that enlightened body of opinion which we represent. *We have decided* that drowning strangers are to be rescued, not laughed at. Lucky for them; they might have got into deep water among the Hottentots, who have made the opposite decision.

Such a way of talking is, to say the least, misleading. In making our 'decision' we are not expressing our royal pleasure as joint sovereigns of a moral universe. The action is not due because we decide it shall be. What we decide, or come to a common mind about, is that it is due. Heaven help the Hottentots; but if we go Hottentot, Heaven will not help us. We decide that the action is due; and even this is not a decision simply about the action. We do not decide that the rescue as such is an obligatory performance; as we get the dog to regard it as due that he should fish out of the pond the stick we have thrown. What we come to a mind about is that our fellow-man is such that we should assist him in danger, whether he happens to enjoy the advantage of our acquaintance or not. And so it is natural to say that we *see* something about him, viz. that his humanity claims our succour.

It is a logical truth that the claim made on us by the drowning man cannot be deduced from any genuinely descriptive statements we may make either about him or about ourselves; but that is not to deny that the claim arises out of his nature and ours. All the logical negative excludes is that it arises from descriptive statement by way of logical implication. It arises, nevertheless; it is not to be deduced, but acknowledged in the way in which basic non-conventional claims are acknowledged. And if we say that we have *decided* such a claim, we mean that we have come to an acknowledgment of it, after whatever contemplation or consideration we may use for getting into a position to be capable of such acknowledgment.

To return, now, to our persuasive argument. If we exercise persuasion on moral Hottentots we are not just spoiling the natives; we are putting them in the way of acknowledging real claims which will else go unregarded. It is a pity, for example, that the strangers in their rivers should drown. But how do we know that they are wrong and we are right? Why shouldn't the Hottentots start working among us? Let them, and let's see who can open the others' eyes to more, the Hottentots or we.

The recognition of our neighbours' claim upon us arises out of our knowledge of them; but is it, in addition, itself a sort of knowledge about them? Perhaps this is a question of words. It does not add to our other knowledge of them, our factual knowledge, that is. 'Claimingness' in the moral sense is not an addition to such a list of characteristics as those of being heavy, yellow-haired, malleable, easily led, and consolable with *aqua vitae*. And yet I do not find I wish to deny that the exercise of a claim upon me by my neighbour's existence is in any sense a fact about him, or to say that whatever fact there is lies simply in response on my part.

It even appears to me that there is a significant analogy between moral knowledge and physical knowledge. My knowledge of the physical properties of things is all, in the end, reducible to my discovery of the ways in which they limit and condition my bodily being and action: to such facts as that I can walk across the floor and not through the wall. I *cannot* walk through the wall, I *must not* override my neighbour. I *cannot* escape the gravitational pull, I *must not* evade the claim of kindred. If the 'active properties' of bodies are any sort of facts about them, why are not the 'claimingnesses' of persons some sort of facts about them?

If such a way of speaking is at all justified, and if the Christian's way of taking his moral life is the right one, then a fact about God is a part of his daily experience. For the personal claim which meets him on every hand is exerted not simply by men, but by God. So the Christian may think; but he must not suppose that such a fact about God can conceivably stand alone. A God who was simply 'the X with the absolute claim' could exert no claim at all. The 'claimingness' of anything is always consequent upon what we take that thing to be. And, as we said in the body of our argument, the God who makes claims upon us through our fellows is taken to be their maker and redeemer. The consideration of moral experience uncovers a point at which the faith of Christians can most easily be seen to bear upon their lives. It is no substitute for examining the faith.

CHAPTER II

THE POSSIBILITY OF THEOLOGICAL STATEMENTS

by I. M. Crombie

(1) *Introduction*

CHRISTIANITY, as a human activity, involves much more than simply believing certain propositions about matters of fact, such as that there is a God, that He created this world, that He is our judge. But it does involve believing these things, and this believing is, in a sense, fundamental; not that it matters more than the other things that a Christian does, but that it is presupposed in the other things that he does, or in the manner in which he does them. This is a fact, but it is in some ways an awkward fact, and for many years some theologians have tried to sidestep it. It is an awkward fact because, for example, if one professes certain beliefs, it seems that one ought to be willing to offer some kind of grounds for them. Yet we all know that it is difficult, and some think it is impious, to offer adequate grounds for the faith. Again – a requirement which has become more prominent with recent developments in philosophy – if one professes certain beliefs it seems that one ought to be willing to map out, roughly at any rate, the extent of the claims one is making by saying what is compatible and what is incompatible with them; and that again, in the case of religious beliefs, is something which is difficult to do, for reasons which will be considered in this chapter. Therefore some theologians have tried to sidestep these problems by denying that the Christian religion involves anything that may fairly be called factual beliefs about a transcendent being. That, it is said, is metaphysics, and religion has no interest in metaphysics. A simple-minded move, that has had its devotees, consists in saying that we do not believe that there is a God; we believe in God. More sophisticated apologists have urged that credal affirmations may, without significant loss, be treated as equivalent to recommendations of the behaviour and attitudes that are agreed on all hands to be their proper corollaries. 'There is a God' thus becomes equivalent, or nearly equivalent, to something like: 'Treat all men as brothers, and revere the mystery of the universe.' Beliefs are said to be merely the expression – the somewhat misleading expression – of an attitude of worship.

But, in spite of the piety and wisdom of those who have been seduced by them, these expedients must be denounced as evasions. The distinction between *believing that* and *believing in* is, of course, valid; but it does not help us, for *believing in* is logically subsequent to *believing that*. I cannot believe in Dr Jones if I do not first believe that there is such a person. Nor is the reduction of credal affirmations to the behaviour of worship and general charitable conduct that ought to follow from them of any avail. For Christian worship cannot be exhaustively described in terms of how the worshipper feels, of what he says and does; it retains an irreducible element of belief. Christian worship is neither a kind of poetry nor a kind of *ascesis*, neither a giving vent to feelings of awe and reverence, nor a cultivation of the soul. Fundamentally it is thought of by the Christian as an entry into relationship with a transcendent being, whom non-Christians do not believe to be there to enter into relationship with. Christian worship, therefore, is not only something which the non-Christian *does* not do, it is something which, by virtue of the difference of his beliefs, the non-Christian *cannot* do, though he can, of course, do something which, in externals, is as closely similar as you please. What the non-Christian does, whether in church or out of it, may be better or it may be worse than what the Christian does, but it cannot be the same, because it cannot share the same credal basis.

There are then certain factual beliefs which are fundamental to Christianity, in the sense that they underlie all Christian activity, and give it its specifically Christian character. The expression of such beliefs I shall refer to as the making of *theological statements*.*

The problem stated

Our problem in this chapter, then, is: how are theological statements possible? For it is a fairly common philosophical position to-day to say that there can be no meaningful theological statements. This view may be loosely put by saying that theological statements are unverifiable, and therefore meaningless; or it may be more carefully put by attending to the rules which Christians appear to lay down for the interpretation of theological statements, and contending that these rules conflict with each other in such a way that no meaningful statements could possibly be governed by such rules. For, it is said, the statements purport to be about a quasi-personal subject, and in that way to be parallel to statements about, say, Julius Caesar; and yet if we proceed to draw conclusions from them, to bring arguments against them, in general to test them as if they were parallel to statements about Julius Caesar, we are told that we have failed to grasp their function. They have, apparently, some kind of special exemption from empirical testing; and yet if one attempts, for this reason, to assimilate them to other kinds of utterances (moral judgments for example, or mathematical formulae) which enjoy similar exemption, one is at once forbidden to do so. How paradoxical this is; and how much easier it makes it to believe that the making of theological statements rests on some kind of confusion than to accept them at their face-value!

My procedure will be to ignore the loose statement of the case (the doctrine that unverifiable statements are meaningless is like the doctrine that cars are fast; not entirely false, but blanketing so many important distinctions as to be useless), and attend to the more careful one. Here I shall not dispute that theological statements have the paradoxical features attributed to them by their

---

* This is, of course, a wide use of the word ' theological.'   In this use theological statements are the kind of statements (' affirmations,' etc., if you prefer) which all Christians make, not only theologians.

opponents, but I shall argue that these paradoxical features need not be regarded as demonstrating the impossibility of meaningful theological statements, but rather as contributing to a grasp of their meaning by giving a partial characterization of their subject. For, I shall argue, their paradoxical features make it clear that these statements are made about no object which falls within our normal experience, or any imaginable extension of our normal experience; and to learn this is to learn something about the nature of religion. Something, but not much. To know that God may not be identified with anything that can be indicated is only the first step in theology. I shall therefore go on to try to define the extent to which we can claim to have any positive grasp of what we are talking about when we make theological statements, and thus to elucidate the sense in which they are meaningful. Very briefly, my argument will be: the inquirer may learn from the paradoxical features of theological statements, that, if they are about anything, they are about a mystery. If he requires further specification (and he is right to ask for some, though if he is wise he will not demand that those who believe in a mystery should offer him a detailed anatomy of it) he must seek it from two sources. Firstly from the affinities and relationships which exist between theological statements and utterances of other kinds (for example moral judgments; to do the will of God is our supreme duty); and secondly by considering whether a sense of mystery seems to be the appropriate response to any part of our experience. If this enables him to see not only what theological statements are not about, but also, so to speak, in what region the mystery that they are about is located, then he may feel that he understands what it is that Christians are talking about, but not why they talk about it; for surely it is self-stultifying both to say that something is a mystery, and also to make 'statements' about it. To this I shall reply that, if we claim to know something of the mystery, we do so because we believe ourselves to possess a revelation, that is to say a communication made in terms that we can understand; and I shall argue that if we reflect on the kind of thing such a communication would have to be, we shall see why theological statements have the characteristics that they have, and how they are to be taken. That is to say, I shall attempt to show that theological statements are meaningful by showing what they are about, and how they offer information about it. For, after all, all that is necessary for an utterance to be a meaningful statement is that it should be governed by rules which specify what it is about, and what it asserts about it. The problem about theological statements is simply that there is a sense in which we cannot know what they are about (a sense in which we cannot know God) nor what it is that they assert. The solution of the problem must consist in defining the sense in which, on the other hand, we can know enough of these things for our speech about them to have an intelligible use.

The critic's case

So much by way of preliminary sketch. Let us begin our argument by considering the case advanced by the critic, as I shall call the man who denies the meaningfulness of theological statements.

He knows of course, that theological statements have many of the characteristics of meaningful statements, in particular that they form a system, within which inferences may be drawn, incompatibility relations obtain, and so forth; and that they command a response, both emotional and moral, in those who accept their validity. What he suspects, however, is that although they form a system, it is a system without reference to anything in the real world. The system maintains itself, not because it is seen to report the truth about certain objects, but because it is causally connected with a set of images and practices which are valued for their own sake, and in particular because it can be thought of in mythological terms. That is to say, one can think of divine judgment in terms of the pictures on mediæval chancel arches; of beings with wings weighing souls in balances or driving them into a fish's mouth with pitchforks; and one may be moved, poetically and morally, by such pictorial representations. Because one is moved by the picture, one wants to believe that it is a representation of something which will really happen at the last day; because one

has the picture, one is able to imagine that one is believing in
something when one says that 'he shall come again with glory to
judge both the quick and the dead'. Now the Christian is perfectly
willing to admit that he does not expect at the last day any event
having any resemblance, in any literal sense, to the events depicted
in mediæval dooms. Whenever a trumpet sounds he knows it is
not the last trump because, whatever the last trump will be, it will
not be the sound of a trumpet. But he maintains that he believes
in something, of which the mediæval doom is a pictorial representation. It is here that the critic dissents. He can understand why
the Christian wants to believe that he believes in something
underlying his mythology; but, in his judgment, there is nothing
there. This judgment he bases on the peculiar elusiveness of
theological statements, once they are stripped of mythological
form.

In its most general terms, this elusiveness takes the following
form: on the one hand the Christian claims that his statements are
concerned with a particular being, God, with particular kinds of
events, such as the creation, the last judgment, the operation of
the Holy Ghost. Yet if you try to pin him down by asking such
questions as 'Which person? Where is He? What events are you
talking about?' he protests that such questions display crude misunderstanding of the nature of theological language. Yet if he
uses words which appear to be proper names, or which appear to
refer to cosmological happenings, or to occurrences in human
personalities, surely such questions are perfectly proper ones to
ask. It is, of course, true that anybody who knows anything about
the more abstract intellectual disciplines is familiar with many
words and phrases whose use is logically much more complex,
whose relationship to their subject-matter is much more devious,
than that of words like 'axe' or 'butterfly'; and the critic is quite
prepared to believe that the words (like 'God' and 'grace') whose
use is peculiar to theological statements may be of this kind, and
also that when ordinary words (such as 'loves' and 'made') are put
to theological use, they also are made to work under similar conditions. But if we consider words of this kind from other spheres,

such as 'electron' or 'Œdipus complex', we see that we can gather what they are about by observing how they are used, by noticing what kind of observations are held to substantiate a statement about an electron, what kind require that it be withdrawn. There are specific laboratory or clinical conditions with which these words are fairly tightly connected. But let us take a word like 'grace', and begin by observing that it appears to be used about certain happenings in human personalities. Now let us go on to try to discover which happenings these are; let us ask such questions as: 'If a man decides to go to church, is that an example of what you call "the effects of grace"?' Always we seem to get an ambiguous answer: 'It might be or it might not. It would be if it were the result of divine influence; it would not be if the decision proceeded from some other cause.' But this will not help us much; it tells us that grace is what God does to a man; but unless we know what God is and what form His action takes, we are no further forward. We tried to break our way into the system of theological statements by taking a concept – grace – which appears to refer to events in human beings in the hope that these parts of the system might be familiar to us and so enable us to understand the rest of it. But when we try to isolate the events in question, in order to discover what is being talked about, we are offered no characterization of them except that they are the results of divine influence. It would appear then that we must begin at the difficult end; if we are ever to discover what theological statements are about, we must tackle the concept of God. But if we ask what the word 'God' refers to, we are likely to be told that God is a transcendent being who cannot be known to us except in his effects.

It appears then that we are imprisoned in a circular maze. Grace is what God does, and God is the being whose action in human souls is grace. How, asks the critic, is anybody supposed to discover what this circular system of concepts is about? Is it not much easier to believe that the system is nothing but the relic of pre-scientific mythology in which God was an almost human being and grace was something concrete, like the prosperity of the

law-abiding; that with growth in scientific knowledge and moral
sensitivity, theological concepts have been progressively detached
from the fictitious celestial being, and real, but insufficiently edifying, terrestrial events, with which they were once identified; and
that the whole system has been preserved, beyond the point at
which it was evacuated of all content, only for what one may
brusquely call sentimental reasons?

Ambiguity of the critic's case

That, or something like it, is the case for the meaninglessness of
theological statements. It is a case which I do not propose to dispute. The premises are sound enough, though the circle is not so
complete as I have let it appear (it is true that the Christian will
never assert positively that this or that thought or action could
only have flowed from divine grace;* but he will claim that faith
hope and charity are supernaturally infused virtues, and he is
prepared to offer, not exactly criteria for the infallible recognition
of these gifts, but some account of what he takes genuine faith,
hope or charity to be). But it is indisputable that there is no region
of experience which one can point to and say: 'That is what theological statements are about.' If you care to conclude from that
that there is no way of discovering what theological statements
are about, then that, too, is indisputable if your meaning is that
one can never know what it is like to be, for example, divinely
inspired, in the way in which one can know what it is like to have
a cold, or even, perhaps, an Œdipus complex. What I do wish to
maintain, however, is that this does not show that theological
statements have no legitimate use; it is simply a partial definition
of the use that they have. For the elusiveness we are considering
is a consequence, indeed an expression, of the fact that all theological statements are about God, and that God is not part of the
spatio-temporal world, but is in intimate relation with it.

To maintain this contention, it will be necessary to look rather
more closely at this characteristic of elusiveness. It derives, we
must begin by insisting, not from the natural shiftiness of persons

* On this see Chapter VI.

who make theological statements, but from the uses for which such statements are devised. If one is to talk about these matters, one has to do so by making use of statements governed by apparently conflicting rules. The formal properties of theological statements (that is to say, the rules determining how they are to be taken and how they are supposed to be related to statements of other kinds) have to be, at first sight, mutually contradictory if they are to do their proper work. We must turn to a more detailed consideration of these antinomies.

(2) *The anomalies of the formal properties of theological statements*

The first anomaly

Since all theological statements are, by definition, about God, then however they are worded, we may say that God is the subject of them all (statements about grace, for example, are not about a commodity which is dispensed from heaven, but about what God does to men). Therefore we may describe the first antinomy in the following terms: theological statements are to be interpreted as if their subject was a particular individual, and yet differ in logical character from all other statements about particular individuals. Let us put it in the following way.

If I say that Tom loves Mary, you can ask me who Tom is, and it is at least logically possible for me to point him out to you. But if I say that the average man falls in love at least once between the ages of 18 and 27, you display that you do not understand the expression 'the average man' if you ask me who he is. I shall put this by saying that while 'Tom' is a *proper proper name*, statements about the average man *have to be reduced;* the first statement, I shall say is *directly* about Tom; the second is *obliquely* about people in general. Now what about the statement 'God loves mankind'? On the one hand the question 'Who is God?' is proper, and on that account the statement appears to be direct and does not have to be reduced; and yet although the question is proper, there is an important sense in which it cannot be answered. There is such an operation as introducing somebody to Tom, but there is no such operation as introducing somebody to God; or rather if there are operations which may, from the standpoint of faith, be so described, it is so only from that standpoint, and they differ vitally from ordinary introductions. If a child asks 'Who is God?' he can only be given statements (such as 'He made us') by way of answer. He can never be brought into a situation in which it is proper to say 'That is God'. The symbol 'God' might therefore be described as an *improper proper name*. It resembles a proper name like 'Tom' in that we are told that statements about God are direct statements about God and not oblique statements about something else, and yet it differs from ordinary proper names in that its use is not based fundamentally, as theirs is, on acquaintance with the being it denotes. It is not easy to see how such a symbol could have a valid use.

There are however other symbols in somewhat similar case; and it may illustrate and sharpen the point to consider some of them. Take first the expression 'point'. The rules governing the use of this expression in geometry require (1) that points be in space, but also (2) that they be not even tiny volumes. Now, one might say, I can understand that something can be sizeless; a thought, for example, has no size. But then it is also not in space. How can anything be both sizeless and also somewhere? Being somewhere is occupying space, and to occupy space one must have size. The expression 'point', therefore, like the expression 'God', seems to be governed by contradictory rules. Or take proper names for fictitious characters. 'Titania' is a proper name, and to ask 'Who is Titania?' is to ask a proper question. And yet it can only be answered by statements (such as 'She is the wife of Oberon'); there can never be a situation in which 'That is Titania' is the right thing to say, and that not because one cannot get to fairyland, but because the idea of a journey to fairyland is a logically incoherent idea. 'Titania', too, is an improper proper name.

In other words, the expression 'God' in some ways resembles words which stand for fictions. Titania is certainly a fiction, and

Plato called points geometers' fictions. But the religious man will of course insist that this comparison in no way illuminates the nature of theological statements. He obviously does not want to give God the status of Titania, and it is equally fatal to give theological statements the status of geometrical statements. For geometry is about spatial relationships; and we tolerate the expression 'point', although in a sense there could not be such a thing as a point (nothing could conform to the definition), because we know clearly enough how talk about points is useful in talk about spatial relationships. If then one appeals to statements about points (admittedly respectable) in support of statements about God, one will be told that statements about points are valuable because one knows how to translate them into statements about sets of volumes; into what are statements about God to be translated? Here of course the religious man must reply that they are not to be translated, and so the point of the comparison is lost.

This comparison having failed us, we are back where we were, forced to admit that the expression 'God', being an improper proper name which is devised for non-fictional discourse, is in a logically anomalous position. On the one hand statements about God are not reducible, and in that they are like statements about Tom as opposed to statements about the average man. On the other hand, although they are not reducible, but have their own distinct subject, in the manner of 'Tom loves Mary', that subject is not an ordinary subject. And yet in saying that God is not an ordinary subject, we do not mean that he is a peculiar or extraordinary subject, like Diogenes, who lived in a tub; we mean to assert something like a logical difference, while at the same time we deny that it is any ordinary logical difference, like that between Tom and the average man. When we say that Tom is not the same kind of being as the average man, we mean something different from what we mean when we make the same statement about Tom and God; and yet we mean more by saying that God is not the same kind of being as Tom, than we mean by saying that my brother is not the same kind of being as my dog. The difference between God and Tom is in some ways like a logical difference, and yet it is not a logical difference. Or, to put the same point rather differently, the impossibility of going to heaven and seeing God is not a technical impossibility, like the impossibility of going to Neptune, and yet it is not a logical impossibility, like the impossibility of going to a state of perfect competition and seeing the economic man. A claim to have seen God is outrageous, without being exactly logically outrageous. The statement to a child 'You can't see God' is not like 'You can't see a virus,' nor like 'You can't see the average man.' The difference between God and other subjects is neither precisely a logical, nor precisely a physical difference. The religious man may claim that the difference is a metaphysical difference, that the point is that God is a transcendent being; but the critic will reply that he could only understand the meaning of these phrases – 'metaphysical difference' and 'transcendent being' – in the light of an example, and that the example offered is of no use to him because he cannot understand what statements about God are supposed to be about. As far as he can see, he will say, the expression 'God' purports to stand for an individual; now some expressions ('the average man' again for example) which purport to stand for individuals do not in fact do so; they are on a different logical level from that on which they purport to be; they are used in speech about classes from a particular aspect, or something of the kind. But this kind of treatment of the expression 'God' is not permitted: 'God' is not allowed to stand collectively for human benevolent impulses or anything of the kind. But if it is claimed that it stands for an individual, what can be made of this claim, when all the normal criteria of individuality are held not to apply in this case? There are no doubt innumerable individuals (perhaps 'the oldest male on Mars' may describe one of them) of which we know nothing, but of these we do not seriously speak. Individuals about whom we do speak seriously are either known to us, or have been known to somebody (Tom, Tom's wife, or Julius Cæsar), or else are uniquely characterized as satisfying some comprehensible description (the man who invented writing, the largest oak in Hampshire). God is not known to anybody, and these descriptions which are sometimes offered as uniquely characterizing Him ('the first cause', 'the necessary being') are such that nobody can say what it would be like to conform to one of them (if one knew what it would be like for something to be a necessary being, then one could say that 'God' stood for whatever satisfies these conditions; but one does not), and therefore have no identifying force. How then can the reference of the expression 'God' be fixed? And if it cannot be, how can this expression be treated as a proper name?

The second anomaly

This then is the first perplexity: it concerns the reference of theological statements – what they are made about. The second perplexity concerns their content – what they say about whatever it is they are about. This perplexity can be divided into two parts. We are now considering the predicates of theological statements, and, generally speaking, these predicates are or can be expressed in everyday words: '... loves us', '... made the world'. Now it is fairly obvious that these everyday words are not being used in their everyday senses. When I make a table I take some tools and some materials, but Creation is *ex nihilo*. Therefore the words which express the predicates of theological statements are presumably being used in an unusual sense, and one may want to know what that sense is. Now the second perplexity, which, as I said, can be divided into two parts, concerns the fact that nothing which happens is allowed to necessitate the withdrawal of theological statements; they are allowed to overrule all factual objections.* The first part of the perplexity derives from noticing this fact (and not making any difficulties about the meaning of the words in the predicate-expression), and consists in asking how, in that case, it can be claimed that theological statements can be regarded as factual statements, which can be true or false. The second part derives from noticing the irrefutability of theological statements, and asking how, in that case, we can ever learn what meaning to attach to the words in the predicate-expression, when

* As I shall argue later, this is only a half-truth; see pp. 51 and 72.

theologically employed. The two parts are no doubt facets of the same point, but it will be convenient to consider them separately, taking the first one first.

(1) Those who believe that God loves us, or that He created the world, believe that these are factual statements. That is, they are comparable to 'Tom loves Mary' or to 'John made a model boat' and not to the large and heterogenous class of familiar utterances which are not to be regarded as factual statements. For example, 'I promise . . .' does not report my promising; it is my promising: 'Shut the door' is a request: '2 + 2 = 4' is a correct arithmetical formula and not an observation about the habits of pairs. None of these can ever be false because, by virtue of being the kind of utterances they are, they are logically incapable of colliding with the facts. They are preserved from falsity, not in the way in which 'John made a model boat' is preserved from falsity when John made a model boat, not by the existence of a fact for them to correspond to or agree with, but by their logical incapacity to agree or disagree with any facts. Now the theist wants to say that God really does love us, that He really did make the world; and he wants to say that these are not edifying stories, or expression of pious attitudes, but statements of fact. But, says the critic, what can be meant by 'fact' in this context? When we say, of an ordinary factual statement, that it accords with the facts, we mean something like this: a statement like: 'The cat is on the mat' delimits a range. There can be very different kinds of cats, very differently disposed on very different kinds of mats. 'The cat is on the mat' therefore does not indicate just one quite specific kind of situation, but delimits a range. There are situations which cannot count as the cat's being on the mat, and situations which can; and learning to draw the line between them is learning the meaning of the sentence. When there exists a situation which falls within the range delimited by 'the cat is on the mat', then a statement to that effect will be true; when there does not, it will be false. Now, normally, to say that a statement is factual is to claim that, by virtue of its meaning, it selects in this manner between possible situations; it has a range, such that some possible situations fall

outside it, and its truth is the existence of a situation which falls within its range. But, in the case of theological statements, the theist denies that there are any situations which fall outside the range of 'God loves us' or 'God created the world', and he denies this without claiming an exhaustive knowledge of all the situations which there are. 'God loves us,' he says, is not an empirical hypothesis about the pious prospering; he is quite content to leave it to historians and others to find out what happens to people in the world; 'God created the world' is not meant to prejudge the deliberations of astronomers; the theist does not pretend to know how the world began; he only claims to know that, however it began, God created it. In other words, says the critic, the theist says what he says, not because he has discovered that there are in fact no situations incompatible with his assertions, but because, in his opinion, there could be none. If you ask him how God's loving us differs from the hypothetical case of God's not loving us, he denounces the second alternative as unreal, because it assumes a modification in the divine nature, whose fixity is the foundation of everything. But then, if no possible situations could fall outside the range of 'God loves us', that must surely mean that this formula is such that, by virtue of its meaning, it is incapable of choosing between situations; that is, that it is a request, performatory utterance, tautology or something of the kind, and in no sense a factual statement.

Here again, it may be worth observing in passing, fictional statements are in somewhat the same boat with theological ones. It is entirely to misunderstand 'Holmes sprang into a passing hansom' to treat it as a request, tautology or performatory utterance, and yet nothing whatsoever can offer the slightest ground for supposing that Holmes did not spring into a passing hansom. And yet once more the comparison is embarrassing rather than helpful to the theist; for the statement about Holmes is preserved from the possibility of a collision with the facts by belonging to a world of make-believe; and the theist does not want to take that way out. But how, in that case, are the theist's statements preserved from the possibility of collision with facts? And if they are not so preserved, how can he assert them without exhaustive knowledge of all the relevant facts? Since he makes no claim to possess this knowledge, surely he must judge it unnecessary, and surely it can only be unnecessary if his 'statements' are not intended as statements of fact, but as recommendations of attitudes, or something of the kind.

(2) So much for the first part of the second perplexity. The second part draws attention to the difficulty of learning what particular theological statements can be supposed to mean. Taking for our example the statement 'God created the world', we can put the difficulty in the form of a dilemma: either this assertion selects from among conceivable alternatives, and as such is a cosmological hypothesis subject to scientific refutation; or it does not select, and in that case it is impossible to say what it means.

For, says the critic, it is agreed that the theist is not alleging any ordinary making when he talks about creation. What he is alleging, then, remains to be discovered. How are we to discover it? Well, the statement is supposed to tell us something about the world – that it was created by God. Let us then take the propositional function ' X was created by God'. Now if we are allowed to suppose that this function delimits a range of possible situations, such that some situations fall outside this range, then the statement about any given thing that it was created by God would convey information to anybody who was apprised of the boundaries of the range. But how can we become apprised of the boundaries of the range? We need to be capable of envisaging specimen situations which fall within the range, and specimen situations which fall outside it. Since, *ex hypothesi*, there can be no actual examples of these latter in this case, the specimen situations from outside the range of 'God created the world' will have to be imaginary ones. Since I have got to be able to envisage these situations, they must consist of familiar elements rearranged. But in that case, what 'God created the world' excludes is a set of possible situations which can be fancifully constructed by taking actual objects or properties, and supposing them arranged otherwise than as they are. 'The cat is on the mat' gives me information, not simply because it is incompatible with 'The cat is somewhere other than on the mat' (one does not know what a sentence means by knowing that it is incompatible with its own negation), but because I can easily envisage situations which agree with the one and disagree with the other. Supposing I have never seen that cat anywhere but on that mat, then I have never encountered any situation excluded by 'the cat is on the mat'; and indeed perhaps there has never been one. But because cats can be in all kinds of places, the class of excluded situations may be said to exist, and I can easily envisage specimens, for example by combining the familiar elements: the cat, being on, and the sideboard. Because I know that being on the sideboard or under the sofa would not be a case of being on the mat, I know what is claimed by 'the cat is on the mat' (the non-existence of all the incompatible situations) and thus what it means. But in the case of 'God created the world', if I am to know what this means, I must have some idea of the incompatible situations, and if I am to be able in this way to envisage them, they must be situations which can be constructed by rearranging familiar elements, and in that case what the assertion we are considering rules out must be something which logically might be the case. But if something is such that it logically might be the case, then it is always possible that some observation, some day, will show that it is the case. Therefore on this view 'God created the world', if we are ever to discover what it means, must be a scientific hypothesis, subject to scientific refutation. Consider, as a fair parallel, 'the universe is expanding'. This is a fair parallel because it is, like the creation statement, completely general. If it is true, then there are no cases of a non-expanding universe, ever, anywhere. Nothing actual is excluded by the statement. When, then, an astronomer makes it, how do we discover what he means? By looking to see what evidence he brings in support of the view, what observations he admits would refute it. Perhaps the spectra of the heavenly bodies are such as they would be if observer and observed were moving rapidly away from each other; if this were not so he would withdraw his claim. We thus know what his claim amounts to. If 'God created the world' is allowed to be in similar case, then we can know what it means, and what it means must be something empirical. If it is not, then we cannot discover what it means, because it cannot literally mean anything, and we must conclude that its efficacy in discourse is not that of an ordinary factual statement. Perhaps it is a myth that we tell in order to inculate an attitude of reverence.

So much for the philosopher's perplexities about theological statements. To summarize them, the first is that these statements purport to be about a particular object, which it is in principle impossible to 'indicate' in any non-linguistic way, and which is thus different from all other particular objects in whose existence we have any ground for believing; the second that while it is claimed that these statements are true, and have determinate meaning, none the less the theist seems not to regard himself as embroiled in scientific dispute; he claims an immunity which belongs properly to persons who do not make statements of fact. In themselves, his sentences are perfectly intelligible. We all know what '. . . loves us' means, and 'God' is a proper name. Anybody, therefore, can understand the assertion 'God loves us' on its own. But as used in theological discourse it acquires formal properties which render it utterly baffling to the critic; the rules laid down about how such utterances are to be taken (e.g. that 'God' is indeed a proper name, but that it is in principle impossible to see God) are such that he cannot see either what its reference can be (the first perplexity) or what its content (the second).

(3) *What follows from the fact of these anomalies?*

The anomalous formal properties of theological statements help to fix the reference of these statements

We must now turn to see what we can do about these perplexities. Let us begin by considering what a theist might reply to such a critic. Might he not say something like this: None of the above arguments are compelling. You show that God is unlike all other individuals and expect us to conclude that therefore there is no such individual. You show that statements about Him are not like ordinary contingent truths and so invite us to class them with tautologies and requests. Admittedly we might do these things, but we do not have to. Is it not clear, from the formal properties of our statements alone, that we believe in the existence of a being different in kind from all ordinary beings, and in some way detached from the events of the spatio-temporal universe; and that, therefore, we shall inevitably make statements having the *prima facie* peculiar, formal properties outlined above? Surely the formal properties of our statements delineate the object of our belief rather than furnish evidence that there is no such object.

For the formal properties of theological statements can themselves be expressed in higher-level statements having God as their subject, just as the formal properties of ordinary statements about triangles (such as that their interior angles total 180 degrees) can be expressed in higher-level statements having triangles as their subject (such as that triangles are not physical objects, but a shape). Thus we can express some of the formal properties of theological statements in the higher-level statement 'God is a transcendent, infinite and incomprehensible being, in incomprehensible relationship with the familiar universe.' Now is not this a tolerable statement of vague undifferentiated theism, not far from the kind of belief in God which we find, for example, in Aristotle? Too vague, indeed, for the needs of religion, but still the essential foundation on which religion must be built?

Up to a point this reply is justified, but we must tread carefully here. If some such higher-level statement is to be regarded as simply recording the formal properties of theological statements, then the words occurring in it must bear no sense beyond what is necessary to express these properties. 'God is a transcendent being' becomes something like 'There exists an object of discourse which is particular but not indicable'. But of course when stated thus, there is nothing religious about the formula. So the position is something like this: the theist may claim that if he wants to talk about a transcendent being, his statements will have to have the formal properties of theological statements, and that, therefore,

there is nothing scandalous about their possession of such properties. The critic may reply that he still cannot see what talk
about a transcendent being is talk about, and therefore the theist
cannot claim that the formal properties of his statements are
sufficient to delineate the object of his belief. The most the theist
can claim for the consideration of the formal properties alone (or,
if you prefer, the higher-level theological statements in which they
are expressed) is that it diverts attention away from all irrelevant
subject-matters; that it makes clear that all non-theological subject-matters are irrelevant – theology is not to be assimilated to
anything else; and that, therefore, if anybody is to understand
what religion is about, he must be willing to conceive the possibility of an object which is neither similar to, nor in any normal
relation with, any spatio-temporal object.

What the argument so far has shown is that there is no direct
inference from the paradoxicality of the formal properties of
theological statements to their meaninglessness. The critic's case
is a *probable* case, and the theist has a probable case on the other
side. The critic, feeling no impulsion to talk about anything which
would have to be talked about in such a fashion, judges it probable that such talk only occurs because theologians, valuing for
various reasons the simple piety of simple people with their
anthropomorphic God and geomorphic heaven, but aware that
they cannot defend these beings against the advance of knowledge,
protect them from scientific criticism by the assertion that they
are beings of a peculiar order. The theist, on the contrary, believing in a mystery beyond experience, traces of which he claims to
detect in experience, contends that he is obliged to use, for the
expression of his beliefs, language governed by paradoxical rules.

The 'affinities' of theological statements help to fix their reference

But the theist cannot really rest there. The critic is open to be
convinced of the validity of theological language, if someone can
show him what such language is used about, and how it succeeds
in communicating truth about it. Let us then continue with the
argument and see how much further we can get towards meeting

the first of these requirements; that is, how much further we can fix the reference of theological statements.

First we might ask the critic to bear in mind the formal properties of theological statements, as an essential negative clue, and then listen to people making use of theological statements. For, we may say, an important hint concerning their reference may be derived from observing the relationships which appear to obtain between theological statements and statements of other kinds. For although we do not regard the divine love as identical in kind with human love, divine creation as identical with human making, none the less the words which are chosen for use in theological predicates are chosen for some kind of appropriateness. Again, although we do not identify the divine activity with any set of finite events, and for that reason refuse to let statements about providence or grace be strictly equivalent to empirical generalizations of history or psychology, none the less we do maintain that statements about grace are about a subject-matter which overlaps at least with the subject matter of psychology.* We do not regard the doctrine of divine love as a doctrine of exemption from suffering, and for that reason evidence to the effect that people suffer is not allowed to over-rule the doctrine that God loves them. Yet the theist must be intellectually sensitive to the existence of suffering; if for example somebody said that our life was one of unalleviated misery the theist would be committed by doctrine as well as by common sense to disagree with him. Against the rule that theological statements, not being empirical generalizations, cannot come into logical conflict with empirical generalizations, not being moral judgments, cannot come into logical conflict with moral judgments, and so on, you must set the rule that, since the subject-matter of theological statements overlaps with the subject-matters about which empirical generalizations and moral judgments are made, theological statements are sensitive to, and have affinities and relationships with statements of other kinds.

Listen, then, we say to religious discussion. You will find that

* Again the reader should turn to Chapter VI.

religion is connected, in this loose way, with ethics, cosmology, history, psychology; that it has nothing very direct to contribute to mathematics, literary criticism or marine biology. Surely, if you do not pitch your demands too high, this will begin to fix for you the reference of theological statements? But first let us amplify the caution against pitching your demands too high. Imagine a game: one player leaves the room, and the rest select an object. On the return of the first player, the others utter the predicates only of true statements about the chosen object, and the first player must guess the object. Thus the players say '. . . invaded Britain', '. . . kept a log', '. . . required his wife to be above reproach'; and the first player guesses 'Julius Cæsar'. Theists are not playing a game of that kind; God is not a familiar object cryptically named, as anti-fascist Italians used to speak of Mussolini as 'Mr Smith'. God is a mystery, and therefore you cannot expect that knowing what statements about God are about will involve anything like having a precise conception of their subject. The most that can be hoped for is something much vaguer, of which the following may serve as an example.

I do not know what a quaternion is; for all I know it may be a measure of time, like a quinquennium, a dance, like a quadrille, a kind of lizard, a poem, an elementary particle, or anything whatsoever. But now suppose I listen (as we are advising the critic to listen) to people talking about quaternions. Fairly quickly I shall discover that they are not dances or lizards, and they hardly seem to be periods of time. Gradually they will place themselves for me somewhere in the region of the mathematical sciences. I shall still be very ignorant indeed of what they are; but I shall know what section of the library to go to to look for a book about them. If you like, we might mark the extreme vagueness of my grasp of quaternions at this stage, by saying that, while my listening has not fixed the reference of 'quaternion' for me (for I do not know what they are), it has fixed the reference-range (for I know what kind of thing they are). Surely, then, we may say to the critic, if you listen attentively to theological discourse, you will come to discover its reference-range?

Now the critic must, I think, concede that negatively such listening may be of considerable assistance. It is at least as useful as attending to the formal properties of theological statements for seeing what theological talk is not a contribution to. But for providing positive identification, it is a very different matter. Crudely put, identification by negation is only positive identification if one has a list and eliminates all the items but one. But the trouble is that God is not on the critic's list and therefore he cannot be enlightened by elimination. Let him put the point thus: the man who, from listening to talk about quaternions, comes to place them in the region of the mathematical sciences, only does so because he knows at least something among these latter, or at least can envisage their possibility. A child or a primitive, who had not yet abstracted the idea of number, could not place quaternions in the region of the mathematical sciences, because he would be absolutely without a notion of them. But, says the critic, with respect to God he is himself in the position of the unmathematical child with respect to quaternions. Nobody has ever taught him how to abstract the idea of God. Furthermore, he suspects that his listening has now made him unteachable; for it has shown him that religion is closely connected with such subjects as history, psychology, ethics and cosmology. Theological vocabulary draws upon words commonly used in these subjects, innovations in these subjects are apt to upset theists and so forth. But if he is asked to find room for a further subject, related to these subjects as theology is apparently supposed to be related to them he simply cannot do it. How can anything underlie moral obligation as the divine will is supposed to do? How can grace be something which occurs in human souls and yet something which the psychologists can manage without? Again, he may say, it is no good saying that the reference-range of theological language is fixed by the language itself. For it is precisely fictions which are created by talking, and theology is not, apparently, a multi-volume novel. The reference-range of 'quarternion' may be fixed for me by listening to mathematicians talking, but it is fixed for mathematicians by the existence of the appropriate mathematical problems. If there were no such problems, there would be no talk about them. Theists cannot therefore content themselves with telling us to listen to them if we want to find out what they are talking about, for if they are talking about anything, then it must be possible to indicate what it is, or talk about it would never have begun. Unless they can indicate what their subject is, it is fair to ask them why they ever started uttering, and how it would matter if they stopped.

To some extent this reply is, certainly, justified. If theological talk has any valid use, then it must be possible to show in what kind of context one becomes conscious of the need to talk in this way; and this demonstration cannot be sufficiently given by disclosing that theological statements cannot be identified with statements of any other kinds, but have affinities and relationships with some of them. In so far as the critic believes that he can show that there could be no other subject-matter related to history, psychology and the rest, in the way in which theology is supposed to be related to them, there is no reason why we should agree with him. But in so far as he merely confesses a personal incapacity to see what this further subject is, he is, of course, perfectly justified. He is also perfectly justified if he stresses once more that the reference-range of theological statements is supposed to be fixed, and yet is not fixed by any normal kind of indication or conceptual description, that this is logically anomalous, and that he has a right to be given some account of it.

What is it that impels people to make theological statements? The short answer is, a conception of the divine. But what, asks the critic, is that? Is it not the remains of primitive myth, adorned by the feeling of awe in the face of natural phenomena? What are we to answer him? As we have seen above, a conception of the divine must be a conception of a being outside space and time, on whom the spatio-temporal universe is in some sense dependent. Given such a being, talk about him will have the formal properties theological talk has been found to have. It will not be possible, in any ordinary way, to indicate such a being, for indicating is select- ing a region of space-time in which certain qualities are manifested. Again, it is natural to suppose that if the universe is dependent on God, then what is true of Him will be, not exactly necessarily true (certainly not tautological) but, so to speak, less contingently true than truths about the dependent universe. It also seems natural to suppose that if God is conceived as the source of the space-time universe, Himself outside space and time, His activity will not be manifested (at least normally) here rather than there (for then He would *be* here rather than there) and hence that statements about His relation to the created universe will not take the form of cosmological hypotheses, verifiable by observing the contents of particular spatio-temporal regions. So far, so good; given a conception of the divine it looks as if we might be able to smooth away the apparent logical anomalies of theological language; to show them to be necessary consequences of the purpose for which it is intended. But are we given such a conception?

We must acknowledge at once that in the ordinary sense we have no conception of the divine nature. We do not know God, and it would be absurd to claim that we know what kind of being He is. In so far as we use adjectives about Him ('omniscient', 'eternal' and so on) they do not enable us to conceive what it is like to be God. Omniscience is not infinite erudition, and what it is must be beyond our comprehension. And yet people, whether they be theists, atheists, or agnostics do normally suppose themselves to know what people are talking about when they talk about God. The critic, of course, has his own explanation of this fact. According to him, what makes people suppose that they can grasp the reference of talk about God is nothing more than the old anthropomorphic conception of a superhuman being somewhere above the sky. No civilized person believes there to be such a being, but the picture serves, in unsophisticated minds, to conceal from us that we do not know what we are talking about.

This is certainly a possible account of how the reference-range of theological language is fixed for most people; whether it is, for you, a plausible account, will depend on your opinion of the critical powers of those who use such language. But our business,

if we want to convince ourselves of the validity of theological
language, is to show that the widespread readiness to attach sense
to the notion of a being outside space and time has a more fundamental and more respectable origin than that.

(4) *The reference of theological statements*

*A 'conception of the divine' being necessary to fix their reference, what
     is this?*

Can we, then, find a more fundamental and more respectable
origin for our readiness to attach sense to the notion of a being
outside space and time, a being whose nature would explain the
anomalies of theological statements? To this we must now turn.
What I propose to argue could be put like this: the conception of
the divine is indeed in one sense an empty notion; but it is the
notion of a complement which could fill in certain deficiencies in
our experience, that could not be filled in by further experience or
scientific theory-making; and its positive content is simply the
idea of something (we know not what) which might supply those
deficiencies. This bald account I must try to supplement, but not
without a warning that what follows will be extremely sketchy and
inadequate. The business of explaining the origin of the conception of God has provoked a very considerable literature, which
passes under the name of natural theology. Often it has been held
to be the task of natural theology to prove the existence of God.
This seems to me to be a task which cannot, in any strict sense of
'prove' be accomplished. What however the arguments of the
natural theologians do do is reveal the intellectual pressures which
lead people to talk about God; and, in so doing, they illuminate
the meaning of such talk. This being so, I must ask the reader to
turn to the classical works on natural theology if he wants a more
adequate treatment of the subject with which the following
paragraphs are concerned.*

   * See for example: Austin Farrer, *Finite and Infinite*; or E. L. Mascall,
Existence and Analogy.

Our willingness to entertain the notion of a being outside space and time (of what I shall call a 'spirit') is perhaps most fundamentally based on our inability to accept with complete contentment the idea that we are ourselves normal spatio-temporal objects.* No doubt the point has often been put in extremely misleading ways, and many quite untenable claims have been made; but it remains true that you cannot adequately describe a human person with the range of concepts which is adequate for the description of a chair, a cabbage or even an electronic calculating machine. And the additional concepts which are needed for the adequate description of human experience – *loving, feeling, hoping,* even *seeing* are obvious examples – all have a relative independence of space, not in the sense that we can think of a loving being that is not somewhere, but in the sense that if you try to anatomize his loving you cannot think of it as rest or motion of parts, while you can think of his walking or digesting in such terms. One can of course think of the organic correlates of loving or hoping in physical, and therefore spatial terms; but while few would wish to distinguish the organic correlates of a psychical state, and the state itself, as two separate things, it remains true that we most of us feel uncomfortable about completely identifying them; not that we suppose that we are here dealing with two distinct, but accidentally conjoined, things, but that a full description of this one thing in terms of adrenalin glands, or whatever it may be, does not begin to do justice to the thing as it is known in experience, and has no logical connexion with an adequate description of the latter. Much, that is, of what goes on in us is describable from two standpoints: the standpoint of the observer, who can see our muscles twitch, observe our brain-pulsations in an encephalograph; and the standpoint of the agent who is directly aware of himself; and what is described from this latter standpoint demands a distinct set of concepts. I would agree with the tradition from Aristotle to Professor Ryle which does not see in this duality of the human person any warrant for describing a man as a committee of two distinct entities, body and soul; but

* On this I must refer the reader to Chapter V.

the duality remains, and is, as far as we know, a distinctive characteristic of our experience. We are not, nor is any part of ourselves, beings outside space and time, or spirits, but part of our experience of ourselves is only describable with the aid of concepts of a non-physical kind. What we should derive from this is not the grandiose view that we are spirits, but the ability to conceive the notion of a being independent of space, that is a being whose activity is not at all to be thought of in terms of colliding with this, or exercising a gravitational pull on that. We cannot of course form any kind of a lively idea of what it would be like to be such a being; but this is not the positive inability with which we are unable to conceive of a being corresponding to a self-contradictory or meaningless description. In the case of 'spirit' we do not know that there could not be a being like that, as we know that nothing could correspond to the description 'round square' or 'asymptotically democratic potato'. 'Spirit' is not an expression which affronts our logical conscience or leaves us with no clue at all. There are many different grades of 'not knowing what is meant by . . .' and our ignorance of the meaning of 'spirit' (that is, of what something would have to be like to conform to the requirements of this word) is not absolute. To say, then, that we conceive of God as a spirit, is to pitch our claims rather high; for the suggestion is of something parallel to conceiving of Tom as a sergeant-major, where there is some body to the conception. But because of the duality of our own nature, and of the applicability to ourselves of concepts which are not needed for the description of the material world, the formal properties of theological statements, requiring as they do that God be a spirit, leave us unable to conceive what it would be like to be God, but do not leave us without any inkling of the reference-range of such statements. It is not a conception, but a hint of the possibility of something we cannot conceive, but which lies outside the range of possible conception *in a determinate direction.*

But the duality of our human nature is of course a freakish characteristic in the world of space and time. If the world of common experience is all there is, then its purely 'material' contents form a sufficiently complete system on their own, with human spirituality a kind of alien intruder like the ornamentation on Victorian furniture. The pressure of this 'sense of alienation', this sense that we are strangers and sojourners upon earth, has led men for centuries to posit, what they cannot imagine, a spiritual world, to which we really belong; so that we are no longer bits of irrelevant ornament upon an independent structure, but the meeting point of two 'worlds', or interconnected systems of beings, to each of which we belong in one of our dual aspects.* Or, if you like, our limited and imperfect spirituality – the fact that we are not spirits, but beings with a spiritual aspect – leads us to think of beings who are perfectly what we are imperfectly; not that we can properly conceive of such beings, but that we are forced to frame the abstract notion of them, by the feeling that the smattering of spirit which we find in ourselves must be a pointer to a pool from which it comes.

But, the reader may complain, I am talking of all this in terms appropriate to explaining the genesis of an illusion. I ought to be anatomizing the meaning of the word 'spirit', and that ought to mean listing those experienceable characteristics which we refer to in using the word. Instead of this I am apparently conceding that the word has no meaning (is used of something we cannot conceive of), and trying to explain why people use it as if it had. This I am doing because, in a sense, the notion of spirit is, not exactly an illusion, but an illegitimate notion; illegitimate because it is a kind of reified abstraction. For the words 'spirit','spiritual', and so forth, come to have specific meaning for us by being con-

* Friendly critics have objected to my use of the word 'aspect' here. While agreeing, more or less, with the arguments of this section, they hold it less misleading to talk, in the traditional way, of spirituality as a 'part' rather than an 'aspect' of men. For, they say, spirituality is at least an essential aspect; we identify ourselves with our spiritual activity in a way in which we do not identify ourselves with such other aspects as our height or weight. I agree that the word 'aspect' could be misleading; I use it for the reasons given below, and I think that if its meaning is confined to that which is required by these reasons it will not seriously mislead. In other contexts, I would quite agree, 'part' is often better.

nected with particular characteristics of, or events in, human beings. We distinguish 'spirit' from 'influenza' or 'digestion' by showing to which aspects of men these words severally refer. 'Spirit' derives from 'spiritual' and 'spiritual' acquires specific meaning by correlation with thinking and other activities which only occur, in our experience, as activities of human beings. 'Spirit', then, is not a common noun like 'mouse', because it is not the name of a distinct kind of being; it follows from the way the specific meaning of the word is learnt that it is an abstract noun like 'digestion', because it stands for activities of beings called men. We should all regard it absurd to speak of beings which were pure digestions; not the digestings of animals, but just digestings. Is it not equally absurd to speak of things which are pure spirits; not the spiritualizing of animate physical objects, but just spirits? Surely it must be a category mistake to use the word 'spirit' as anything but an abstract noun, or aspect-word?

Now, against a claim that we know what we mean by 'spirit' in the way in which we know what we mean by 'digestion' or 'smile', such an objection would be decisive. In the sense of 'meaning' in which the meaning of a word is those experienceable characteristics to which it refers, anybody who knows the meaning of 'spirit' can infer that, just as smiles can only be arrangements of features, so spirits can only be characteristics and activities of men. But I am not claiming that we 'know the meaning' of 'spirit' (in the theological use) in this sense. In Berkeley's words, I admit that we have no idea of spirit, and claim only that it is extravagant to say that we have no notion whatsoever of how the word is used. How the word is used (and this, of course, defines such meaning as it has for us) in the theological context is by the deliberate commission of a category-mistake under the pressure of convictions which require us to depart from normal language-practice in this way. For if a man believes that there are beings, or one being, who are comparable to us only in so far as we are spiritual, then the following two things would appear inescapable: (1) that he cannot have any clear and distinct conception of the object of his belief; and (2) that, to express it, he will require some such noun as 'spirit' which will (*a*) retain specific meaning by connexion with 'spirituality' as the name of a human aspect, but (*b*) be governed by a rule declaring that this noun is not to be taken as an abstract noun like 'smile' or 'bad temper', but as a concrete noun like 'man'. If you are prepared to accept the view that belief in the existence of purely spiritual beings is simply the result of logical illusion (like the belief in universals as independent entities), that theism is simply a category-mistake, then you need not sully your tongue with a word whose syntactical behaviour is incompatible with the way in which its meaning is learnt; but if you feel that you might entertain the view that there are purely spiritual beings, then you have to have the word. It does not seem to me at all plausible to regard theism as a category-mistake, for it is not pressures derived from logical theory that make people theists. People do not believe in *greenness*, existing independently of green things, until they have been subjected to philosophical reasoning, and told that, if A and B are both green, then there must be a common something in each of them, viz. the universal *greenness*. This is a pressure derived from (mistaken) logical theory. But theism has a quite different origin; we do not believe in God as a pure spirit because we are told that if Smith and Brown are spiritual beings, pure spirituality must exist – or anything of the kind. The notion of God as a spirit is indeed a category-mistake, or category-transgression, but one deliberately committed to express what we antecedently feel; and, if we antecedently feel something, the category-transgression we deliberately commit to express that feeling has some meaning – that, namely, which it is designed to express. Disagreement with this conclusion must rest, I believe, on one or other of two general principles, for neither of which can I see any compelling argument: (1) that there can never be good grounds for committing category-transgressions; and (2) that there can be no 'meanings' which do not correspond to clear and distinct ideas.

Let me add, as a pendant to this discussion of 'spirit', that the sense that, in one aspect of our being, we belong to a country in which what is imperfectly realized in us is fully and perfectly realized, is not, of course, a compelling argument for the existence of such a country. I claim only two things; the first, that it does not rest solely on inadvertence to logical grammar, but can even survive a clear realization of the logical anomalies of such a belief; the second, that it is this belief or feeling which fixes for us the reference-range of 'spirit' and related expressions as they occur in theological language.

But God is not only a spirit, but also Infinite Spirit. We have so far been discussing the noun; what of the adjective?

Here again an adequate discussion would be equally beyond my space and my powers. But by way of further illustration of the way in which the reference-range of theological language is fixed for us, I shall again venture something.

When we speak of God as an infinite being we are not, of course, using the word 'infinite' in its strict mathematical sense. We mean, negatively that He is unlimited; or, more positively, that, being the source of all limitation, there is nothing whatsoever to which He is conformed, or to which He must conform Himself. 'Infinite', therefore, comes to very much the same thing as 'necessary', 'omnipotent', 'creator of all things', and other words of the same kind which we use about God. Now it is characteristic of all these words, that, in so far as they have any precise sense, they cannot be used about God. For, since we do not know God, they cannot acquire a precise sense by reference to His properties; if then they have a precise sense they must acquire it from reference to the properties of something else; and, since nothing else can be an adequate model for God, in so far as they have a precise sense, it cannot be applied to Him. Suppose we say, then, that what we mean is something rather loose and vague, loosely and vaguely connected with the normal uses of these words (or, in the case of a word like 'omnipotent', with the result of combining the normal forces of their components). Even so, we have many difficulties to face. Take, for example, the formula I used above, that God is 'the source of all limitation', and that, therefore, 'there is nothing whatsoever to which He is conformed, or to which He must conform Himself'. Now even supposing it is admitted on all hands that we cannot expect to have any idea of what it would be like to be, or encounter, such a being, we may still be asked to provide *some* sense for the phrase 'source of all limitation'. What can we say? Limitations are due to natural laws, natural laws to the natures, behaviour patterns, or whatnot which things have. If then God is the source of all limitations, He gave things their natures, or created them. But although we can push the counters about in this way, and travel by 'bastard inference' from *infinite* to *creator*, where have we got to when we arrive? What does a doctrine of creation amount to? If you think of God anthropomorphically, creation is all very well. He took some raw material, and by compounding and arranging it, gave it the properties we see around us; He now sustains it, and will one day put it on the bonfire. But if you think of God anthropomorphically, who made God?

So far are we, in fact, from being able to argue from the contingency of the world to the necessary being of God, that we cannot see how to attach a clear sense to the claim that the world is contingent. The logical sense of the word will not do: in that sense parts of the world may be said to exist contingently – that only means that if x exists, it might not have done so, and that only means that from what we know of the rest of the world we cannot strictly deduce that x exists. But the world as a whole cannot be contingent in this sense. We cannot sensibly say that, from what we know of the rest, we cannot strictly deduce that the world as a whole exists, for there is no 'rest' for us to have knowledge about – unless indeed the rest be God. Yet although we cannot find a clear sense for 'contingent' 'created' and so forth in this context, the fact remains that people do persist in having beliefs for the expression of which they call upon such terms. To some extent, no doubt, these beliefs rest on theoretical errors. Thus people may hold that there must be a God because, they say, the world can't have come from nothing, for *ex nihilo nihil fit*. If you reply that either it is possible for a thing to 'come from nothing', or it is not possible, and that in the former case the world may have 'come from nothing', and in the latter case God cannot have done (so that by parity of reasoning we must ask: 'Who created God?'), you may or you may not dislodge the belief. If it rests merely on the theoretical error of applying the principle *ex nihilo nihil fit* to the entire universe, on the ground that it may be legitimately applied to particular portions of it, then no doubt you will. But in some people on whom you employ this reasoning, you may encounter an obstinate conviction that none the less this is in fact a created universe; a conviction which involves the belief, not that, as a general 'truth of reason', everything whatsoever must have an origin outside itself (in which case God must, too, *ad infinitum*), but rather that *this* universe is something about which one is prompted to ask where it comes from, with the corollary that there might be something about which one was not prompted to ask this question.

What those features of this universe are which make us feel that it is not its own origin, I am not going to enquire. Many of the classical arguments for the existence of God are designed to draw attention to these features. Nor, of course, am I suggesting that because people feel that there might be a being about which one was not tempted to ask 'What is its origin?', therefore such a being must exist. My claim is only that if you want to know what is meant by such expressions as 'infinite', 'omnipotent' or 'creator' when applied to God, then the sense that this is a derivative universe, with the corollary that a non-derivative being might exist, is the nearest you can get to an understanding of their meaning.

'Finite' and 'infinite', 'contingent' and 'necessary', 'derivative' and 'non-derivative': all these are pairs. When we use either member of any of them in the theological context we cannot anatomize the meaning to be attached to it. When we speak of the world as finite we do not mean that it can be counted, or travelled across; when we speak of it as derivative, we do not think of it as extracted from its origin by any normal kind of derivation. But the meaning to be attached to the second member of each pair is to be got at by seeing what kind of judgment about the world is intended by the use of the first. The kind of judgment intended

by the use of such expressions (or by the parallel use of less metaphysical language, such as 'There must be something behind all
this passing show') is an intellectual dissatisfaction with the notion
of this universe as a complete system, with, as corollary, the
notion of a being with which one could not be thus dissatisfied.*

That is, you may say, of a being who could claim one's adoration. And many will hold that, to fix the reference-range of
theological statements it is better to attend not to what religious
people feel or say about the world, but to how they dispose
themselves towards God – that is, to learn what worship is. It is
the contrast between the attitude of worship, and the attitude
which religion commends towards creatures (always to be valued,
but never, absolutely, in themselves) which illuminates what
religion takes the infinite-finite contrast to be. It was the ban on
idolatry which taught the Jews what God is. Indeed, it may be
said that the sense of contingency is psychologically a correlative
of the attempt to worship; one does not begin to feel a sense of
finitude until one has made an effort of self-surrender. I do not
want to quarrel with any of this; I have tried a more theoretical
approach, because I think one should be possible, and because
one ought to be suspicious of the possible abuses of appealing to
what a man does for the elucidation of what he believes. But I
have no doubt that if any vividness of apprehension of the meaning of such terms as 'infinite' is required, then the activity of
religion may best supply it.

Let me try to sum up this part of the argument. We are considering how the reference-range of theological statements is
fixed – how we know what statements about God are about. The
problem is posed by the fact that we neither know God nor know
what kind of a being He is. God is neither 'that being', nor 'the

---

* Professor Findlay's article: 'Can God's existence be disproved?' (*Mind*,
1948; reprinted in *New Essays in Philosophical Theology*, ed. Flew and
MacIntyre) depends for its disproof of God's existence on taking 'necessary'
in 'Necessary Being' in the logician's sense; but seems to me to provide a
very fair characterization of the theist's sense, by its characterization of 'the
religious attitude'.

being such that. . . .' More positively, we want to say that God is
a being beyond the reach of our conception. Very well, then: God
is inconceivable. But, it may be said, that is only a clumsy and
misleading way of saying that the expression 'God' lacks meaning.
We cannot *mean* inconceivables, for the meaning of any expression can only be those conceivables by reference to which we use
it, by indicating which we could teach its use to others. I have
tried to define a sense in which we *can* mean inconceivables, and
that is when we use a word to refer to the postulated, though
unimaginable, absence of limitations or imperfections of which
we are aware. It is a little as if I were dissatisfied with a sentence I
have written; it is inelegant, and somehow it does not express my
meaning. Now the expression 'the correct version of that sentence' is not entirely without meaning to me, although, alas, I
cannot at the moment conceive what it stands for. But I should
recognize and welcome it if it came, and it would remove a fairly
specific dissatisfaction from which I am suffering, or at least a
dissatisfaction about a specific subject. This analogy must not be
pressed;* but it may shed some little light on the sense in which
it may be claimed that such an expression as 'Infinite Spirit' has
meaning for us. Such expressions stand for the abstract conception
of the possibility of the removal of certain intellectual dissatis-
factions which we may feel about the universe of common
experience.

The critic complained that he could see neither what theological statements were about – how their reference-range was
fixed – nor how they could be regarded as making statements
about it – how one could extract their content. I have been trying
to deal with the first problem, and must now pass to the second.
But before I do so I have a caution to offer. In trying to fix the
reference-range of theological statements I am trying to fix it *for
the critic*, that is for the man who says that he cannot see what
religious people are talking about, and does not believe that there
is anything which can be talked about in such a way. It is only to

* There is no difficulty about the *sense* of 'the correct version of that
sentence'; but only about its *reference*.

him that one would ever think of answering the question 'What does "God" stand for?' in such a way. To the religious man the natural answer to such a question is ' "God" is the name of the Being who is worthy to be adored'. And, as I have said, that is perhaps the most illuminating answer one can give. The answer I have given is one which would only be given to a man from whom the other answer would provoke the retort that, as he did not know what 'adoration' referred to – certain actions apart – the phrase 'the being worthy to be adored' could serve as no kind of identification for him. I have been trying to offer a neutral account of what 'God' stands for, one which does not employ any notions whose understanding presupposes a religious outlook. To put it another way, I have not been trying to describe what the Christian takes God to be, but merely to answer a logical challenge, to the effect that theological statements cannot be meaningful because they employ a proper name which seems to be such that it is logically impossible to indicate to an inquirer what it stands for.

(5) *The content of theological statements*

Very well, then, says the critic, I will allow for the moment that 'God' may be regarded as an indicating expression; you may call it a proper name if you wish, of a logically intelligible kind, although its referent is such that it is impossible to become acquainted with it in any normal sense, and cannot be regarded as falling under any stateable class-concept. It still seems to be impossible to say anything about it, for you would know neither what to say nor how to say it. Let us suppose that people do form the conception of a being corresponding to an ideal sketched out by lamenting the imperfections of our nature and our world, and supposing them removed. That gives them no right to say even that there exists a being corresponding to such a conception, let alone to make specific statements about it.

That, of course, is true; the conception of God, alone, can give rise to religious poetry and religious aspiration, but can supply no warrant for religious belief. For the latter one needs to be able to find, within experience, positive indications of the reality of God. There must be, within the space-time world, persons or events whom one is impelled to treat as having a divine origin. For the Christian, of course, the history of Israel, the life and death of Christ, and the life of the Christian community are, in their varying degrees, to be treated in this way.* Why the Christian treats Christ (and Israel and the Church as seen in Him) as having a divine origin, I shall not here enquire. But a difficulty may be raised as to what it *means* to treat something as having a divine origin. To this I can only reply, summarily, that to believe in our Lord's divinity is to believe that no convincing and genuinely adequate account of Him can be given in naturalistic terms, because He seems to us to be in all ways greater than nature; and that, since the notion of God is the notion of a Being greater than nature, who is worthy of adoration, such a judgment is a judgment of divinity.

Christ, then, is the word of God to us; both the evidence of the reality of God, and also the declaration of Him to us. Being the declaration of a mystery He is to be taken both as comprehensible (or it would not be a declaration) and as incomprehensible (or it would not be a mystery); that is, as the visible, tangible, intelligible image of what stands outside our comprehension. Since He is, in His person and in His teaching, a declaratory image, it follows that the doctrines in which we communicate the image, since they are made in human language, must be inadequate to the mystery they concern, but must at the same time command our trust.

It is here that we must look for the resolution of the critic's logical difficulties concerning the content of theological state-

---

* To those who find my introduction of 'revealed theology' abrupt, I must plead the demands of reasonable brevity, and make reference to Dr Farrer's chapter on Revelation in this book and to the significant agreement between Professor Flew and Professor Mackinnon in *New Essays in Philosophical Theology*, p. 183.

ments. Christ provides the answer to his challenge that we have
no right to claim that there exists a being corresponding to the
conception of God, for we ascribe to Christ divine origin; and He
also provides the answer to the problem how we know what to
say about God, for He is the image or declaration of God to us.
But there is a specific logical difficulty which the critic raises,
which requires a specific answer. It is this: the critic complains
that, even if we are justified in calling upon the deeds and words
of Christ as evidence that there is a God, and that He loves us,
he still does not see how the words 'loves us' are to be taken when
they occur in a sentence with 'God' as subject. For, he says, you
do not suppose that God is a human person, nor therefore does it
make sense to attribute human feelings or dispositions to Him.
On the subjective side – what it is in the lover – the so-called love
of God is not like human love. But it is not from the objective
side either – from what it means to the loved – that the meaning
of the word 'love' in this context can be learnt. That is to say, the
claim that God loves us is neither that God undergoes certain
feelings towards us, nor that our life is lived under certain conditions, which sufficiently resemble those which one might expect
from benevolence on the omnipotent scale to be described as
divine love. One can say that the English climate is kind, without
ascribing to it certain feelings; but in doing so one does ascribe to
it certain effects – the provision of tolerable conditions for an
unusually wide range of animal and vegetable life. But if the
ascription of love to God were logically parallel to the ascription
of kindness to the English climate, then that God loves us would
be an empirical hypothesis referring to certain standing conditions
of human life, and falsifiable by a change in those conditions.
Notoriously the doctrine is not to be interpreted in this way.
Repeatedly we are told to cleave to our faith in God's love whatever happens. But then if God's love is comparable to human love
neither subjectively nor objectively, how is the meaning of the
word 'love' in this context to be learnt?

The answer must be that we are to start from the meaning of
the word in its everyday sense; or rather in its least crude everyday

sense. To love somebody is to care for his well-being. How you express this care, whether in gentleness or in severity, will depend on your conception of well-being in general, and his well-being in particular. As the starting-point therefore of our understanding of 'love' in the theological context we must assume a sense of the word compatible with biblical criteria of well-being. If some people use the word in such a way that you can only love what you fondle, that sense must be put aside. That precaution being taken, we have an 'everyday' sense of the word in which it is evidently true that Christ loved His fellows. Since we believe that in this, as in everything else, He was declaring the divine being to us, we must accept His love as an image of the Father's. What it is an image of, we do not need to know, since we believe that the image is faithful. Now we see in a glass darkly, but then face to face; now we know in part, but then shall we know even as also we have been known. We do not know what it is in God that we are talking about when we talk about the divine love, nor what it will mean in our lives; except that since we take the image or parable of the loving father to be faithful and true, we are obliged to believe that whatever is allowed to happen to us can be turned to our well-being. Similarly, if we think of the wrath of God we are not to suppose that God is in any literal sense like an angry man; nor are we to suppose that if we incur the wrath of God it will go with us as it would if we had incurred the wrath of a human potentate. Quite early, prophets and psalmists realized that that was not so. But we are to suppose that, if our conception of anger is the most exalted we can rise to, then it is a faithful image of the truth to think of God as capable of anger. If you like you can say that the things which are said of God are parables.* The point of a parable is that you do not suppose that there is any

---

* I have said more about this use of 'parable' in my contribution to *New Essays in Philosophical Theology*, pp. 118–23. Perhaps I should say here that my use of 'parable' does not seem to be exactly equivalent to Dr Farrer's in Chapter III ; for I would say, what he would not, that to speak of God as a Person is to speak in parable. I do not think this represents any disagreement of substance.

literal resemblance between the truth which is expressed and the story which expresses it, but you do suppose that if you accept the story, not as a true literal account, but as a faithful parable, you will not be misled as to the nature of the underlying reality. The psalmist believes both that God is angry at sin, and that the wicked often flourish as a green bay-tree. Because it is a faithful parable to think of God as a man capable of righteous anger, these two beliefs conflict, and a reconciliation of them must be sought. If the psalmist simply told himself that when we use 'anger' of God we do not mean what we mean when we use the word of human beings, then, since he would have nothing else with which to peg the word down, he would have had no means of testing his beliefs against experience because his beliefs would merely be formulæ, capable of meaning anything he pleased. The formula 'The cat is on the mat' has fixed meaning for us because we know its situation-range, and therefore know when to assert it and when to deny it. We do not similarly know the situation-range which is to be correlated with the formula 'God is angry at sin'. It is precisely for this reason that the critic says – and in a sense rightly – that such formulæ are empty of content and can be neither true nor false. They acquire content, however, not by being correlated with their own peculiar situation-range, but by being treated as parables. That is to say, the content of 'God is angry at sin' is the content of the same statement with a human subject, this content being thought of, not as the literal truth, but as a faithful parable concerning God. It is in this way that theological statements acquire fixed meaning, and religious discourse is freed from irresponsibility to the facts of experience. Because he thinks of human anger as an image of a divine disposition the psalmist can ask himself how it is that God's anger against the wicked manifests itself, since it does not manifest itself in material adversity.

Two things follow from this account of the content of theological statements. Firstly, it follows that we must believe in some kind of resemblance or analogy between, say, human and divine love. We must believe that what we now see in a glass darkly we shall then see face to face, and shall know that what we then see face to face is the same thing which was faithfully represented to us in the image of a father's love. But although we *believe in* the analogy, we do not *use* the analogy to give a sense to 'love' in the theological context. We postulate the analogy because we believe the image to be a faithful image. The sense the words bear within the image or parable is drawn from thoughtful experience of human life. The second consequence is that although it is a formal property of theological statements that they are not empirical hypotheses and hence cannot come into logical conflict with facts of experience, there is another formal property or interpretation-rule according to which facts of experience can count as objections to them.* As we have just noticed, if words occurring in the predicates of theological statements were thought to have special 'theological senses', then since we should have no means of teaching the situation-ranges with which the special senses were to be correlated, we should have no means of telling what kinds of facts constituted an objection to which doctrines. The theist could then blandly ignore all *prima facie* objections, and nobody would listen to him, nor would he advance in understanding of his doctrine. Since, however, theological statements are parables and the words in their predicates bear their ordinary senses, we do know what constitutes an objection to them. Thus the theist cannot simply ignore the fact of suffering when asserting God's love. Suffering, indeed, is not in itself an objection, but utterly and irremediably pointless suffering would be; the Christian therefore is committed to believing that there is no such thing. Because he must believe this, his faith will be continually tortured by what he sees around him, and in this process of torture his faith should be purified and his understanding of life deepened. In the process of testing faith against experience one is to grow in the understanding of each by the reaction of one against the other. This is only possible because we know what the words in the predicates of theological statements mean, and this we know because we take these statements as human images of divine truths.

* See p. 51.

We may now pick up some threads. The reader may remember that we twice found ourselves comparing theological statements to fictional statements; that is to the statements with which we build up a make-believe world. At the time we shied away from the comparison, but now we can look it in the face. Again the critic was always ready to concede that he could understand theological statements if he could take them anthropomorphically. At the time we agreed with him that he was not to take them so. But in fact it is not all that wide of the mark to take theological statements anthropomorphically, even, if you like, to take doctrine as the creation of a make-believe world; so long as you assert, with the utmost emphasis, that these anthropomorphic statements and the 'make-believe' world they 'create' are intended in plain earnest; are intended, not as improving fables about the things in this world, but as divinely given images of the truth about a transcendent being. If you are to understand theological statements in the sense which their users intend, it is essential to do equal justice to each of three propositions. First that the theist believes in God as a transcendent *being*, and therefore intends what he says about Him to be referred directly to God and not obliquely to this world; second that the theist genuinely believes God to be *transcendent* and therefore beyond our comprehension; and third, that since on the one hand God is a mystery, and since, on the other hand, if a man is to talk at all he must talk intelligibly, therefore he only talks about God in images.

The conception of theological statements as images or parables is, therefore, important, but in one respect it can be misleading. One often thinks of an image or parable as a device by which one illuminates, or compendiously expresses, something already comprehensible. Thus, to some extent at any rate, with some of the parables of the kingdom in the gospels. The seed which fell on stony ground in the parable of the Sower is an image of something which could be expressed without an image. There cannot be much development in apprehension of such an image, for it is lucid from the start. A better parable for my purposes is one which happens to be told in actions rather than words, namely, the entry into Jerusalem on an ass, that is in the habit of the Messianic King. For here one is obliged – in the light of the events of Holy Week – to ask what on earth this claim to be the Messianic King can mean, what kind of kingship is here laid hold upon. 'For as yet they understood not the scriptures'; and Christian doctrines are things in whose understanding one advances.

The point might be put by describing at least some doctrinal assertions as bases for meditation. In the case of some doctrines, perhaps, one must be content to take them as images, and not to hope to advance in understanding of them. Others are a kind of higher-level doctrine which delimits a range within which lower-level assertions must be confined; thus in the doctrine of the Trinity we are not perhaps expected to understand in any sense the triune nature, nor required to torment our imagination for an image of it, but to use the doctrine as a caution against what the Church holds to be misleading images.* But there is a third kind of doctrine, in whose apprehension we ought to grow. Take for example the belief corresponding to the petition: 'that we may evermore dwell in Him and He in us', the belief in the presence of Christ in the believer. Now what on earth, one may say, am I to make of such a doctrine as that? For local presence is obviously not meant, and mere metaphorical presence (like seeing his father in an infant) is said not to be enough. What then can be the force of ' in' here?

The doctrine in question is one which intimately concerns ourselves, and it should be possible to make something of it. After all if there is any truth in it, then something which can be called the presence of Christ ought to be detectable in believers. But how is one to know what to look for? The answer must be that one is to meditate. That means to think, reflectively, without haste, and without expectation of unravelling the mystery and finding it was only a conundrum after all. For religion is nothing if not the assertion of the existence of objects and situations which are either

* What exactly is the logical relation between a dogmatic formula and the parables or images which it sanctions or forbids? On this see Chapter IV, esp. pp. 110–112.

right outside our ordinary experience, or at best very much overlooked in our ordinary interpretation of it; and therefore it must
assert that there are things of which we have no direct experience
and cannot comprehend, and other things perhaps which we may
be capable of experiencing, but only if we are prepared to widen
and deepen our apprehension. But how do we begin? Well, we
begin in this case by noticing that local presence and metaphorical
presence are not meant; so it must be something else, which we
will call spiritual presence, for the sake of a name. If, then, we are
to believe this doctrine, we must so conceive of human nature that
we can find room in it for the possibility of the spiritual presence
of Christ. What we are to find room for is still of course positively
an unknown; but negatively we know something about it – we
can think of many things which it would be meaningless mystifi-
cation to describe in this way. This may be enough to set us
looking; it may, for example, be enough to suggest that our conception of human personality is too flat or two-dimensional to fit
any such notion to it. Thus we may come to reform our conception of human personality; and it may be that, having done so, we
find that we now have a better understanding of what men are,
even apart from the strictly religious context. With our deepened
conception of human personality may come a hint of an inkling
of what spiritual presence might be. But, of course, it is not enough
just to cast around in our minds for illumination; we must try to
practise the Christian life, so that we may come to experience
better in ourselves what we are trying to understand. Then we
may be ready for a new attack on our conception of human
nature; and so on. What I am here describing is familiar in
experience to the Christian; the point of this bald account of it is
to remind ourselves of the complexity of the process, with its
intertwining of thought and practice. What must be insisted upon
is that by such a complex process many most perplexing doctrinal
assertions may and do come to have meaning to the believer.
'And do'; for just as Christianity would hardly have survived if
people had not found answers, which did not seem to them mere
evasions, to the obvious objections to the doctrine of God's love,

so it would hardly have survived if, in what it maintains about the spiritual life, people had not found verification and, with it, understanding in experience. To find this verification and comprehension we must use doctrine in the way I have tried to sketch; casting about to find a possible fact which could do justice to the words, that is, explain why, given their ordinary meanings, they should have been chosen to express this truth; not expecting in the end to arrive at a position of full comprehension of what the fact is, but hoping for a clearer grasp of what our words refer to; reforming on the way many of our ideas about human life, where they seem to stand in the way of giving sense to the doctrine. We begin from the normal meanings of the words we use; and their religious meaning is defined by the increase in comprehension to which they give rise, and which we still employ them to record.

This last point needs elucidation and underlining. The saint, we believe, comes to know, at least in part, what the indwelling of Christ is. This he does, both because he understands more of what goes on in all men (for his mind has been stretched and suppled for the grasp of divine truth), and also because more is given to him now than was given in the beginning. He has both a better understanding of the soul, and a larger experience, and therefore understanding, of grace. But now that he sees, comparatively speaking, face to face, he still finds appropriate the language which once enabled him to see in a glass darkly. Now that the rectification of his thought and the enlargement of his experience have given him a use for language about the indwelling of Christ, he does not reject the language as inappropriate; for the fact is what the language was trying to foreshadow. In doctrines concerning the spiritual life this kind of relationship (verifying and clarifying) can be *known* to subsist between the beginning of the process of understanding and its end; and it is this kind of relationship which is *believed* to hold between our earthly understanding of all doctrines and the understanding which we look for when we shall know even as also we have been known.

Much more might be said about how theological language works; of how we extract meaning from theological statements, how we put theological ideas into words; how we pass from theological to empirical statements and *vice versa*; and so forth. For this is a subtle and complex subject. But it must be looked for elsewhere in this book, and in other books. My task has been the defensive one of trying to hold at bay the wolf who would devour, as meaningless, all theological statements in one meal. I have tried to show that there can be ways in which these statements can be validly used. To establish this I have had to give a sketch map of some of these ways. But to understand them, one must study them in use. Just so with psycho-analytic concepts, for example. You will come to understand the concept 'Œdipus complex' best by watching it in psycho-analytic employment. The abstract explanation of the kind of concept it is can do little more than break down initial prejudice against the existence of such a condition, based on mistaken interpretation of the logical nature of its name. Similarly it is from reading theology, not meta-theology, that one can come to understand how theological statements work, and thus to believe that they do work.

(6) *Summary of the argument*

Let me try to sum these conclusions in an example. Let us suppose the critic to say that he is prepared to entertain, even, perhaps, favourably, the doctrine of creation, provided he can be told what he is to entertain. So far, he protests, he is given only an account in Genesis of the order of events at the beginning of the world; an account which science has disproved, and which he cannot accept. What can we offer him to take its place, not in terms of vague generalities, but in terms precise enough for assent or dissent to mean something? We shall tell him, perhaps, that he is to think of the world as something which has been made in every detail by an intelligent being, to compare it to a work of art; that he is, therefore, to think of what happens in space and time as produced by a supreme intelligence. This, we shall say, is enough to give the thought some determinate character. He will now know, for example, what counts as an objection to the doctrine of creation. Suffering, waste (these limitless tracts of nebulæ and emptiness) and all kinds of futility are obstacles to this article of faith; sanctity, intelligence, the production of valuable things are comforts for it. Next we may invite him, in order to obtain further specification of the nature of this doctrine, in order to expose the doctrine more to the risk of falsification, to consider it along with other Christian doctrines, such as God's fatherhood of man, or His redemption of the human race. Thus he will see more of the *kind* of Creator whose existence is claimed, and may discern more accurately what can count in favour of the existence of such a being, what can count against. Thus he will learn, for example, that the nebulæ are comparatively weak evidence against the doctrine; for the creator whose existence is asserted is said to be intimately concerned with the production of a society of spiritual beings, and if such a creator cares to produce millions of light years of empty space, who shall search His purposes? But if we can detect ultimate futility in human affairs, if true piety does not prosper, in the sense that the desire to know and enjoy the God who is the centre of the society of spiritual beings is ultimately rebuffed, then we have powerful evidence against the doctrine of creation, then we have reason to suppose that whatever gods there be are powerless against blind forces of nature.

Very well, then, he may say, I now know something of what I am to believe, in the sense that I have some idea (and you tell me that if I think resolutely within the charmed circle of theological doctrine I shall acquire more) of the kind of picture of the world that I am to form. Admittedly I am now in a position to assess the realism of this picture, of its conformity to life, rather as I can assess the conformity of Hardy's conception of existence, or Dostoevsky's, to existence as it actually is. But all this is in the world of make-believe; I am to think of the world 'as if'. What more is required of me than this? For it is possible for a novelist to illuminate life by distorting it. People do not behave in real life quite as they behave in the books of Hardy, Dostoevsky, Kafka, Huxley; and yet it is possible for a man's understanding of real life to be deepened by reading their books. But what we learn from Kafka or Huxley is not that the real world is like the world they create; rather, having travelled in imagination to a very different world, when we come back to the real world we see it a little differently, and the difference seems to be gain. The unlife-like element in the fictional world is a device which makes us see things which are present, but overlooked, in ordinary experience. Granted, then, that we might discover that our understanding of life was deepened by conceiving of it in Christian terms; in that case the Bible could be regarded as a work of 'serious' fiction. The Christian interpretation would vie with the Dostoevskian or Kafkaesque interpretation. It might indeed surpass them all. But success, even supreme success, in interpreting life could only confirm it as an interpretation of life. It would still be open to me, the critic may say, to admit its validity as an interpretation, but none the less to regard all reference contained in it to things beyond experience as simply the device by which the illumination is thrown. Is it enough, he may ask, if he admits this much?

Of course it is not enough. The critic is not only asked to conceive of the world *as if* it were the work of a supreme intelligence, but also to believe that it *is* the work of a supreme intelligence. Creation, Redemption, Judgment are not to be accepted as illuminating fables, but affirmed as faithful parables. That these parables deepen our understanding of the world is one of the *grounds* for affirming them; it is by no means the whole *content* of that affirmation. To believe these doctrines is not only to believe that they illuminate the facts which come within our view, but also to believe that they do so because they are revelatory of facts which lie outside our view. Formerly we asked the critic to think himself into the content of the parables in order that he might be in a position to admit that there is something there which could count as an interpretation of life, something to which life could conform or fail to conform. Now we ask him to do something more. If he can agree that the world as known in experience does conform to, is illuminated by the parables, we ask him to affirm them. This is a further step, and one he may refuse to take. He

may demand our reasons for believing these parables revelatory
of the unknown, and these we must try to give in due season –
this is the work of apologetics. But before he is prepared to listen
to reasons for assenting to such claims, he may ask to be dis-
abused of what seems to him a conclusive reason against such
assent. 'For', he may say, 'I simply cannot believe that the world
was devised and executed by an intelligent being, because it is
evidently not the object of operations of creation or sustaining in
any familiar sense. However one may wish to believe in an artificer who made the globe or an Atlas who sustains it, it is just
simply the case that no vestige of such a being can be found; and
the desire to believe in one can only be denounced as an infant-
ilism of the imagination'. Ah, but, we say, you say that no
artificer or Atlas can be found because you are looking for a finite
creator, who might be the object of particular experiences; the
creator we believe in is a transcendent being, an infinite spirit
whose relationship to the universe is spiritual, not physical, who
cannot in principle be detected by scientific investigation and
whose existence cannot therefore be refuted by the failure to
detect him by such means. But now we shall be told that this is a
retreat into verbiage; a device to preserve the doctrine from
falsification by clothing it in meaningless expressions. The critic
is prepared to concede that there may be beings of which we have
no experience and whose relationship to the familiar universe
cannot be known to us. But we cannot have it both ways; the
relationship of such a being to the universe can either be incomprehensible, in which case we cannot attach a word to it, or it can
sufficiently resemble sustaining to deserve that name, but in that
case some process of being sustained must be somewhere detectable. Let there be an X such that the universe is in some relationship sufficiently like being sustained to it; then, for us to know
that this is so, it must be possible for us to point to the sustaining.
If it is not, then however much we may be justified in claiming
that there may be any number of X's standing in any number of
relations to the knowable world, we cannot be justified in giving
names to these relations; for, in the absence of a detectable resem-

blance between the relation named and the relation which the chosen word normally refers to, the choice of the name must be entirely arbitrary and its use entirely equivocal.

In reply to this there are two things we must do. Firstly, we must have it both ways; we must confess that we do not understand the relationship in which God stands to the world, but we must also claim the right to name it 'creatorship' or 'sustaining'. The choice of the name is not arbitrary, although, since we do not understand the relation named, its use is in one sense equivocal. That is, to understand what we are claiming and therefore what may count against the claim, we must think of it as if it were sufficiently similar to ordinary making and preservation. If the most honest and patient scrutiny fails to discern what seem to be the effects of intelligent design, then the claim must be confessed paradoxical. But, while we believe the relationship to have some, as yet incomprehensible, similarity to ordinary making, we cannot expect it to have sufficient similarity for it to be possible to detect actual creative operations. But although the use of the name is to this extent equivocal, the choice is not arbitrary. Our use of this image, and therefore our choice of this name for the thing imaged, is based on two things: firstly on the fact that we find ourselves impelled to regard the events recorded in the Bible and found in the life of the Church as the communication of a transcendent being, and that the image is an essential part of this communication; secondly on the fact that the more we try to understand the world in the light of this image, the better our understanding of the world becomes. These two things conspiring together are our authority for the use of the image, and for our affirming it.

So the first thing we must do is to insist on having it both ways, and to offer some such justification as the above for doing so. Only so can we explain how we both profess to believe that this is a created universe, and simultaneously confess that we cannot comprehend what creation is. But there is something else that we must do, whose necessity I will try to indicate in three ways. Firstly, I have said that to 'affirm the parable' is not only to believe that it is true (as a novelist's Weltanschauung may be true) of the knowable world, but also true of the other, unknowable term of the relationship. Secondly, I have spoken of 'confessing' that we cannot comprehend what creation is; but this is not so much a confession as a boast, for we want to say that we proclaim a mystery, not that we propound a cosmological hypothesis. And thirdly, in claiming that our use of the creation image is not arbitrary I have argued that we are impelled to use it because we find it embedded in what we take to be the communication of a transcendent being. In all these three ways our explanation so far has assumed that we can attach meaning to the notion of a transcendent being. In speaking of the other, unknowable term of the relationship, in asserting that we proclaim a mystery (and so warning the critic not to try to probe the mystery with a telescope or a geologist's hammer), in using the notion of a transcendent being to express the authority conceded to Scripture in the adjective 'Holy', I am using language which could be denounced as merely empty. Nothing, the critic might say, is warrantably meant here but negation. 'The other, unknowable term to the relationship' is simply an expression used to deny that one is talking about any spatio-temporal object; 'mystery' simply means 'what a scientist can't discover', and 'Holy Scripture' or 'the Word of God' simply means 'the writings to which I take up an attitude of unquestioning reverence.'

To convince the critic that this charge is unfounded we must show him the kind of meaning that we attach to such expressions as 'transcendent being' or 'infinite spirit'. Unless we can do that he is justified in believing that 'God' is for us merely a proper name which occurs in the parables, but for which we do not seriously believe in a correlate in reality. Since our experience is only of finite beings, we cannot pin down these expressions by indicating the object or objects to which they refer, because the object cannot be indicated. Nor can we lay down the conditions to which a being would have to conform in order to deserve such titles, except by indicating the 'imperfections' in experience the (unimaginable) removal of which is intended by their use. This is what we have to try to do; and if we can proceed in these ways, we are justified in claiming that it is logically possible to 'affirm the parables'. For we have laid down rules as to how they are to be interpreted, and we have specified what they are to be taken as referring to. Having given a reference-range for theological statements, and said how they are to be taken (therefore what they may conflict with and so forth), we are justified in claiming that they are meaningful. For, in order that an utterance be meaningful, what more is necessary than that speaker and hearer know, or can find out, what it is being made about and how to determine the extent of the claim which is being made about it?

CHAPTER III

REVELATION

by Austin Farrer

I

THERE is nothing superficially less attractive to a philosophical mind than the notion of a revealed truth. For philosophy is reasonable examination, and must resist the claim of any doctrine to exempt itself from criticism. And revealed truth is commonly said to be accepted on the mere authority of its revealer; not on any empirical evidence for it, nor on any logical self-evidence contained in it. The analogy used to substantiate this difficult idea is that of human statements taken upon trust. It is pointed out that we often do, and must, accept without evidence the self-disclosures of our friends about their past histories, present sentiments, and future intentions; and it is asked whether it is not even more necessary and proper to accept the self-disclosures of God. More proper, for He neither errs nor lies; more necessary, for whereas we may guess the minds of our equals by many indications, we can scarcely hope to guess the mind of our Creator, beyond establishing the visible nature of His creations. But:

what eye has not seen, nor ear heard, what never entered the heart of man . . . God has revealed to us by the Spirit; for the Spirit searches all things, even the deep thoughts of God. For who among men knoweth the thoughts of a man, save the spirit of a man that is in him? Even so the thoughts of God none knoweth save the Spirit of God. But we have received not the spirit of the world but the Spirit which is of God, that we might know the bounty devised to us by God. . . . Now the natural man receiveth not the communications of the Spirit of God, for they are foolishness to him; he cannot know them, because they are spiritually judged. Whereas he that is spiritual judges all things and is himself judged by none. For *who hath known the mind of the Lord that he should instruct him?* But we have the mind of Christ (1 Cor. ii. 9–15).

It will be seen that St Paul works from the analogy between divine self-disclosure and human self-disclosure. But he is unable to make a straightforward development of it. For whereas our friends disclose their thoughts to us by speech, none of us claims to have heard the tongue of God, or even supposes that He has a tongue. St Paul avoids the difficulty by introducing artificial language. Instead of saying that no one knows a man's intimate thoughts except the man himself, he says, 'save the spirit of the man', a tolerable phrase for the man's self-consciousness, or for the man *quâ* self-conscious. But the word 'spirit' is magical; it is commonly used not simply for 'mind', but for 'mind' conceived as capable of extension or transference from one person to another. And so St Paul's readers are led to accept the suggestion that whereas the 'spirit' of our friends is communicated to us by speech, the Spirit of God communicates itself to us by infusion or direct transference, leading us to utter, rather than to hear, the words of God. The result is that no one who does not share the supernatural gift can pass judgment on what we say; for that would be a case of the creature presuming to instruct the Creator. The 'natural man' has a creaturely mind; the spiritual man has the creative thought communicated to him. So high a privilege it is to share the mind of Christ.

St Paul's text puts the whole scandal of revelation in a clear light. 'Revelation' means 'personal self-disclosure', but the analogy from our friends' utterances will not bear a plain application to God. And, even if we let that pass, we are scandalized by the conclusion based upon it, a conclusion which appears to foreclose enquiry. The divine mind is known by infused supernatural wisdom, and all attempts of natural reason to estimate it are beside the point and doomed to failure.

We are not here concerned with scriptural exposition, but for the credit of the cause let us recall that biblical writers are not philosophers. They do not put in the qualifications as they go along; we have to look for them on other pages. And St Paul's way of reasoning elsewhere might lead us to interpret him somewhat more liberally here than the words by themselves suggest. Perhaps his text expresses Christian confidence rather than exclusive dogmatism. The Christian is in fact assured that he is admitted to the secrets of divine compassion and that he has nothing to fear from the pretensions of secular criticism. But this need not mean that he withholds his credentials from examination, or how shall he convert the world? The 'natural man', indeed, will not understand them so long as he insists on fixed 'natural' standards; but there is always hope that he will allow his mind to be stretched by 'spiritual' considerations; and in so far as he does so, he will cease to be a merely 'natural' man.

Whatever is the exact bearing of St Paul's words, they are no part of an address to the 'natural' mind. He speaks here to the converted; he dwells on the centre of faith, where the believing heart is at one with the self-disclosing God. The 'natural man' stands on the circumference, looking in. He is not convinced of divine revelation; he is at most aware of certain phenomena in which he is invited to recognize it. And what are these phenomena? Not simply the order and fabric of the world, for while St Paul would claim that they show the Creator's power and existence, he would deny that they contain His self-disclosure. No, the 'natural man' will be directed to certain utterances and actions carrying the authority of God Himself, and he will feel a 'natural' rebellion against the whole idea of authority. Once granted the divine speaker, and that He is speaking here, His authority, no doubt, is axiomatic. But the 'natural man' has granted nothing of the sort, and so the authority which is claimed appears to him to inhere in formulæ sanctified by custom, or narratives traditionally accepted; these are, it seems, being tricked out with a supernatural aura, like the conventional rays spreading from a framed text on an old cottage wall. And this seems wildly irrational to him.

If the 'natural man,' in his reasonable indignation, rejects all authority as such, he takes too wide a ground and opens himself to the attack of a platitudinous apologetic. It is easy to show the rebel against authority that his only course is to return to the jungle and live on berries. If we do not allow our elders and predecessors to persuade us in favour of our cultural heritage we have no more stock-in-trade than the gorilla and our personal achievement will be scarcely more considerable than his. Humanity is an inherited deposit taken on trust.

The argument is a rejoinder to what is said; it is no refutation of what is meant. Those who protest against 'belief upon authority' are not founding their rejection on a general refusal of their cultural heritage, but on enthusiastic acceptance of what they think the best part in it. Now to be human we must accept the traditions of the tribe, but to be more human we must discriminate among them; to say otherwise is to canonize barbarism. The rebel against authority takes his stand on science. He sees that the principle of authority as it is upheld in religion works quite differently from any authority which is acknowledged in science. He sees that in former days scientists conceived of authority on the religious model, but that their science was strangled and stultified; and he is contemptuous of a theology which is still in the old authoritarian mist. When a Catholic theologian demonstrates that the divisibility of the Church into separate communions is a doctrine unknown to the early centuries of Christendom, he is still thought to be making a hit, whether or not it can be countered. But when Edward Topsell argues against a disbelief in unicorns as being a mushroom heresy no more than 300 years old, his modern readers are hit by nothing but the folly of the Jacobean Age; and they may go on to wonder whether the theologian's appeal to the Fathers of the Church is any wiser. If we can find no unicorns, fossil or animate, we shall not believe in them. If the 'inviolable' unity of the Church is found to have been broken, the inviolability is a myth, whatever St Augustine or St Chrysostom may have said.

Is that the end of the argument? Would it not be better to

reflect a little on the nature of religion, with a view to seeing whether authority has, or has not, any special and inevitable place in it? But before we plunge in, let us put ourselves on guard against an irrelevance. In so far as a religion is a society, it may set up a practical or disciplinary authority; but we are not talking about that, we are talking about authority for believing. It is the more necessary to beware of confusion, because the two sorts of authority overlap in practice. Disciplinary authority may concern itself with the latitude of opinion which the Body can tolerate. In the systems of Catholic Christianity, discipline determines the articles of a creed which you must be able to profess if you are to qualify as a member. But theological tests are no more the cause of faith than medical tests are the cause of health. Catholics do not believe the creed because discipline requires it. At the same time, one of your reasons for believing may be that the Body believes. The belief of the many, headed (let us hope) by the wise, and in continuity of life with saints, has weight with you. And the fact that the Body exacts a certain profession of belief as a matter of discipline is evidence, not only that the Body holds such a belief, but that it holds a belief about that belief: holds, indeed, that the articles it contains are vital to the religion the Body professes. At this point authority exacting belief and authority for believing coincide. But the philosopher will have no difficulty in distinguishing them.

We will say no more about disciplinary authority, except to ask the reader to consider how far a confusion with it contributes to the unpopularity of the other authority, authority for belief. It is inevitable and tolerable that we should be bullied into obedience, but it is intolerable that we should be bullied into an opinion. If, then, we operate with a confused notion of 'authority' in general, we may, because of the disciplinary sort, think of it as something which forces us; and when we hear of authority for belief, we may suppose we are being told that belief is to be forced.

In taking up the subject of authority for belief, it will be convenient first to state what there is in common between authority in religion and in science, and then to proceed with the differences.

What they have in common is quickly said. The scientist and the religious believer must both attach so much weight to the precepts of their predecessors as to act upon them; and the precepts, in being acted upon, must be put in peril. If they will not bear being acted upon, they must ultimately be modified or abandoned. If they will bear it, they are in so far confirmed.

Such is the formula of concord, but how wide are the differences it covers! In natural science the very use of the word 'authority' is little better than rhetorical. It reduces to the platitude that we get nowhere unless we start where our predecessors left off; it confers no sanctity on their conclusions. The classic formulations of scientific theory may be the products of genius, but they derive their authority from the experiment which verifies them, not from the vision which discovered them; and such authority is no authority at all. The experiment, once invented, can be repeated by anyone who sees both how it goes and understands what it is about; it requires equipment, competence, and care, and where these are forthcoming the tiro can make himself independent of the master by repeating his results, or refute him by showing them to be unobtainable.

In spiritual 'science' the situation is not like this. The religion we derive from saints and prophets lays down precepts by which we are to live, and unless they can be lived by, they will cease to be accepted. For faith is not the blind belief that certain attitudes and policies, utterly unremunerative in this world, will be inexplicably rewarded in another. Faith assures us of everlasting salvation, but only because it is a way of life here and now; a way which must convince us, not indeed by easing life, but in some way by deepening it. Yet the proving, in life, of those things delivered to us upon authority is nothing like physical experiment, nor does it in like manner free us from dependence upon the authority accepted.

The simple feasibility of physical experiment follows from the Cartesian principle of dividing the question. No one can put a whole physical theory, or 'natural philosophy', to the test at once. We must be able to divide the question about it into distinct questions of manageable size, and then to define an experimental test proper to the decision of each. But no one supposes that a religious faith can be divided and tested thus. We cannot, for example, reduce the faith to the creed, divide the creed into articles, and knock them off one a week, by arranging spiritual experiments to test, in turn, the truth of each. Nature is tested by masterful violence, but if God is to be known, it is by humble obedience, and by patient waiting for Him; nor is there any prediction possible about the time it will take a man to obtain an experimental assurance of God.

In natural science there is a dead level, a minimum of competence in the experimenter, which will secure a result of (to all intents) a standard decisiveness. In religion there is nothing like this. No one has the spirituality to prove anything absolutely, and the spirituality of the ordinary believer is a negligible equipment compared with that of the saint. What is received on authority must be proved in action, and yet it can never be so proved, that it could not be proved more. And so there is never a moment for ceasing to lean on the authority which first commended what we perpetually prove. The scientist may have a moral certainty of having excluded disturbing factors from his experiment, but the believer has no such assurance of excluding folly and sin from his attempt at co-operation with Divine Grace.

The religious mind, incapable of proving faith in seventy years of imperfection, adds the years of others to its own and extends experiment by proxy. We live and feel through the friends we know, or through the saints and apostles we read. And now the balance swings the other way. Instead of valuing what we have received as a prescription for the experiments we may make, we begin to value our own experiences as clues to a labyrinth of spiritual history. The schoolboy set to make hexameters begins by regarding Virgil's text as an authority for his painful work, but it is to be hoped that he will come to find in his work a clue to the poetry of Virgil.

History and, indeed, hearsay or the reading of imaginative books are an extension of our experience through that of others;

the point is a commonplace. But in the exploration of spiritual history, as the believer views it, there is a unique factor. History in general extends our lives into ages and places in which we shall never live, and enriches our knowledge with variations on the human theme other than any that we shall ever play. There is no one constant thing which man throughout his history has experienced, except himself; and what he has experienced of himself has been the historic alteration. That is the view of secular historians, but spiritual history sees a constant object, God. And so by going into the ages behind us we do not shift our eyes from the object before us. It is not I to whom God is revealed, it is the people of God in all their persons, times and places, and if I will not look with them I need not hope to see.

When faith claims that in all ages God is one, she does not deny in religious history a fabulous and absurd variety. In one way of viewing it the figure of man has been far more constant than the figure of God, for man has kept at least his human lineaments, but God has been a beast, a vapour and a star. The history of man is the variation of a given unity; God has no history, but the history of religion exhibits a phantasmagoria of scattered vision slowly unified into an acknowledgment of divine perfection. If we are to look through the eyes of our predecessors we will choose those of men to whom we believe God was already as known as He can be to us. If we look further back, we will discount the imperfections of the revelation by the standard of what has been since revealed. Even if we use the eyes of those whose light we acknowledge to have been brighter than our own, apostles or Christian saints, we find colours in their vision peculiar to their times, and unacceptable to ours. Yet it can still substantially convince us as being what we still are able to see. How such conviction is possible, experience may discover.

The bent of current philosophy inclines students to demand the practical implications of the statement that God is a, or rather the, transcendent person. Will it be any sort of answer to point to the religious facts we have been retailing? God is a person, so we hope to know Him by dealing with Him: by obeying Him, for example, or trusting Him. He is the 'transcendent' person, His personal being does not, that is, consist in such things as the dealings with us through which we know Him. Neither does He undergo historical changes; His actions everywhere express a simple and unvarying perfection. But again, His transcendence means that His perfection does not find an expression sufficient for the needs of our religion in our solitary dealings with Him. The recipient of His revelation is redeemed mankind, not any member of it in isolation.

Such a phrase has its obvious dangers; for whatever may be true, a democratic account of revelation is not. All men may be equally the objects of divine compassion but they cannot be equally the instruments of divine revelation. What is for the many is through the few. What God does for mankind is made known by those who have, or to whom He gives, discernment. The validity of revelation may depend upon a possibility of wide appreciation, it cannot depend upon a general and shared discovery. That is not the sort of thing that happens.

II

In the last few pages we threw up two principles which need to be brought into relation with one another. To do this shall be our next attempt.

First, we said that the religious history of mankind differs from the merely cultural in this, that it claims to have a constant object, God. But second, we have said that when God is conceived as a person, it is understood that He cannot be properly known except through our dealings with Him; or, to speak more religiously, through His dealings with us. And these principles do not, on the face of them, appear consistent. For when we think of an unchanging object of human experience throughout recorded history we think first of something quite impersonal like the general nature of physical substance. Here indeed is an unvarying fact, and mankind has been always wrestling with it, trying various holds and throws, not all equally successful; but it has remained the same. When, on the other hand, we speak of a person, of someone able to be known through personal dealings, we think of someone who exists in a series of successive actions, some of which are sampled by those who deal with him. But if God is known in this way what becomes of His changeless unity? What is that personal dealing or active policy of God in our regard which can be recognized as the single intention of a constant mind, or even as having the sort of unity discernible in one inconstant finite life, from the cradle to the grave?

It may seem that we are faced with a dilemma. Either we assert the unity of God, or we assert a personal knowledge of Him. If we assert his unity, we must equate the experience of Him with the experience of whatever factors in human life are simply unchanging; and then perhaps the divine will reduces to an amalgam of two constituents: the physical or psychical nature from which in no circumstances can we ever escape; and the grand platitudes of valuation from which in no circumstances ought we ever to escape. If, on the other hand, we stand by the assertion of a God personally known through His personal dealings with us, we may attribute to His will our personal destiny and individual calling; but then there will, so far as our knowledge goes, be as many persons of Godhead as there are human destinies. Every man, as an ancient Greek might have said, will have to reckon with his own *daimon*, and the relation between the *daimones* of us all and any transcendent Godhead there may be, will remain problematical. As between a polytheist and pantheist solution there is hardly a cash difference: whether we agree that our various *daimones* are external to the supreme God, or whether we allege that the one divine nature has the remarkable property of manifesting itself in infinite *daimonic* variety.

It is probable that many pious persons use the following escape from the dilemma we have posed. God, they think, in His dealings with us is something like a good schoolmaster or a good priest. He is not involved in our individual histories beyond the involvement of kindness and compassion. He has a distinct way of dealing with each of us according to our case, and yet there is a family resemblance between His handlings of us all. They are all the policies of one heart and receive their supreme direction from one interpretation of the human aim.

This solution is, in what it asserts, acceptable to almost any religious mind; but it is difficult to believe that it is as self-contained as it professes to be. Does it not presuppose the Christian, or some other particular revelation? The family resemblance between God's ways with us all is readily recognizable, if we have all put ourselves into the hands of the Christian system, and interpret God's disposal of us as His application to us all of one flexible model, that of Christ. But if not, then what is this family resemblance? No one wishes to dispute that there are broad commonplaces of aspiration which give some community of direction to most spiritual minds. But it would be mere rhetoric, surely, to call this broad convergence of direction a personal dealing of God with those who respond to it. Everything you would wish to call 'personal' would have to be additional to it.

The Christian method of dealing with this difficulty has been already hinted at. The Christian believes that God has given Himself a personal history in relation to us; a history which does not consist merely in scattered dealings with individuals or in a general direction of our spiritual evolution. It consists in the life of a single man, but this life has a divine significance for all men, because God has made it His own. Human history which, considered in itself, has no theme, no centre and no goal, receives from the Incarnation an orientation. In so far as previous events are seen to prepare for, and converge upon this unique event, they allow the unity of Providential Government to be discerned. Once in the world, the revelation remains; it is a living force, a Church, a faith, and all human things subsequent to its beginning bear upon it, and it on them; so the visible unity of God's operation continues. He deals, indeed, with each of us, but always by extending to us the action of Christ.

The philosophical reader may well have viewed this pious discussion with mounting impatience. The method of argument may seem to him radically vicious. First, he will complain, we wallow in the embarrassments resulting from the naive application to God of a model or parable borrowed from human personality; then we invoke a *deus ex machina* – Incarnation – to pull us out of all this quite unnecessary mire. There is no need of a magical solution – a logical solution will do. It is enough to point out the unreasonableness of first forcing the parable, and then lamenting that (without magical aid) it will not fit. Why should it fit? All we have to do with any parable is calmly to observe how far it fits, and how far it doesn't.

Nothing sounds more reasonable than this comment; and yet it is not clear that it applies to the case in question; for it is not at all certain that 'personality' is, in the sense that would justify the comment, a 'parable' about God. Not, anyhow, a parable as other parables are. To call God 'Father' and to say that He deals with us as sons is a parable; it asserts an analogy between what fathers do, and what God does. 'What God does' is outside the parable; it is that to which the parable is referred. And the phrase 'What God does' places God's action in the personal category; it is taken to be the same sort of phrase as 'What Henry does' and not at all the same sort of phrase as 'What prussic acid does'.

Very well, the personal interpretation of 'What God does' stands outside the parable about fathers and sons. But that need not mean that it stands outside all parables. There is nothing to prevent us from referring a parable to what we suppose is a literal description, and then coming to see that the description is itself parabolic after all. And there is much to make us think that 'God's personality' is a case in point; none of us in fact ever thinks that God's personality is identical in kind with our own, and the most obvious account of what we mean in ascribing personality to Him is that personality as we know it in ourselves is a tolerable parable of what He is.

The trouble about the suggested formula is that it is absolutely sterile. A God about whom we can say no more than that He is something to which personality offers an analogy is of no interest to anyone. He is not even the creator of heaven and earth,

or the first causal agent; for to create or to cause is to do something, and there is no such thing as 'just doing'. All theological
parables are about God's doing, and they all suppose that His
doing is of the personal sort. And if we try to treat God's *doing*
as a parable of God's *something else*, we are powerless to supply
any suggested description of this *something else*, which does not
turn out to be a mere synonym for 'doing'.

If anyone likes to call 'personality' a parable about God he
may,* so long as he recognizes that we cannot treat it as we treat
other parables, by referring it to a stated reality lying outside it.
What we do is something different. Unable to content ourselves
with a mere equation of God's personality with our own, we have
recourse to negative qualification. 'Personal – but not as we are,
by identification with a single pattern of physical action.' 'Active –
but not by proceeding from inaction to action as we do' and so
forth. The negative qualifications are drastic enough, and yet they
must not be allowed to remove what they qualify, or we are left
talking of nothing.

It remains that if we talk theology at all we are committed to
'personality' language. It is the very substance of our discourse,
and we must suspect of a watery sophistication any theological
statement which tends to dilute it. In a philosophical arena
theology itself is under discussion; but the more seriously the
personality of God is asserted, the more there is to discuss; and if
the faith of the Incarnation gives the fullest value to language
about the personal action of God, it may fairly claim to be *the*
religious faith *par excellence*. All others by comparison sound
somewhat half-hearted.

The self-incarnation of God gives the highest reality to
'personal' language about God, but that is not to say that we can
work out *a priori* from the verbal notion 'a personal God' the
consequence 'self-disclosed in the mode of incarnation'. For
though the personality-language may not be parabolic in the
common sense, it is not literal enough to allow of such an *a priori*
demonstration. We know that the assertion of divine personality

*Such would appear to be Mr Crombie's usage: see Chapter II, pp. 70–72.

is at grips with negative qualification, and we can scarcely have an *a priori* certainty where the qualifications will stop, or (to put it the other way round) which aspects of personality as we know it remain uneroded by qualification and capable, therefore, of sustaining the deductions we propose to hang upon them.

The picture of an *a priori* religiosity, sweating with conviction of a personal cause, and not knowing in what manifest acts of God to find that personality actualized, might seem completely unreal if the fact were not encountered. To reach conviction that the personality of God must be taken with full seriousness does not advance us an inch; we are no nearer towards determining what acts or events would be needed to justify the 'full seriousness' of the personal language. Only God can justify it, by doing the acts or by causing the events.

Undeterred by the current discredit of apriorism, the philosophical critics of theology follow down the slope. The argument may proceed like this*: 'God is the absolute case of a personal agent? – Yes. – That means He is omnipotent and good? – Yes. – Does omnipotent goodness have practical consequences? – Yes. – Will a good person who has the power prevent harm from befalling the innocent? – Yes. – Then will not almighty goodness prevent all harm from happening to all the innocent? – Mm. –Is there a single verifiable generalization about visible misfortunes which God will, or will not, permit to befall any definable class of people?'

Here is a pretty piece of discussion, but it is not a discussion about what anyone believes. The counter-attack may take the following form. 'For reasons already given it is not logically possible for you to deduce the way almighty goodness would have to work and then look round for factual verifications. But I can point out to you a self-revealing action of God in which He justifies His claim to almighty goodness. I am not prepared to discuss your risky deductions from metaphysical formulations

* Cf. Antony Flew, 'Theology and Falsification' in *New Essays in Philosophical Theology*, ed. Flew and MacIntyre, p. 96.

but I am prepared to defend the biblical affirmation that God is love.'

When St John said that God is love he was not engaged in cashing out a notion of supreme personality; he was finding a summary formula for what the action of God in the Christian story discloses. 'The God who has given his creatures a vestige of his likeness and who intervenes with incarnation and redemptive sacrifice to save them from natural perishableness and unnatural perversity, what is he shown by such actions to be? He is shown to be pure love.' That a premature and painful death is the likely consequence of 'accepting divine love' in the world of his day, St John knows and tells us in so many words. And yet the saving acts of God, in St John's eyes and in ours, give a full value to the analogical statement that God is love.

The impossibility of deducing the form of God's personal dealing with us from the mere notion of a supreme personal Being personally known, is a logical aspect of Revelation itself as Christendom understands it. To believe in God is doubtless to believe in a supreme personal Cause; yet His 'personality' is subject to negative qualification, and conviction dissolves in ambiguity when we try to decide how deep the qualifications go. But (our religion holds) while we are immobilized by logical mist, God sends us his *Logos*. We cannot fit our human similitudes on God, but God can, and does, take the human similitude on Himself, and in that form deal humanly with human creatures.

If Christ is called Word or Logos, it is not meant that he is the lucid instance of general ideas, but that he is the self-enacted human parable of Godhead. The Christian's last ditch of dogmatism about divine personality is this: God must be in such sense a personal agent that he can be said voluntarily to adopt and really to use the human forms of life and action. A Christian who admits difficulties about incarnation from the divine side stands his theology upon its head. What positive knowledge has he of the divine personality which could exclude incarnation? On the contrary, the divine personality is for him defined by incarnation; self-defined, indeed, and therefore 'revealed'.

We may call the Incarnation the self-enacted parable of God-head, to express the belief that the existence and action of Christ are the divine translation, almost the symbolization of the transcendent Life in human terms. But the phrase 'self-enacted parable' seriously misrepresents our faith if it suggests a play having no action outside the frame of the stage, except by working on the spectators as plays do work. Oberammergau plays the Passion of Christ, but the Passion of Christ was not an Oberammergau. The self-enacted parable of Godhead is parable relatively to the divine Being, but it is the very stuff of ours. If we act a parable of heavenly things we put it on a stage because we are not our own creators, and all we can make is an artificial arrangement. God is our creator, and what He makes is the creature. Man is in any case a reduced similitude, a parable of God; but in being this he is a natural man. And if it pleases God to deal with man through a more perfect similitude, through a man in whom He personally lives and acts, then what the Man does in the human sphere is no play but simple earnest. Christ does not save us by acting a parable of divine love; he acts the parable of divine love by saving us. That is the Christian faith.

III

If, in attempting to discuss revelation, we fall into writing sheer theology, it is not to be wondered at. 'The possibility or nature of revelation in general' appears to be the philosophical topic; but, as we have seen, it evaporates when we come to consider it. What we can show in general is not the possibility of revelation, but the impossibility of our forecasting the nature or bearing of God's personal action until He reveals it. Revelation is what God manifestly does, and is shown to be possible by His doing it. All we can do with it is to unfold it, to explain by any means we have what is said to have been received by those who claim to have received it; and this is just Christian, or some other, theology. There will be as many theologies as there are (supposed) revelations; and rival theologies, like the rival serpents of Moses and the magicians, will try which can swallow the rest. For every revelation which makes serious claims, claims universality, and no revelation doing that can leave rival claimants in the field. Either it must deny them, or it must annex them to itself as preludes, approximations, deviations. Here a vast field of comparative study opens; but this is evidently not the time to explore it. We already have too much on our hands if we confine ourselves to the revelation in which we believe.

The difficulty is, having once started, to stop anywhere. For if it is true that the mere notion of revelation is empty apart from the specification of a mode of revelation by the act of God, it is no less true that the specification of the mode is empty apart from the full particularity of its embodiment. The Christian idea of incarnation carries no conviction; what alone can convince us as reasonable, saving and divine is what incarnate Godhead does; and to expound this requires a whole theology. But at whatever risk of unreality we must pick a question. We cannot attempt a theology of what God Incarnate does; we will ask how what He does is received or recognized.

We may say this much about the Christian doctrine of salvation, that it concerns God's dealing with us. Now 'dealing with' involves two parties who must both be aware of one another's action. God is believed to dispose of us and of our destinies at all times, but that is not to say that He deals with us but rather (if the phrase can be tolerated) that He deals in us; it certainly does not mean that He is revealed to us. If Godhead had been incarnate under a complete incognito, what could have been the result? Those who had to do with Him would have to do with their Creator, but only as children who take it for quartz may handle diamonds; it is no handling of diamond to them. His companions would have felt the impact of divinely good life, and perhaps passed on the influence. It would have dwindled as it spread and left at length not a ripple on the surface of history.

The incarnation must be acknowledged. How can it be? There is no special difficulty in seeing how a number of persons should come round to the belief that one of their number is divine. We must agree that it has happened more than once (though with reservations on the meaning of the word 'divine'). The difficulty is to see what would make any one such belief or acknowledgment valid.

The question is ambiguous. In one sense what makes it valid is what the angelic spectator sees – that the fact is what it is taken for. In the other sense what makes it valid is what we can hope to appreciate – the criteria of validity. But what are they? In most fields of enquiry it is possible to set up models of argument and canons of proof. The usefulness of such aids varies greatly from one field to another. In the matter of revelation it must surely reach a vanishing point. If there is no *a priori* model for the form of God's self-disclosure, how can there be *a priori* canons for the marks of its authenticity? There is no major premiss which lays it down that every child virginally born, or every good man making divine claims, or every crucified man raised from the dead, is a Person of Godhead. There existed in the minds of Christ's contemporaries certain premisses about the supreme human instrument of divine intervention. The Gospels devote a surprising amount of space to the demolition of them.

We can nevertheless speak of criteria, and list them as preparatory, intrinsic and relative. The preparatory criteria are simply those of other sciences, such as history, which undertake the examination of the factual evidence. Yet even these do not operate with complete autonomy in the field of revelation. There are crucial pieces of evidence – say, for the Resurrection of Christ – about which the most believing historian will scarcely claim more than that they are very hard to explain away. He cannot call them historically conclusive. It will always remain open to the unbelieving historian to weigh the improbability of delusion or fraud on the part of the witnesses against what is to him the supreme improbability of the miracle, and to find the second improbability the greater. The believer's mental scale tips the other way. And why? Not because he is a more, or a less, scrupulous historian, but because to him the miracle, though naturally improbable, is divinely appropriate. His predicament is much like that of the apostles whose faith he shares. They knew that the return of the dead is the proverbial case of that which does not occur, and that those who meet the departed are deemed to see visions or to suffer delusion by spirits. Yet they allowed themselves to be convinced, not only because the event had the marks of reality, but also because it was the divinely appropriate conclusion to a train of events in which they had begun already to recognize the divine.

They were moved, that is, by the *intrinsic* criteria of revelation. These are nothing other than the character and structure of revelatory fact, not merely as first encountered, but as added up and gone over in every part. In the case we have referred to the intrinsic criteria enter the arena of the preparatory. Their first business is in their own; not, that is, in establishing certain parts of the evidence but in estimating the revelatory character of it all. *Intrinsic criterion* is a sort of oxymoron: it means that our decision, denied the aid of ready-made criteria, must be reached by a scrutiny of the thing itself; as happens, perhaps, when we judge the merit of any great and original work of art.

The *intrinsic criteria* are scarcely separable from the *relative* – we should not find revelation intrinsically convincing if everything else made nonsense of it, and it made nonsense of everything else.

When any of us believes, he believes a gospel which has been believed already. Our belief continues or prolongs the belief of others. It is difficult to think of an absolute first belief; but that, presumably, is the moment of revelation *par excellence*. The Christian scheme, in a sense, avoids this difficulty, or swallows it up in a greater. For the recognition of revealing action begins with Christ; He first, and in Himself, acknowledges divine presence. And if he was in truth the Divine Son it seems absurd to ask how he knew it; how could he have been ignorant of it?

What we are, however, driven to ask, even on the Christian hypothesis, is in what terms it was possible for Him to possess divine self-knowledge. For to be really a man at all He must be a

man of a certain time, race, and condition. A man-in-general is no
more to be met with than a beast-in-general. And in fact Christ
was a Galilean carpenter, a man deriving his mental stock from
family piety and Pharisaic preaching. If his thoughts were not
expressed in some individual modification of his cultural tradition
they were not human thoughts. To judge by the only evidence
we have, His reported words, they were so expressed. And here
is the paradox for believers: the stock of popular Jewish theology
provided no set of terms in which incarnation or metaphysical
divine sonship could be stated. And so his knowledge of what he
was scarcely could, and so far as we can see, never did, take the
form of definition. It was an ability to converse with the Divine
Father in the manner proper to a Divine Son; an ability to grasp
and communicate the function which was his among men. Can we
venture to apply a fashionable distinction and say that it was more
like a knowledge how to be what he was, than a knowledge of
what he was? Only if we observe the limitation of the distinction
when applied to a case like this. A knowledge how, and a knowledge that (or what) are perfectly distinct in such cases as the
performance of shots at tennis; to know how to make the shot is
to be able by paying heed to make it, and implies no power at all
to describe the movements one executes. But if we are to execute
a function which is both personal and not physically obvious, like
that of a man towards God, or towards men viewed in their relation with God, we may do very well without definitions, but we
shall not manage without some notions which represent to us our
standing in these relations. So far as we know, Christ found such
notions in the language of Jewish expectation about the Kingdom
of God and its visible head, King Messiah. Even so, He was not
content with it, but in using it greatly modified it, and so prepared
the development of Christian theology.

According to St Paul's words which we began by quoting, the
extension of the revelation beyond the person of Christ Himself,
involves the extension of 'the mind of Christ' to His disciples;
and this extension is not simply their taking of His words to
heart, it is the operation in them of a divine presence. Such is the

apostle's teaching, and it is suicidal for Christian theology to go
back upon his claim to direct inspiration. If the apostles of Christ
were not inspired the Christian is helpless. His knowledge of
Christ is through apostolic interpretation, and if the way to Christ
is by stripping off the interpretation rather than by applying it, the
Christian is left with no object of faith but an exegetical puzzle.
Again, apart from a claim, however modest, to a divine gift, the
Christian can say nothing rational about the fact that he believes,
while his perhaps equally well-instructed neighbour does not.
If the Gospel is credible to him it is that some touch of the
supernatural presence which the Gospel describes acts in his
mind.

In writing as we have done we have put things the wrong way
round. Belief in the inspiration of Christians, and to a higher
degree, of saints and apostles is no after-thought, no additional
article necessary for buttressing a faith already received. It is the
Christian's starting point. If he is confronted (as he believes) with
the divine, it is not in a historical figure whom he cannot directly
reach, but in a living and speaking faith which he encounters. To
him, Christ speaks through His apostle and both through living
Christians and also through the new believer's own heart. Every
part of the chain bears its own weight and no part can dispense
with the rest. The pull is felt as one divine action; subsequent
reflection separates the links and tests the strength of each.

And this is not all. If inspiration extends the mind of Christ in
His disciples, it seems we shall have to say that it had foreshadowed
the mind of Christ in his forerunners. For the thoughts of Christ,
as we have said, were built out of elements from older prophecy,
which He himself acknowledged and which He set Himself to
fulfil. The divine self-disclosure in the human mind never starts
from nowhere; even where the novelty is in a manner absolute,
as with Christ's knowledge of what He is and does, it is still out of
revelation that revelation grows. In looking through the eyes of
the prophets Christ was Himself illuminated; how much more His
apostles, in looking through the eyes of Christ.

Leaving Christ Himself aside there are still two degrees of

illumination, that of the ordinary believer and that of the prophet
or apostle. The illumination of the believer is his believing. The
faith proposed to him applies to his life and acts in his mind
sufficiently for him to believe it. He adds nothing to the content
or definition of the faith. To enlarge revealed truth is the function
of special inspiration. If it be asked how such inspiration is
possible there is, once more, almost nothing we can say that is of
general application. *If* God extends His self-disclosure by way of
inspiration He will convince His chosen instruments of the truth
they are to deliver. And if it be asked 'But how?' the dogmatic
answer must be 'Anyhow'. For God is not a particular 'cause' but
the 'First Cause' behind all 'causes', and all means worthy of Him
are in His hands. So it is vain to ask what is *the* means of His self-
disclosure to, or through, His prophets. If, on the other hand, we
turn from dogmatic principle to empirical enquiry, we open up a
fascinating field, but a field which contains all the variety of
particular biography and of cultural climate. It will be hard to find
any generalizations which have a genuine universality.

If we are approaching the histories of specially inspired men
we may nevertheless usefully look for the two phases, reflection
and ecstasy. By reflection, prophets have loaded their minds with
the divine truth they already claim to know, and with the present
standing of the people of God in God's sight as they are able to
conceive it. By ecstasy they experience in one of many forms that
condition of fertile passivity out of which new ideas and images
are commonly born. The crudest of the prophets worked themselves into a holy intoxication or used a means of divinatory pro-
jection comparable with crystal-gazing. The more advanced in
spiritual refinement needed no such aids; they could wait and
'listen' till the word came forth; or the moment fall on them
unexpected and unsought.

To suppose that the successive occurrence of such mental
motions guarantees divine revelation would be folly. The pattern
we have outlined is common to many processes: poetic invention,
intellectual discovery, personal decision. What is distinctive of
divine inspiration must be sought in the subject-matter, the pro-

duct, and the conviction of divine origin which accompanies it and which it is able to communicate.

Even so there is no intrinsic guarantee of validity. What is most precious has most counterfeits; the history of revelation is largely the history of false prophecy and a sifting of much sand to find a grain of gold. A number of complementary filters have gradually operated: the 'discernment of spirits', or scrutiny of the effect produced by the supposed revelation on the man who utters it; efficacy, or the tendency of his message to produce godly states in his hearers; orthodoxy, or the mutual support of all prophecies commended on other grounds; rationality, or agreement with conscience and good sense; and above all, applicability to fact.

The revelation which has won our acceptance has not been concerned with mere disclosures of things invisible or systems of supersensible being, but always with what has happened, is happening, or will happen; events in which the prophet claims to trace the hand and purpose of God. Before Christ, inspiration dealt with the calling and destiny of the people of God, and any prophecy casting Israel for a role which history disallowed was either crushed or new-minted by fact. In Christ Himself the duality between supernatural understanding and the fact to which it refers appears to be bridged, in so far as His teaching reveals the significance of what is accomplished through Himself; for He who declares the interpretation makes the fact. Yet by thus coalescing in one person with the fact it declares, the Word does not evade the hard control of factual necessity: the impenitence of the Pharisees, the interest of the Priests, the policy of Pilate. The Apostles of Christ and the Fathers who followed them were tied to the facts of the Gospel and controlled by the developing destiny of the Chruch.

Not that prophecy has ever been a mere attempt at divining facts to come, or describing facts present and past. Of past and present it gives not a natural description but a supernatural interpretation. The natural facts must bear it out but they cannot simply demand it. As for the future, prophecy hopes not so much to predict it as to shape it, by directing the course of the people of God. If they disobey they can still justify the prophecy by incurring the sanctions.

We placed the control of fact among five complementary checks on the validity of apparent revelations. But the operation of the checks is, to the believer, as much a part of revelation as any other, since the whole process is in the hands of God. It is thus that the canon of Scripture, and the Catholic creeds, come to be received as summaries of revealed truth. A long process of sifting and shaping went to the formation of both creed and Bible, and to the fixing of the sense in which either should be read; the refinement of interpretation never ceases.

It should be noted that the title of 'inspired' is conferred upon some considerable part of the Scriptures retrospectively. The Israelite law of property and the detailed story of Saul's battles are not, on any apparent evidence, the product of inspired pens. But the Church believes she has been inspired, or guided, to canonize what is required for the understanding of revelatory events.

'The Church believes.' Whatever sentences with this preamble may be, they are not philosophy. As we said before, he who attempts to philosophize about revelation will have nothing to philosophize about unless he first listens to a good deal of positive statement. If we have done nothing else, perhaps we have offered some raw material. If it is found to be indigestible and to repel rather than to tempt a philosophic appetite, let us hope that the fault does not lie in the exposition. It is no part of our business to commend our faith otherwise than as it commends itself, or to disguise difficulties which may serve to prompt philosophic reflection. We are not here to throw sand in anyone's eyes.

CHAPTER IV

HOW THEOLOGIANS REASON

by G. C. Stead

I

OUR present debate between faith and philosophy revolves upon the language of religion rather than its activities or institutions, and in particular on those religious pronouncements which appear to be statements about God or other transcendent beings, but which, it is said, cannot really function as statements because there is no possible or even conceivable method of testing their truth. It is convenient to refer to them as theological statements, and in a former chapter it was argued that despite its figurative and parabolic character there is a real sense in which such language can be said to state facts. But to complete the inquiry we shall have to pay some attention to that kind of religious discourse which is theological in the more precise sense, and consider the technical language of theology and the methods of argument used by theologians. If we can show what they consider valid reasons for belief in a religious doctrine, we shall no doubt also discover what they consider invalid reasons for belief, and again what they consider valid reasons for disbelief; and it may then appear that theologians, and ordinary believers, too, insist that what is in fact believed would have been refuted if certain conceivable events had occurred:

> Had Christ that once was slain
> Not burst his three-day prison
> Our faith had been in vain;
> But now hath Christ arisen.

This inquiry of course must be a co-operative affair. For who is to assess the meaning of theological expressions? Is it the philosopher, who alone really knows how words are used, or the theologian, who alone really knows how *these* words are used? Obviously we are putting a false antithesis. The philosopher is conversant with general theories about the significance of symbolic expression, of which theologians have little experience and simple believers still less. He advances broad schematic explanations of possible ways in which theological statements might be significant, which are attractive because they are relatively clearcut and seem to shed *some* light on a puzzling and only partly explored field of human behaviour. The theologian will always feel that such diagrams leave out important lights and shades; and sometimes, no doubt, that the philosopher has simply blundered for lack of knowledge.

Perhaps, indeed, we have already over-simplified the matter by talking of 'methods of argument used by theologians'. For whom are we to take as theologians? St John? St Athanasius? St Thomas? Calvin, Hooker, Barth? It would indeed enormously simplify my task if I could construe 'theologians' to mean 'those modern theologians whom I find congenial': but for reasons I hope to explain I shall not do so. But if we consider the giants of the past, we shall often be reluctant to say that *their* theological discourse amounts to argument. It's not what we call argument. St John is a particularly good example, since he habitually uses extremely simple, indeed primitive, modes of thought to express religious ideas of considerable subtlety. When, for instance (ix. 7), he makes Jesus say to the man born blind, 'Go and wash in the pool of Siloam, which is by interpretation Sent', the last five words are not an etymological digression; they are put there deliberately. We can, if we like, distil from the saying an argument to the effect that since none of the Lord's words were without inner significance, they show that spiritual cleansing is to be gained through baptism in the name of Jesus, who is ὁ ἀπεσταλμένος, the heaven-sent Messiah of Isaiah lxi. But how far is this an argument presented by St John? It is clear, from his use of irony elsewhere, that he aims at exploiting commonplace remarks in the interest of a symbolic meaning: they are, he would say, σημεῖα, signs.

The theology is profound, but the convention is archaic: it has the elusive, inexhaustible quality of poetry; it cannot be reproduced in prose.

Theology as a form of human culture resembles art, and to a lesser extent history and philosophy, rather than science, in the attention it invites and the authority it claims for its great historic exponents. Their personal insight and the tradition they inherit may well give theological value to writings phrased in an antiquated theological idiom, or whose theological purpose passes unnoticed. The theological work of one stage of early Christianity simply was to exhibit the life of Christ in a certain light. But it is unilluminating to say that all religious language is theological. Theology is marked off, not so much by the kind of language used as by the use made of it. Religious language becomes theological where there is a deliberate intention to support, to qualify or to relate the symbolic expressions of unreflective piety, though without necessarily abandoning the symbolic form. In Christian theology some classic controversies have turned on the questions, whether Christ was pre-existent; whether He was created; how He could be both God and Son of God: questions which arise naturally out of reflection on passages such as Col. i. 15; Prov. viii. 22; John x. 30. A formula used in answering the last question, that Christ was 'consubstantial with the Father' may serve as an example of the theologian's technical diction. It was adopted only after a struggle, in the course of which repeated attempts were made to state substantially the same doctrine in non-technical language drawn from the Bible. Part of its function is to lay down rules which govern the use of the original metaphor: Christ's sonship resembles human sonship in that it implies likeness of nature, but differs in not implying juniority. The formula has some resemblance with the scientist's descriptive apparatus, in that it connects this metaphorical expression, 'Son', with other metaphors for the relation between Christ and the Father, such as that of one lamp kindled from another, 'Light of Light', or a stream flowing from a fountain; it rules out certain natural inferences, such as that Christ is the Father's 'image' in the sense of a dim reflection or inferior copy; but it is not alleged to avoid all elements of metaphor or to afford precise insight into the subject to which it refers.

The dislike which even religious people often feel for theology is no doubt provoked by its technical language and summary statements; the dogmatist, with his pat verbal answers to perennial human ponderings and strivings, seems to be making light of ultimate mysteries. Religion without theology has often been proposed, and the proposal is still tempting to the spiritually-minded empiricist, whose fresh appreciation of the non-descriptive uses of human discourse encourages him to think of religious language as a mythology which embodies valuable emotional attitudes and perhaps some genuine insight into spiritual possi-bilities: yet in an elusive, individual, poetic idiom which cannot be reduced to logic. For him, the dogmatic theologian fails at all points: the magic and mystery is lost in his dusty prose, the symbols and metaphors are concealed but not reduced and no real precision is gained. And if religious documents such as the New Testament embody theological arguments (as St Paul and Hebrews certainly do), then so much the worse for them.

But to eliminate, not theological technicalities, but theological activity itself, we should have to go much further. We should, for instance, have to sacrifice the Gospels, for modern scholars have rightly emphasized the theological aims especially of Mark and John; indeed there is hardly a book in the Bible which is not coloured by a deliberate effort to comment on, or align itself by, some earlier form of the tradition. Suppose, then, we simply ignore the theological aims of religious writers and refresh our souls on a devotional residuum? The devotional use of scripture is all-important; but to make it the only use, and demand that religious language be not sifted or criticized, is open to two objections. First, it argues lack of appreciation: if the biblical writers them-selves are influenced by theological motives, you cannot under-stand them if these are not considered. Secondly, it is impossible to sustain in practice: interpretations and assumptions spring up unawares, and if there were no such thing as truth and error in religion, decisions would still be needed to prevent individuals and churches drifting into divergent theologies. Theological controversies have in fact generally turned on a divergence which was held to be intolerable in a community professing 'one faith'. Indeed they often turn precisely on the question whether some text in the Bible is to be taken literally or not. Are we to press Paul's phrase πρωτότοκος πάσης κτίσεως (Col. i. 15) and if so, in what sense? Is Christ simply the first in the series of created things, as the Arians taught, or is He 'begotten before all creation'? But if we do not press it, if we dismiss it as a mere devotional compliment, we are not avoiding a theological decision: we are already fellow-travellers with the Adoptionists.

But clearly it is not enough to show that some form of theological activity is inescapable for religious people. We need to defend technical theology, for instance by showing that summary, credal statements have a logically legitimate function; at least, as controlling and checking the use of religious imagery; if possible, as themselves the starting-point for fresh, and less technical, outgrowths of religious thought. They may not in themselves afford any insight; but they can be unpacked into statements that do.

But are they themselves really statements? Most modern theologians, no less than St Athanasius, would certainly conceive themselves to be arguing for propositions. Creeds and articles, if they are to do their job, must be what they appear to be, namely carefully phrased assertions. Whether or not they treat of supernaturalia like God or the future life does not greatly affect their setting in theological discourse. They are intended partly as models, partly as tests* of the language of actual worship. This is not to deny them any expressive or declaratory functions at all; these are indeed attested by the devotional use of the Creeds; but theologians would regard the latter as a mere application of their primary assertive and regulative use.

* Cf. the commonly accepted view that Creeds originated within the baptismal service and developed into tests of orthodoxy. See e.g. J. N. D. Kelly, *Early Christian Creeds*, pp. 205–07.

How should the philosopher react? He cannot be expected merely to endorse the theologians' account of their activities, and assume that the considerations they advance in support of a doctrine amount to arguments for it, or reveal its logical functions as those which these arguments actually justify. But his theories must be controlled by a sound working knowledge of how theological statements are actually used. Consider, for instance, the theory that they are 'really' concealed exhortations. What is it intended to assert? Presumably it is an attempt to assess theological statements purely from the point of view of their logical effect, without paying any attention to literary-critical categories. Whereas the theologian professes to use symbolic statements, making obscure but would-be informative references to heavenly mysteries, and having ethical overtones, the sceptical philosopher regards the mythological elements as logically non-significant; so that the ethical residuum is the only element he can recognize. This is rather as if one should say of a machine whose function one does not appreciate, that all it does is to generate a little heat by friction. This is understandable, but may be misleading. It will not do to say that a roulette-wheel is really a kind of stove.

On this assumption, too, one can make nothing of the *texture* of theological argument, which purports to use statements of belief in support of moral counsels, and to support these statements by further reasons. Suppose the philosopher approaches St Paul with the presumption that 'God loves all men' really means 'Love for all men is the supremely valuable quality' (or 'is a disposition I hereby avow'*), what is he to make of the considerations which are used to support it, for instance the argument about rains and fruitful seasons reported in Acts xiv. 17? He might consistently reply that the real function of the latter is to illustrate the disposition commended by means of a familiar myth; but the unplausibility of this suggestion is at once disclosed when one compares the text with Matthew v. 45, which could lend itself to such a sceptical interpretation. St Paul is clearly

* So, most recently, R. B. Braithwaite, *An Empiricist's View of the Nature of Religious Belief*, esp. pp. 18, 19.

arguing. He may indeed be operating with mythological conceptions whose only obvious use is to commend φιλανθρωπία, but his language is not the language of commendation, and does not entitle us to infer that his mythology is baseless. The argument, again, may be a weak one; it is in fact much the same as figured in the recent parable of the Invisible Gardener*; but no one has ever supposed that this was concerned with an argument that it is good to look after gardens.

It seems to me quite evident that the whole class of statements used by theologians do not show any significant logical similarity: we should not dream of approaching, say, history or economics with any such assumption. But I am also very doubtful whether it is possible to make useful logical generalizations about the more limited category of statements about God. Let us approach this point by considering how such statements stand up to a well-known verificationist difficulty, the so-called 'double-think' argument. It is said of many religious affirmations that if taken in a literal sense they are clearly false, but if so qualified as to avoid falsity they lose all significance: the 'analogy is eroded': and the believer is represented as oscillating between a literal acceptance of religious symbolism to gain substance for his belief, and elaborate qualification to protect it from disproof.†

This argument was worked out in connexion with the statement 'God is love', which is presumably a statement common to the theologian and the simple believer. We are told that, as ordinarily interpreted, it conflicts with observed facts (such as innocent suffering); but that, when taxed with these, the believer is liable to qualify or dilute his statement rather than abandon it: 'Ah, but *God's* love doesn't necessarily imply. . . .' A supporting argument is that the believer himself professes that his belief in God's love would be maintained in any conceivable set of circumstances; but if *nothing* would disprove it, then it denies nothing, which is to say that it affirms nothing. In this case the counsel for

* See John Wisdom, *Gods*, in *Logic and Language*, Vol. I, pp. 192–4.

† See Antony Flew in *New Essays in Philosophical Theology*, pp. 96–8, 108.

the defence will naturally dwell on the scope of divine operations: in a scheme so vast, many apparent cruelties may consort with a beneficent whole design. It may, indeed, be enough to point to an ambiguity in the phrase 'any conceivable set of circumstances'. Any conceivable set of circumstances is at least theoretically reconcilable with divine love, *provided it is not the whole story*. But not, of course, any conceivable total history of the universe.

But if we take the specimen article that 'Christ is of one substance with the Father', this seems to derive its justification and use from a more limited range of facts. It seems primarily intended as a comment on remarks about Jesus, such as 'Truly this man was the Son of God' (Mark xv. 39). Both text and comment, as Christian writers fully acknowledge, are analogical statements which could be taken in a sense which is irrelevant and absurd rather than obviously falsifiable. But the original text is one to which particular historical data are relevant. It is unlikely, but theoretically possible, that evidence should turn up that Jesus was a bad man. Certain other admitted facts, e.g. his suffering, raise difficulties and suggest further questions. Is God then capable of suffering? Is there something more in Christ than the 'He' that suffered? Should we draw distinctions within the term 'suffering', which might perhaps also apply to the saints? The exact positive content of the text is hard to specify: it characterises Jesus in terms of already-accepted notions of Divinity; does it also imply that the universe is governed by a personality akin to Jesus?

This discussion suggests to me not only that theological statements are logically rather heterogeneous, but also that they possess in a high degree the characteristic of 'open texture'.* The theologian is concerned to state things, and it may be essential to the usefulness and suggestiveness of his statement that its connotation is not precisely delimited. 'God is love' raises insoluble difficulties if 'love' is taken to mean 'unlimited kindness': but not because there is a different and exactly definable meaning of 'love' which is the right meaning. The religious thinker is still experimenting: in the face of suffering he reflects that love is sometimes

* See F. Waismann, 'Verifiability,' in *Logic and Language*, Vol. I, p. 119.

exercised by stern discipline: there is loving correction. Yes, but *innocent* suffering? Then one might liken God not to a conscientious disciplinarian but to the parent sending his child away to school. For the sake of the child's development he is prepared to relinquish some of his control. Perhaps this image in turn will need modification, so we shall not trust it implicitly. Meanwhile it is perhaps enough to show that the religious thinker's response to a challenge is not always a withdrawal: he reinterprets his statements by envisaging fresh analogies as well as retracting weak ones. How far this procedure is analogous to scientific theorising I must leave it to the expert to decide.

II

I have stressed the value of classical theology; but it would, I think, be unreasonable to expect it to be accurately trained to meet the modern empiricist's attack. Much of it is indeed argumentative and controversial: but in such cases it has been mainly concerned with objections that Christian doctrine is false or unproven – together of course with complaints that it is trivial, harsh, impracticable, enervating or whatever else its opponents may have urged. Theologians have seldom encountered the charge 'This is not an assertion at all', 'There is nothing here that one can either believe or disbelieve'. They have, of course, seen that assertions about unobservables raise special difficulties, but not that they raise *these* difficulties; so the methods by which they have sought to justify or criticize beliefs about God are not very sharply marked off from those which they use in other cases. One finds the same basic ingredients, appeal to tradition, appeal to scripture, appeal to non-Christian writers of repute, and so on.

This diversity of sources is characteristic. Theology has in the course of its history developed into a complex of studies integrated by certain traditional assumptions about the world and God but not penetrated by a common method. It has always drawn a large part of its material from outside sources. In the Old

Testament we find a borrowing of pagan myths, such as the flood story, which is re-told as a lesson of God's indignation, mercy and faithfulness, and a borrowing of tribal legend, which under the assumption of divine intervention becomes the record of the wars of the Lord. In patristic times we find wholesale borrowings of Platonic-Stoic natural theology and ethics, which eventually found a place in the scholastic synthesis and may presumably be treated as more or less permanent endowments of Christian thought. But this borrowing extends to methods as well as material; and nowadays a great number of specialized techniques, with their own distinctive employments and rules, become theological when they are applied to the Church considered as a divine institution and the Bible considered as the Word of God. So theologians rub shoulders with atheists in the discussion of history, archæology, anthropology, philology and philosophy, and it is hard to say at what point in these studies their theological convictions prompt them to take a distinctive line.

This situation finds its characteristic expression in the doctrine that there are two sources of religious knowledge, namely Reason* and Revelation. The two need not be absolutely separated; if speculative thought be conceived as the exercise of man's *God-given* talents, it takes on some of the attributes of Revelation; and Revelation, it may be said, requires reason for its apprehension. But Revelation, as traditionally interpreted, indicates certain specific channels of God's self-disclosure. Three such are commonly recognized, namely scripture, tradition, and the believer's own religious intuition and experience so far as it is penetrated by God's grace, or by the Holy Spirit.†

Theologians differ widely in the relative weight which they

* The rejection of human reason as a source of religious knowledge is characteristic of the Barthian theology, but not of Protestantism as a whole: see A. M. Paterson, *The Rule of Faith*, p. 94; E. J. Bicknell, *The Thirty-nine Articles*, pp. 52–3, and books referred to, *ib.*, p. 449.

† The still simpler and commoner grouping of scripture, tradition and reason as the three sources of theological knowledge perhaps under-emphasizes the individual's responsibility for spiritual judgment, which is recognized by so judicious a conservative as Bicknell, *op. cit.*, pp. 273–4.

assign to these various grounds of theological argument. In practice, however, it is not always possible to present a reasoned case based on any one of them taken singly. If to my question 'Why accept this?' you answer 'Because the Church teaches it,' I may counter 'But why accept the Church's authority?' You may then quote scripture, relying on my accepting the authority of Christ and also your interpretation of his words; or else you may appeal to my reasoned judgment on the Church's actual achievements. These seem to be reasonable and apposite replies; so it does not look as if, in 'Why accept the Church's authority?' we have reached an *impasse* like 'Why do your duty?' On the other hand, if you lead off with 'Because the Bible says so,' I may counter by challenging your choice and interpretation of biblical texts, inquire what kind of authority you claim for scripture, and so on; and here again you may be ready to reply.

It is indeed often possible to classify theologians according to their working principles of decision. They are traditionalists if they regard the question as to the Church's authority as a *chose jugée*, so that the practical criterion is whether a given practice or belief conforms to the tradition of the Church. They are biblicists if they assume that questions can be settled (according to some established convention) by consulting scripture. They are (shall we say?) modernists if they hold that tradition and scripture are mainly instruments for recording and conserving religious ideas which are imparted and acquired, under God, through the believer's experience. But many theologians, and perhaps the greatest, will not fit easily into any such class; who could claim exclusive kinship with Augustine? And the methods used to establish the initial propositions of a theological system are not necessarily the same as are used for settling 'domestic' issues within a general scheme of Christian presuppositions.

Let us try to examine these principles one by one. The theologian writes from within a religious tradition, and considers himself the servant of that tradition and the community to which it is entrusted. But by adhering to that community of believers he throws in his lot with simple and primitive people, and assumes responsibility for expressions couched in simple and primitive language. Although he may claim a teacher's liberty to interpret and revalue traditional dogma, his rights in this matter are restricted. The philosopher may, if he chooses, reject his predecessors' theories as mistaken; and if natural piety urges that it would be folly to ignore the teaching of so much greater and wiser, though less experienced, a predecessor as Plato, yet this allegiance is not part of his duty as a philosopher. The theologian, however, believes that God has revealed Himself to and in his predecessors; he accepts this belief in various formulations, themselves theological and traditional (e.g. God's choice of Israel, the Holy Spirit's guidance of the Church) and by it he is committed to treating the primitive experience and formulations as revelatory and authoritative for himself.

Over long periods in the Christian Church there has in fact been no overt recognition of the possibility of progress in theology, and theological debates have often turned on whether a doctrine conforms with the decision of an authoritative body; thus whereas the Nicene fathers were criticized in their day for going beyond scripture, a mere hundred years later the Christian teacher would commend his doctrines as simply republishing the faith of Nicaea.* Innovation has generally been discountenanced, and perhaps this may be defended on practical grounds in matters where so much is obscure: new revelations can look after themselves, it may be said; the main function of a religious institution is to defend and preserve the doctrines already received against dilution or corruption.

Nevertheless it is clear that theological thinking does not stand still. Not all apparent change is significant; some of it may be explained as mere defensive manœuvring to support what is substantially the same position against attacks from another quarter. But change there is, and the progress of historical research has tended to prevent the anachronistic reinterpretation

---

* See Athanasius, *de Decretis* I, and the note in Robertson's translation; also the documents translated in T. H. Bindley, *Œcumenical Documents of the Faith*[4], pp. 209, 221, 223, 232, 234.

of earlier writers which disguised it in the past. One cannot now maintain *tout court* that the Church is merely republishing the faith of the Fathers. How then is one to reconcile this apparent change with the traditional claim to a final and sufficient Revelation? One answer, favoured by many Roman Catholics, is a theory of doctrinal development which recognizes new formulations of doctrine made under the guidance of the Holy Spirit. They are said to be 'explications' of what was implicitly taught in the primitive tradition; which, if true, avoids the objectionable charge of adding new *doctrines* to a faith that was thus formerly incomplete. Officially, however, this view has been disowned, and the Roman position is that the beliefs that have recently been made obligatory were always part of unwritten Christian tradition, even though nowhere attested in Scripture or in the other earliest Christian writings.

So far, for simplicity's sake, we have been discussing the notion of tradition as something handed down *within* the Church; should we not perhaps rather think of it as something handed over *to* the Church: the original saving message of the death and resurrection of Christ?* Christianity is the interpretation of certain historical events; to add to them would be presumptuous, to supersede them would be to introduce a new religion. And verbally speaking I think there would be very general agreement among Christians in acknowledging one unchanging Revelation, a *depositum fidei* entrusted to the keeping of the Church which the theologian has to expound anew to each generation. But this appeal to the original message, or the original events, though an important and distinctive characteristic of Christianity does not enable us to step outside the field of religious tradition in its ordinary sense. For Christ's life was lived within the religious traditions of Judaism; it was from the first interpreted as the fulfilment of Old Testament prophecy† and our earliest reports of it are framed in tradi-

---

* See G. L. Prestige, *Fathers and Heretics*, pp. 1–22, and other works noticed in R. P. C. Hanson, *Origen's Doctrine of Tradition*, pp. 31–39.

† By Christ Himself, according to St Luke iv. 21, 'This day is this scripture fulfilled in your ears'.

tional language by a worshipping community for the purpose of teaching and commending their faith. The attempts of historical critics to cut away this 'dogmatic' matrix have involved them in unsupported theorizing and have generally failed to carry conviction. But Christians, too, have their problems of interpretation. Here is a life which revolutionized the Jewish tradition, yet which could not have been significant without the interpretative terms which that tradition itself supplied. To it all Christian tradition must submit, yet we must to some extent defer to that tradition before we can approach it. How can one do justice alike to its claim to absolute authority and to its relevance to its historical setting, and again to its continued representation in the Church's teaching? It has always been easy to lose grip of the Incarnation, to see it as a mere incident in the long process of divine self-disclosure to Israel and Christendom; or alternatively to confront it with too stark and individualistic and subjective an appraisal, neglecting the lessons which other generations of Christians have been better able to read.

One logical point must be made here. The question 'What agrees with tradition?' may be a question for decision as well as a question of evidence. To take a rather simple example, the Western Church used to worship in Latin when Latin was the common speech of everyday life. Does one follow their tradition by retaining the use of Latin, or by adopting the common speech of to-day? Here the changing circumstances force us to choose which of two features we shall perpetuate. The choice is not an arbitrary one; it is made in the light of evidence; for instance, the fact that the Roman Church itself spoke Greek until about A.D. 200 is a precedent for change; and the Roman communion of to-day, which still officially regards the Latin Vulgate as the only authorized version of Scripture, has gone some way along the path struck out by the Reformers in enjoining worship in the common tongue. Similar problems may arise in dealing with early documents, the Scriptures included, where translation itself forces us to choose which of various nuances we shall reproduce. The simplest text will not *automatically* give us a theological decision or moral ruling in terms of to-day; and more serious problems arise when we have doctrines formulated not merely in a dead language but in terms of an obsolete metaphysics. Thus even such a crucial decision as the dogma that in God there are *tres personae, treis hypostaseis,* cannot of itself determine how we are to *expound* the apparently obvious translation, 'three persons', or what we shall say about God in terms of 'personality'; and a contemporary debate about the Trinity can be presented as a debate about the 'true modern equivalent of the Greek *hypostaseis* and Latin *personae*'.* Such a question cannot be settled by history and lexicography alone, though God forbid we should discard them; we still have to argue, and therefore to restate, the 'essential' or 'permanent' force of the original definition, which in turn calls for an artistic sense of the likely force and effect of possible modern formulations. Whatever else the theologian is, in aligning himself by tradition he must be something of a historian, something of a philologist and something of a literary craftsman.

For reasons such as these, theology not only does not, but cannot, stand still. Thought and labour are needed to preserve the Christian tradition from corruption and loss, to ensure that it is still understood and explained. Can we go further and admit that it may be *better* understood and explained? This would seem logical if we allow the contribution to theology of human reason. Men do not become wiser or more intelligent, but they may gain in experience, and have notably improved their means of recording and exchanging information. The modern theologian stands far from the Incarnation compared with Paul, his spirituality pales beside Augustine's; but he may well be (through no merit of his own) a far better scholar than Jerome, and there is no reason for him to undervalue the gifts which Jerome so evidently sought.

There is thus nothing controversial about a 'development of doctrine' understood simply as a process of reformulating traditional teaching and relating it to contemporary language. And we should maintain that the Church in its work of reinterpretation is

* See L. Hodgson in the *Journal of Theological Studies*, N.S. V, April, 1954.

not using its resources unaided but under divine guidance, subject always to its essential continuity with the teaching of Christ. Nevertheless controversies are bound to arise when it is actually claimed that the Spirit has guided the Church, or some part of it, to make a new and authoritative exposition of the original Revelation. For by what tests can one distinguish legitimate explications of doctrine from mere novelties or aberrations? The notion of organic development will not help us much: the Church belongs to no species, so there is no criterion for normal as opposed to pathological growth; and the metaphor of growth itself tends to suggest that any change is allowable provided it comes about gradually, and to deny that truth may be recovered by comparatively drastic movements; as, at some cost, we believe it was at the Reformation. We cannot discuss this problem at length, except to say that the claim that some doctrine or institution is a proper or right *development* of primitive practice depends largely on one's historical judgment of primitive institutions and teaching. We are here in a position familiar to historians: a puzzle about the right reading of the known facts is aggravated by large uncertainties due to gaps in the evidence. It is only rarely that one can convict an opponent of positive errors of fact, or that new data turn up to cut short the debate. In default of these, historical judgments have to be appraised as 'fair' or 'legitimate' or 'inadequate' or 'partial' rather than as simply right or wrong; and the criteria used in settling theological problems in the light of tradition are probably more like these than like any other, and involve the same appeal to learning, humility, fairmindedness and respect for the facts. Given these qualities, to share the life of the Church to-day will make one a better judge of what that Church has thought and experienced in the past; and the Church, which lives by its history, should always harbour and respect these gifts.

The claim that the Church may now decide that certain doctrines formed *part* of the original tradition raises rather different problems. It is common ground that the original Christian message was propagated by the spoken word; and even those who hold that its essential elements were incorporated in the New

Testament might perhaps admit that other authentic beliefs continued to circulate as oral traditions during the early centuries. One would expect such a pool of unwritten tradition to be limited in its content, and to be progressively decanted into written documents, while it would be unwise to discount the growth of mere legend; and in fact we find that whereas the writers of the second century such as Papias and Irenaeus attach importance to oral traditions within the Church, they do themselves commit them to writing; and further that from the third century onwards the emphasis falls more and more on the sufficiency of Scripture, and 'tradition' comes to mean something like 'the Church's accepted understanding of Scripture'.

If one now claims for a doctrine such as that of the bodily Assumption of the Virgin* that it was preserved as an authentic oral tradition, the claim is in principle a simple one, but it is almost entirely unsupported by evidence. The doctrine is ignored by a vast mass of early Christian writings, many of which profess to summarize the essential truths of Christianity. The claim has to be supported on *a priori* grounds, which means in effect that we argue backwards from theology to history. 'But don't all Christians do this?' Yes, to some extent; such considerations are widely used, for instance, in arguments about the Virgin Birth. But it is one thing to argue thus for a belief accepted by a great weight of undisputed Christian tradition in the light of acknowledged early and scriptural testimony; it is quite another matter to postulate a tradition, unsupported by early evidence, on the ground, it would seem, that the doctrine coheres with the rest of the Church's teaching and is therefore true, and that what is true must always have been believed. To most of us such arguments seem forced and unreal. But it is only right to observe that a large body of Christian opinion is prepared to argue for doctrines beyond the range of scripture or acknowledged tradition on the grounds:

* There are, of course, two distinct questions: Is the doctrine true? and, is it an essential truth in which belief should be demanded? Some Anglicans (e.g. Dr E. L. Mascall) would answer 'Yes' to the first, but 'No' to the second.

(a) that they have been endorsed by 'the true Church', which is *ex hypothesi* the authorized interpreter of doctrine, (b) that their truth is attested by their devotional usefulness, and (c) that they have been confirmed by visions which the Church has accepted as authentic; though even here Roman Catholic apologists will be concerned to show that they are at least consonant with the teaching of Scripture.

The controversy may be traced back to differing conceptions of the Spirit's work in the Church. One party attaches preponderant weight to the doctrine of an infallible Church as a necessary guardian and interpreter of divine Revelation, and is disposed to see consistent historic tendencies (e.g. the growth of Papal authority, or of devotion to the Virgin) as divinely guided developments, even if they tend away from primitive practice; or alternatively, to argue that primitive practice must have been more 'developed' than the evidence appears to suggest. At the opposite extreme are theories which attach no importance at all to tradition, which see the Spirit as working through the impact of Scripture on the individual believer, and which are prepared to redefine the term 'Church' in non-historical terms, as a community of 'faithful' (which implies 'like-minded') people. Anglicans believe that the Holy Spirit has indeed guided the historic Church, but that its guidance does not simply overrule all frailty and liability to error. They assign supreme authority to Scripture, as we shall see; and next to it, to the pronouncements of the *undivided* Church as its interpreter: but (with much weight of tradition on their side) they argue that God has not willed to reveal all that human curiosity pursues, but what is necessary to salvation. And all that is necessary to salvation may be proved from Scripture.

III

Our discussion of tradition has, we hope, served to explode the notion of Scripture, tradition and Christian experience as three independent witnesses. Tradition seems rather to be an inclusive

term for the Church's worship and thought, whereas Scripture is
the focus of tradition and the authoritative source to which it
recurs. But the concept of Scripture needs further discussion.
The early Church, together with its preaching about Jesus and
the Resurrection, inherited a body of scripture from Judaism,
and a tradition of exegesis in which the contemporary Jewish
insistence on exact literal examination was modified, first by the
freer exposition adopted by Jesus and next by allegorizing
methods already current among the Stoics and their Jewish
imitators. As the 'good news' about Jesus and its early explications
came to be written down, a body of Christian literature came into
being which was ultimately isolated and accorded the same sort of
authority in the Church's life as the scriptures of the Old Testament already possessed; and the resulting documents, with
relatively minor disagreements (e.g. over the status of the
Apocrypha, or the relative authority of the Hebrew, Greek and
Latin versions) have been regarded as divinely inspired by all
branches of the Christian Church, and the source of its essential
doctrines.

Now the doctrine that all the essential truths of Revelation are
contained in Scripture requires in its turn a logical assessment. It
can be used as a plain statement of policy; in this sense, it attests
a determination to accept as essential truths only those doctrines
which scripture contains: and for the moment we may pass over
the possible disagreements, already noted, on the form and content of scripture, and also the attempts made on controversial
grounds to enlarge the sense of what is 'contained' in scripture
or 'may be proved' from it. But the doctrine usually has wider
implications; for the biblicist usually wants to claim that he
stands within the stream of Christian tradition, and to justify his
selection of 'essential' truths in the light of what the primitive
Church regarded as essential. Hence he holds that all the elements
of the primitive Christian message which were regarded as
essential were incorporated into the New Testament; he opposes
all theories of tradition which stress the importance of extra-
biblical doctrines in the early Church. This is in the main a

historical judgment. Clearly there can be no *conclusive* empirical test of a doctrine's being generally recognized or regarded as important; scholars, for example, may differ on the importance attached to the Roman See in the Second Century, although a great many facts are agreed, and perhaps no completely coercive piece of evidence could be imagined. But new evidence may at any time appear to strengthen or weaken such claims; even such a detail as the original Greek of certain passages in Irenaeus would be worth knowing since many Christians would attach considerable weight to Irenaeus' views, as representing a large body of orthodox opinion.

It would take too long to enlarge on the subject of Scriptural exegesis, which is a concern of every Christian community and has a complicated history. Theories of verbal inspiration, which justify deductions based on the precise wording of scriptural phrases, have enjoyed wide popularity, and the working method often survives where the theory is discredited. Other well-known landmarks are the allegorical method and the theory of progressive revelation. The present-day theologian who wishes to present a rationale of his use of scripture finds his task complicated by philological and archaeological techniques adopted from other fields of study. For,

(1) He is, he thinks, in many ways better equipped than his predecessors to understand what the biblical texts meant to their writers; but his findings may therefore conflict with interpretations which the Church has long used and valued. (This difficulty is not in principle a new one. A classic case is the rendering of Isaiah vii. 14; St Justin, *c*. A.D. 150, is already combating the argument that the Hebrew original does not support the rendering 'a *virgin* shall conceive'.*)

(2) He is interpreting what is in part a historical record, and has to determine how far it is essential to uphold its historical accuracy. Practice here varies very widely; very few theologians would now wish to maintain the literal historical accuracy of the whole Old Testament; however there are certain facts (for

* Justin, *Dialogue with Trypho*, p. 67.

example, the main outlines of the life of Christ) which all theologians would feel pledged to uphold.

Now the point is often made that it is one's *prior* convictions
which determine one's attitude to the evidence. The easy retort
is that of course this is so while the existing evidence is indecisive;
but new evidence does in fact come in, which sometimes confirms
and sometimes shakes the conclusions of orthodox theology. But
one must admit this does not entirely dispose of the argument,
which may be discussed in its wider implications.

It may seem that the theologian's work is vitiated by the fact
that he is pledged to arrive at orthodox conclusions; his declara-
tions of faith and the stigma attached to apostasy make it hard to
see how he can weigh the evidence impartially; or it may be felt
that, although he is unconscious of conflict, yet his worship
prepares him to accept a kind of satisfaction which is not the
intellectual satisfaction that convinces the ordinary doubter.
From the orthodox side it can be replied that religious conviction
quite properly depends on participation in religious activities:
religious phenomena are simply not accessible unless one makes
some kind of (at least provisional) assent to religious doctrine;
(as will be argued,* they can only be described in theistic terms).
Again, that although Christian theologians are often less quickly
shaken by sceptical arguments than the sceptic would like (and
after all, no one who has a complex and far-reaching system of
beliefs will quickly abandon it), yet they are not simply imper-
vious to difficulties and objections; so it looks as if they share the
intellectual values of their critics.

From the practical apologetic point of view, of course, it is
important that Christians do make an effective contribution to
science and philosophy and history, and appear to import the
same standards of critical accuracy into their theological work.
The sceptic presumably regards them as candid and able men who
have just this one unfortunate perversity; and it is by way of a
partial answer to this charge that I have been at pains to point out
the part played by the ordinary intellectual disciplines within

* In Chapter VI.

theology and the extremely complicated interplay between ordinary logic, technical expertise, critical assessment, experience and moral decision that many of its arguments demand.

Now the same basic view of religion as a closed system of thought that cannot be penetrated by rational processes, but only by an initial and irrational decision, underlies a similar criticism which is presented from the point of view of the inquirer. We said earlier on that arguments about the Church may lead to questions about the Bible, as the record of its commissioning, and arguments about the Bible may lead to questions about the Church in its role of authorized expositor. Does this not result in a circular argument? It has become apparent that the question is misleading: Church and Bible are far too closely interlocked to be treated as two independent witnesses confirming each other's story. But it is worth reminding ourselves that no process of proof can silence an ingenious objector. So we may represent apologetic arguments as attempts to conduct an inquirer from a point where his agreement may be presumed towards assent to the historic Christian affirmations; agreeing within limits on the goal to be reached, but differing very widely in their initial presumptions and the kind of judgment they require. A simple argument from testimony assumes that he will assent to the suggestion that Jesus was a man of outstanding spiritual insight, whose judgment on spiritual matters must commend respect: the next step is to show that he claimed Divinity: *aut Deus, aut homo non probus.* If this argument be represented as not only persuasive but valid, it presupposes that the inquirer has some means at least of recognizing a wise and spiritual man. The traditional scheme of Revelation and Reason has rather different expectations and may be presented so as to consort with an institutionalist-authoritarian religious praxis; the inquirer is challenged on the plane of rational argument; from accepted opinions and visible phenomena he is led on to certain basic doctrines of theism; but specifically Christian doctrines are not commended in this way; they are described as revealed, which carries the implication that they are not open to argument *ab extra*, although notoriously they are the subject of argument among theologians working within a scheme of Christian presuppositions. At the opposite pole, the evangelical preacher clearly presupposes a directly religious judgment. He stands in the tradition of the prophets; he calls upon his hearers to recognize the Word of God, of which his preaching is but the instrument.

The extraordinary difference in these methods of approach is due, I think, to their being simplifications which are necessary and allowable for practical purposes but which are inevitably selective and may well misrepresent themselves from the epistemological point of view. The first pattern of argument assumes in practice that the inquirer has inherited a basic pattern of Christian theological judgments without the belief in Christ which is their historical focus; a man brought up in an entirely different religious tradition would simply fail to appreciate an argument presented in this form, and in his case the debate would have to begin at a quite different point. In the last case the preacher assumes a 'notional' assent to the Bible which however lacks depth and conviction: his intention is to bring the text forcibly before his hearers' imaginations: he does not, and cannot, simultaneously explain that what he is in fact preaching is one among a number of possible interpretations of scripture, for which there are historical reasons and theological justifications of varying worth. And the traditional arguments of natural theology can of course be presented fairly simply; but they cannot be made both simple and relevant in the way in which they were first propounded. The thoughtful modern critic does not naturally raise the same difficulties as his medieval forbears and will hardly respond to the traditional arguments – unless one can convince him that he *ought* to share the presuppositions on which they are based. And this is indeed attempted by some modern defenders of scholasticism. But if one simply cuts the knot by taking 'reason' to mean 'what the Church has traditionally understood by reason' and uses the Church's authority to commend a particular brand of philosophy, this is only a roundabout way of arguing from the authority of the Church. Our assumption has been that 'reason' must indicate an attempt to meet the honest inquirer on his own ground; to meet his intellectual difficulties at the same time as one tries to enlarge his experience and deepen his sympathies. But to attempt a rational justification of the '*philosophia perennis*' in this sense is a complex and heroic undertaking; no less complex, in fact, than the rather more radical reconstruction attempted in this volume of essays.

One of the most important features of modern empiricism is its determination to grapple honestly with difficulties and complexities in our use of language and to avoid over-simple solutions. This essay is an attempt to show what theology looks like when regarded from this point of view. From this point of view it must appear complex. But philosophy is not everything. Philosophy, like theology, is a vocation in which we have duties and responsibilities; but it is not the whole of our life.

CHAPTER V

THE SOUL

by J. R. Lucas

THERE is a certain sense of uneasiness nowadays in talking about the soul. This for three reasons. It is partly that our way of using the word is an unfortunate one which invites misconstruction. Our first attempts to think clearly about the soul are liable to be vitiated by unconscious analogies. Our attempts end in confusion, and we assume that this must be because the concept itself is unsatisfactory. It is also partly due to a set of arguments maintained by philosophers from Hume to Ryle, the general tenor of which has been that the notion of the soul is logically improper, and that the use of the word ought to be discontinued and replaced by other, more aseptic, circumlocutions. Partly, again, it is due to a very different difficulty, namely that the soul is a sophisticated notion and there are no knock-down proofs of the utility of the term to those who do not feel the need for it. Babies are not conscious of their bodies at first, nor do boys much want to talk about their minds: likewise only gradually do men feel the need for the word 'soul', and flat exposition cannot convey the meaning of the word to those who have not felt the want for some such term.

This last point I shall not further discuss. I shall leave it as an article of faith that people do exist as well as things. I shall be concerned to show only that the term is permissible, not that it is obligatory. It will be with the second point therefore that I shall be chiefly concerned: my contention will be the negative one that the arguments of the philosophers who wish to deny the existence of the soul are not valid arguments, and rest upon a series of mistaken assumptions which I shall in turn expose. At the end of the essay I shall attempt a more positive account of what we mean in our different uses of the word 'soul'. But I shall also be elucidating the meaning of the word throughout the paper in the course of my examination of the various arguments; for many of these turn upon a misconstruction of the sense of the word.

Consider, for example, the question that springs naturally to our minds when the word 'soul' is mentioned, the question 'Do we have them?' Do we have souls? – the question invites misconstruction. It is dangerously like 'Do we have noses, legs or kidneys?' or like 'Do we have bodies?' We liken the soul to a part of the body, so that it would make sense to ask whereabouts in the body the soul is to be found, whether in the liver or in the heart or in the brain or perhaps in the pituitary gland. And as it is permissible to speculate upon the condition of people who have no nose, or are without legs or have lost a kidney, so we might consider the hypothetical case of a man who would resemble other men in all respects save that he did not possess a soul, and wonder whether it might not be found advantageous in the course of evolution for us all to become like him.

We might then guard against these and similar attacks by explaining that the soul, although like part of the body, is itself imperceptible, immaterial, and non-bodily. The antithesis suggested in the phrase 'body and soul' reinforces this account that the soul is just like the rest of the body except that it is itself non-bodily. This line may silence the biological sceptic for a time, but in the end the latent contradiction will work out into the open, and we are forced to conclude that souls, that is non-bodily bodies, do not and cannot exist.

The confusion may be compared with the one that arises around the word 'meaning' or rather, the fused phrase 'have meanings'. Words have meanings; they also have syllables, some only one, others more than one; words also have sounds, or, in the case of written and printed words, shapes. We can consider the possibility of a word's losing a syllable much as we can think of a man losing his nose or a limb; sounds, like bodies, are not dispensable: a word which can never be uttered is in the same bad way as a man without a body. But meanings are indispensable to words in quite a different way; we are tempted to make a false assimilation and to construe meanings as ghost-words, inaudible verbal genii which shadow each their own word, being exactly like it in all respects save that they are not sounded; and to construe meaning as an unsounded sound is no easier than to take the soul as a non-bodily body. Nor only in their characteristic confusions are the two assertions similar; they also serve similar purposes: in the one case we are using the assertion to make a deep distinction between words and other, meaningless, sounds: in the other case we are distinguishing men from the rest of the created world: some sounds, we are saying, are differentiated from the rest in that they are uttered by human beings according to regular and acknowledged conventions, as a result of which it makes sense to ask of them whether they are Latin or English, archaic or slang, elegant or ugly, or synonymous or non-synonymous with another word; and some material objects we separate off, to be treated with tenderness and respect, capable of being sympathetically understood as well as merely observed, people of like passions with ourselves, who can be talked to and can love and be loved, and of whom it is permissible to predicate not only terms denoting weight, size, and colour, but words like 'generous', 'intelligent', 'spiteful', 'sorrowful', 'saint', and 'sinner'.

Part, then, of what is meant by the assertion that the soul exists is that discourse about personal qualities and experiences and emotions is as legitimate and meaningful as discourse about things. Just as part of what we are trying to convey by the proposition that words have meaning is that when we are talking about words we can ask what their synonyms are, how they should be rendered in another language, what their logical force is, whether they have stylistic peculiarities or idiomatic uses, and how best they can be defined, and that these questions, when words are the subject of our conversation, are as respectable as the simpler considerations of pitch and tone, duration, intensity and euphony, which can still be raised when we are talking merely about sounds. The doctrine that the Soul is a Substance in part means only this: that persons can be the subjects of a discourse in which there are predicated of them attributes and qualities which cannot properly be predicated of things.

This distinction of language – about what can and cannot be said – is grounded upon a distinction of fact: in the one case that words occur only within a system, and are subject to rules of utterance and use, whereas other sounds are not: in the other case that men do behave in ways very unlike those of animals and inanimate things. The questions then suggest themselves: How deep are these distinctions? Is either distinction a difference of kind or are both merely differences of degree? And what are the relations, if any, across the differences? – is the meaning of a word entirely different from its sound, its tonal properties and pitch, or are they to some extent connected? Is the ascription of non-physical, non-physiological epithets to a man in any way dependent upon phenomena a physicist or physiologist could observe?

These questions are so phrased as to extract answers with apparently alarming corollaries: it is incontestable that our only criterion of difference of word-type is difference of sound – if all words sounded alike we should be unable to distinguish them – and, therefore, it would appear that all considerations of meaning and style must in the last analysis be resolved into differences of sound; so that all philology and logic is, really-speaking, a branch of hypothetical acoustics. Likewise epithets reserved exclusively for humans will be resolvable into sets of 'straight' descriptions of observable behaviour; meaning is just a pattern of repeated similar sounds, mind and soul are just patterns of behaviour.

The shocking thesis with which we are then confronted, known as Logical Behaviourism, is one which seems to eliminate the soul, explain it away, analyse it out in terms of behaviour patterns. One's soul is no longer one's inmost self which may long for God with a desire like that of the hart for the waterbrooks, but, rather, a pattern of behaviour or responses that can be correctly classified by housemaster or confessor by some 'spiritual' epithet; which epithet, one must remember, is not a categorical but a semi-hypothetical* term.

* See G. Ryle: *Concept of Mind*, p. 141.

Not all this thesis ought to shock: in so far as it is merely a repudiation of a deep dichotomy between body and soul it is true; behaviour may not be an infallible guide to the state of peoples' minds and souls, it may not be so complete an account as some philosophers think, but it *is* a guide, and the one we normally use. Words like 'generous', 'conscientious', 'proud', 'slothful' can be used to characterize behaviour, and their application to persons is in the first instance grounded in those persons' language and behaviour. Even in the last instance when a sight of a man's face or the sound of his tread is enough to convey the impression of great holiness or great suffering, there is *some* observation of physical appearance, language, or behaviour. Barring a few experiments in psychical research, we are no more able to make assessments of men's souls without having met them, or heard them, or read what they write, than we can of their minds. And even if we could, we should still ultimately rely upon behaviour as *the* criterion: however many allowances we make for temptation, natural difficulties, lack of opportunity, etc., we should refuse to describe a man as generous upon the criterion of telepathy or insight alone, if he never took available opportunities of being generous, and always talked, looked, and acted, ungenerously. As St Paul says* behaviour (ἀναστροφή) is the proper criterion of spiritual qualities, and showing forth the requisite behaviour patterns is a necessary condition of a person's being a Christian. By their fruits ye shall know them.

The shocking part of the thesis is in part due to the belief that if the criteria of applicability of a term be given, the meaning is thereby explained, and that if the criteria are behaviouristic, a reductive analysis of spiritual concepts has thereby been obtained; and in part due to a simple confusion in the use of the word 'behaviour', which is sometimes used inclusively to cover linguistic as well as non-linguistic behaviour, and sometimes used for the latter as opposed to the former. Now for the revelation and communication of our inmost thoughts and feelings far the most important method available is language: if we cannot talk to

* Eph. iv. 22.

someone then we do feel cut off from really knowing him; knowledge of another person which is based on behaviour excluding
language is very much a second best: we cannot be sure our views
are correct – they are only shaky inferences we have not been able
to check – without speech man becomes an animal – we feel we
really should know what animals were like and felt like, if only
they could talk to us. Hence, to say that the criteria for the
applicability of spiritual terms are behaviouristic criteria, is
capable of shocking us, because, if we resist it, it is construed in
the first and wider sense and is forced upon us as a truism, and
when we accept it, it is interpreted in the narrower sense, in which
it suggests that human beings are as inscrutable, because as
inarticulate, as animals, and that there is no essential difference
between speech-privileged men and dumb beasts.

It may be asked 'Well, what *is* the difference? What is there
about language which makes such a deep division between
linguistic behaviour and non-linguistic behaviour? Conceded that
linguistic behaviour is more finely grained and so capable of far
greater complexity, is not the real difference one of degree only
and not one of kind?'

The short answer to this is to say that language *presupposes* a
special status for speakers and hearers: that one could not profit-
ably discuss the nature of discourse without having first settled
between what, or rather, as *we* should say, between whom,
discourse can obtain. Linguistic, but not only linguistic, behaviour
is of this sort: there are many types of activity besides talking,
activities such as smiling, caressing, giving to, hating, hitting, and
spitting at, all of which would be pointless except upon the
supposition that the persons to whom these activities were
addressed were *persons* and not automata or things; that our
relation to them was an I-Thou relation and not an I-it.

To the tough-minded philosopher this may seem to be merely
a dogmatic reformulation of the earlier position it was adduced
to support; and such a philosopher may again claim that really
we always deal with the external world by means of an 'I-it'
relation, and it is only a minor matter that with the very complex

objects we know as human beings we tend to postpone the satisfactions we like to obtain from them, using them not merely as means to immediate gratifications of our own, but also as means to ultimate, or at least delayed, gratifications, that are none the less selfish for having been postponed. Such a position is in a sense unassailable, because it is in a sense a possible outlook: the sin of Pride can go even to these lengths, making a fundamental cleavage between us and all other men, alienating us and isolating us utterly. That this lonely position is, so far as logic goes, tenable, we do not wish to deny: what we seek to do is to distinguish this from the other positions one may take up, and to resist any logicians' attempt to assimilate them to it. Sin may cut us off from all communion with God and communication with other men, but logic hardly shall.

The actual arguments advanced by some modern philosophers are not watertight. It is not only that they are informed by certain basic, though unrecognized, presuppositions which makes them much less philosophically neutral than they are professed to be, but that certain specific inferences are invalid; and it is usually just on these inferences that the upsetting consequences depend. Professor Ryle, whose *Concept of Mind* is by far the best exposition of that thesis, can be castigated* for having three preconceptions, namely that philosophical analysis is best reductive, that the world is composed of simple, manageable, material objects, and that extroversion is a Good Thing; which are indeed defensible suppositions but are nowhere in his work defended or even acknowledged: here, however, I shall attack him for an unfortunate doctrine about the nature of language, which seeks to divide concepts into a set of mutually exclusive category-baskets, divided from one another by a great gulf so that words that wanted to move from the one category to the other could not do so; and for an equation of meaning with method of verification, which does less than justice to the sense of words.

Ryle's thesis is valuable in pointing out that there are differ-

* See S. N. Hampshire, *Review* in *Mind*, 1950, pp. 238, 255 etc.; Iris Murdoch, *Sartre*, p. 35.

ences between words, which may be called category differences, and that the unconscious neglect of these may lead to a dangerous kind of nonsense; but he is wrong in assuming that there are definite and exclusive categories, so that if a word is sometimes categorially different from another word it is always so; that is to say that if in some contexts it would make nonsense to replace one word by a certain other word then there are no contexts in which such a substitution would be acceptable. The inference thus stated is clearly invalid; and that the conclusion is in fact false can be seen by considering Ryle's own examples*: thus while it is a mistake to bracket with the colleges and libraries the University if we want to *see over* them, it is perfectly permissible to bracket them together when one wants to address letters to them; I can indeed write letters to Christ Church, the Bodleian Library, the Ashmolean Museum *and* the University, and *per contra* there is no logical impropriety in my receiving payments from Merton College, Balliol College, and New College, *and* from the University as well. Similarly, though John Doe cannot be godson to or meet the Average Taxpayer, he can be better paid than him, more highly taxed and more disgruntled. Thus although it is true that my soul cannot meet your soul in the High, nor weigh two stone more than yours does, whereas my body can do both of these *vis a vis* your body, it is not *therefore* true that every conjunction of the two terms is categorially improper or that the prayer book phrase 'Our souls and bodies' is a logical pun on a footing with 'In a flood of tears and a Sedan Chair'.

Categorial impropriety in such cases has not been proved, though this is not to say it necessarily does not exist. Whether a conjunction or disjunction of two terms is categorially permissible or no is a question which must be decided in each case individually: we need a trained nose for nonsense, which cannot be reduced to the application of a few rigid rules: speaking about it generally, we can say only two things: first there is a presumption against any conjunction or disjunction that men have been inclined to use being nonsense; usually they have some motive

* *Concept of Mind*, pp. 21–23.

for saying what they do say, and could, if challenged, explain what they meant in other, less felicitous terms; and seldom is there no respect in which two concepts can be contrasted and compared, and so with regard to that respect conjoined or disjoined: and secondly one's determination of nonsense will vary with one's most fundamental beliefs and basic outlook; the materialist will find nonsensical that which to the mystic enshrines the deepest truth, and every rival metaphysics engenders an inability to understand the terms of its competitors. It was predicted and is only to be expected that the terms the Christian most wants to use will appear foolishness to the Greeks.

The crucial doctrine of *The Concept of Mind* and of all reductive analyses of the soul, is the equation of meaning with method of verification: that since the way to verify an assertion about somebody's mind or soul is to discover or observe his linguistic and non-linguistic behaviour, this is *all* that the assertion can really mean. This doctrine is false. But it is not obviously false. It is *prima facie* plausible, and the onus of disproof is on those who would refute it. There seem to be four reasons why we must reject the equation here, and insist that it is not simply behaviour we are describing when we use spiritual epithets, but rather the nature of the man who is behaving so. These four reasons are: the coherence of our experience of other people; the inexhaustiveness or open texture of mental and spiritual concepts; the intuitive insight which enables us on occasion to 'get inside' other people and understand them 'from the inside'; and our own introspective experience which, for ourselves certainly, and for others possibly, shows that mental terms do sometimes denote 'mental' occurrences as well as dispositions to behave in an observable fashion.

The first two of these reasons are exactly similar to ones which have been urged in order to establish the real existence of material objects: Logical Behaviourism is on a level with Phenomenalism; and the reasons for rejecting the latter may be turned also against the former. Leibniz* urged 'la liaison des phénomènes' as demand-

* *Nouveaux Essais:* IV, Ch. 2, § 14.

ing the notion of substance to explain it, and we may urge that the
extreme diversity of sorts of behaviour we are prepared to accept
as criteria for the application of a single mental or spiritual epithet
would be unreasonable except upon the hypothesis of some
unifying principle: we will say that a man is proud or that he
lacks faith or that he is intellectually dishonest on evidence which
varies very much from case to case; yet we feel it is the same
quality which is being discovered to us under these various
guises; there is an intuitive feeling of consistency about our
varying judgments.

Very similar is the second reason for rejecting the reductive
analysis of mind and soul to bodily behaviour which is the
inexhaustiveness of the criteria for the application of mental and
spiritual epithets. Dr Waismann* has pointed out how the 'open
texture' of material object concepts rules out the possibility of any
translation of them into the language of sense-data. The same
difficulties apply in far greater measure to any attempt to give the
logical equivalent of a mental or spiritual concept in terms of
descriptions of behaviour. There is no set of statements about
behaviour which *entail* or *are entailed by* any statement about
mental or spiritual characteristics. However carefully, fully and
exactly we specify our tests beforehand we shall never be able
decisively to discriminate between τὸ εἶναι δίκαιος and
τὸ δοκεῖν εἶναι δίκαιος, being honest and seeming honest. For the
heart is deceitful above all things, and whatever criteria we
adopt, it always *may* succeed in conforming outwardly to our
requirements while inwardly repudiating the standards we have
set. There is as it were a Naturalist Fallacy, or rather a Cephalus
Fallacy, in any proposed definition of mental or spiritual concepts
in behaviouristic terms; the definition, though often true, is true
only *ceteris paribus*; and it is always possible by considering
unusual circumstances to find exceptions to it. The same pattern
of behaviour can always be construed as revealing the most

* F. Waismann: 'Verifiability,' *Proceedings of the Aristotelian Society*,
Sup., Vol. xix, pp. 119–50, reprinted in A. G. N. Flew: *Logic and Language*,
I, pp. 117–43.

subtle cunning or the strictest integrity; the most incompatible readings of the same person's character can be built up upon the same evidence with equal plausibility: there is an ambiguity of tie between the man and his behaviour which should rule out for ever any hope of an easy equivalence between the two. And if it really was *patterns* of behaviour and not the character of the behaver that we were chiefly interested in, our rules for the application of the relevant terms would be very different from what they now are. The tie between the two is much more tenuous than philosophers like to think. In fact it is difficult to interpret people's behaviour, to penetrate to the springs of their action. Most men's motives are opaque. We manage well enough for practical purposes, and though we seldom get to the bottom of anyone, we feel that we are not always utterly mistaken about everyone. Though sometimes we wonder.

These two grounds for hypostatisation are the same as those on which we defend our belief that material objects exist: we are motivated by a general nisus towards the greatest simplification of our thought and discourse, and unification of our conceptual structure; on these grounds we talk of persons as distinct from what they do in the same way as we talk of things and not merely how they appear. The other two grounds are peculiar to persons: they are our untutored intuitive insight into other people, and our more self-conscious introspective self-knowledge, with our conscious extension of it by the analogy of feeling.

We have already alluded to our intuitive understanding of other people as one of the ways in which we gather together diverse and inexhaustively variable patterns of behaviour as manifestations of the same mental or spiritual quality. We are able, on occasion, by the exercise of a certain sympathy – συμπάθεια – to penetrate behind observable behaviour and to put ourselves in another's shoes and to see, to feel, to understand, what we would ourselves do if situated in his circumstances. Sometimes we can do this, sometimes – often – we cannot. That we sometimes can is a fact of the highest importance, strangely overlooked by philosophers, though well known to, and appreciated by, historians, critics, novelists, and poets. This intuitive sensibility is not, as it is sometimes misleadingly put, a sixth sense; it is not a parallel to, nor a rival of, the ordinary five senses; even those who are most gifted with insight cannot know what other people are like without *any* observation; they are not possessed of some sort of telepathic power, but rather are marked by an ability to understand relatively much on a relatively small basis of observation; they can read a man's character in his face or in his posture and can discern his inmost fears from a chance word or a casual phrase. Their advantage over us is not that they can make observations which we cannot make and so can assert simple categorical statements which we are not privileged to assert, but rather that they are possessed of a well of singular hypotheticals in themselves, so that given this and this expression, stance, or behaviour, they can sense which of other actions, attitudes, and responses, would 'go with' this one. This intuitive flair consists of not an extra sense but extreme sensibility: *nihil est in intellectu quod non fuerit in sensu, nisi ipse intellectus.**

Philosophers, who have for the most part been hag-ridden by the belief that all intellectual operations of repute must be either deductive or inductive inferences, have tended to neglect the phenomenon of intuitive insight, and when they have had to take notice of it, to construe it as a set of finely grained unconscious inductions. This view is, like all explanations in terms of unconscious processes, hard to refute. Nevertheless it is to be rejected, partly for technical reasons, partly because it squares neither with our experience of ordinary life nor with the evidence of great literature. The explanation does not save the phenomena: it does not accord with our own private experience – that was hardly to be expected – nor does it accord with what we know in general about men and about intuitive understanding; if intuitive understanding were just a matter of unconscious inference based upon subconscious memories, that is, if it were just a distillation of sense-experience, then it should increase proportionately with the increase of each individual's total sense-experience; but, though

* Leibniz: *Nouveax Essais*, Bk. II, Ch. 1, § 2.

insight certainly is increased by experience (in a sense wider than that of 'sense-experience'), it is not totally dependent upon it; witness the fact that different people with the same backgrounds and very similar experience have different sympathies, and find it easy to be in tune with and understand respectively different sorts of persons.

The evidence from great novelists and playwrights also tells against the claim that our intuitive insight is just unconscious inference: here we have people part of whose genius it is to make appear consistent behaviour which hitherto would have been incomprehensible: if it were just a matter of observation it is difficult to see why Plato or Augustine or Shakespeare or Dostoevski were peculiarly well-placed observers; nor why we, whose walks of life do not usually lead us into the strange situations that they are accustomed to relate, are able to follow their lead and find, upon their pointing it out, an innate plausibility in conduct we previously would have considered implausible; nor, if we were confined to constant conjunctions of observed instances, why reading great authors should crystallize our views so much, nor why, after having read them, we should look upon the world and see people with eyes so different from those we had before.

For these reasons it seems to me best to accept the findings of ordinary experience and common sense, and acknowledge that we often do exercise a peculiar facility for understanding other people and interpreting their behaviour; and consequently to allow our normal ways of speaking, which will not have it that our knowledge of other people is 'flat' and all on a level with our knowledge of sticks and stones, but gives it a sense of depth and profundity; a feeling that we can penetrate deeply into people, and with human beings get behind their superficial appearances, not by the use of eyes other than our physical eyes, by our physical eyes indeed, but using them to observe acutely and actively, rather than waiting passively and dully for sense-data to occur.

Our final reason for repudiating the reductive analysis of mind and spirit to patterns of behaviour is our own first-personal experience. Exception may be taken to the language of intro-

spection and privileged access in so far as these metaphors suggest
an inward eye peculiarly well placed for seeing through an
internal aperture to an internal screen beyond. But that each
person is not in a privileged position for self-knowledge, that
when we have twinges of pain they are not 'mental occurrences'
but, basically, dispositions to give certain sorts of answers to
doctors' questions, and that our temptations, our agonies of
indecision, and our final resolutions, are discoverable to us only
by the same methods as they may be detected by other persons,
to this doctrine, if seriously maintained, we can only say, with
St Augustine, *Da veniam, non credimus*. We concede, of course,
at once, that introspected mental occurrences are not always
necessary conditions for the application of mental or spiritual
terms; that drivers, once they have ceased to be learners, can
drive carefully though unselfconsciously; also that sometimes
introspection may not even be possible. We concede also that,
for obvious reasons, the criterion for the applicability of terms in
a public language tends to be overt and publicly observable
behaviour rather than private and unsharable experiences. But
this is not to say, and we do not concede, that the significance and
point of such language is therefore thus restricted: rather our
whole interest in and need for such language is through its
correlation with private experiences, and this is the best, although
inadequate, means open to us for expressing and communicating
what we alone can feel. As applied to ourselves at least, then, we
reject the behaviourists' analysis; and so, arguing by what is
sometimes described as an analogy, we reject it when applied to
other people too. For, observing that in all overt particulars, other
human beings resemble ourselves and applying simple scientific
procedure, we conclude that if they are really mere automata
then we must be automata also, and all our experience an epi-
phenomenal illusion: 'Either I allow' we say 'that other people
have souls, or else I begin upon a systematic elimination of 'I'.'

We have given our grounds for maintaining that men after all
do have souls; it is important to realize that the word 'soul' does

not have the same meaning in all its uses and contexts. Thus in the fused phrase '– have souls' we may or may not be using the word 'soul' to include 'mind'. In the preceding arguments we have been using the word in the inclusive sense, and have been discussing what philosophers call the problem of Other Minds, the question whether other people are conscious beings like ourselves or are merely automata – 'little bits of paper blown about by the wind'. If we do not believe that people have souls then we shall not do by them as we would be done by, except in so far as expediency dictates; we shall not hesitate to use them merely as means and not at all as ends; and we shall not hope to understand them from the inside, but only as an experimental psychologist can: whereas if we believe that they do have souls we shall respect their interests and their integrity, we shall enter into personal relations with them, we shall feel that the humanities are different in kind from the natural sciences. People who believe that animals have souls regard them as therefore possessing rights, and savages who hold that trees have souls always ask a tree's permission before cutting it down. In these cases Soul includes Mind, and is being contrasted with Body: in other senses the contrast is between Soul and Mind; if we ask whether a particular man has still got a soul, or has lost it, we are not wondering whether he is become insane. 'The good of one's soul' is defined by exhaustion. For all the other goods external criteria can be given, in terms of cause and effect, of physical euphoria or measurable abilities, or of what other people think; whereas it is what is good for one, yet not because it is good for one's reputation, career, pocket, estate, body or mind, but just good for one, good for one $\dot{\alpha}\pi\lambda\hat{\omega}s$. This definition by exhaustion is characteristic of the concept of the soul: we approach by, as it were, a *via negativa*, always knowing and being able to specify what it is not, always contrasting it with some other concept that we know: when we are dealing with the bodies of men we feel there is something behind the body: when we have understood and are able to assess the intellect of man we realize that there is something more besides: and when we consider character and realize how it is shaped by circumstance and how far it is formed by other men, we see that this cannot exhaust the real man, the man himself whom we seek. The soul is beyond personality. It is beyond morality too: the soul slips through the net of obligations that forms the moral law. To discharge one's debts and to do one's duty, however willingly and however scrupulously it is performed, is a chilling achievement, is merely to be a Pharisee: there is a feeling that such a man is not being quite natural, quite honest with himself, quite spontaneous, – a suspicion that he is guilty of *mauvaise foi*: there is not the spirit, the liveliness, which we seek, and which we do find in the self-expression and self-fulfilment of the creative artist. They are live individuals. Creative artists, we feel, do have souls. And we should like to believe of all men that each in his own life was a creative artist. We yearn, not for a new law, but for a personal morality beyond the Law, beyond Pharisaism: for no other morality, however rational and however lofty, can ever really get a grip upon the soul; only the love of God is adequate to win it, and perhaps only God is capable of loving one, not for some external attribute, but for oneself and soul alone.

We are peeling the onion. Every attribute and quality of man, as soon as we recognize and understand it, becomes detached from the essential man himself: 'soul' often means 'self'. David loved Jonathan, his friend, his ἄλλος αὐτός as his own soul.* Often we can translate 'soul' by self, but in the active nominative rather than the passive accusative. The *ego* rather than the *me* or the *id*: and whereas when we try to peel the qualities off things to reveal the essential substance underneath we are engaged in an impossible and unnecessary task, when we turn to know ourselves and one another it is not so clear that the task is futile or that the urge to accomplish it ought to be resisted. Certainly it can be begun: this the paradox of consciousness shows, that however self-conscious one is, it is always possible to go to a further stage. Provided we do not adopt the flat and superficial interpretation of the universe there is no reason to believe that it should be possible to exhaust the soul into a limited number of definitive qualities.

* 1 Samuel xviii. 1. Cf. Aristotle: *Nicomachean Ethics*, IX:4:5, 1166a 31.

But only provided. We might almost say, though we have not proved it here, that belief in God was a necessary and sufficient condition for belief in the soul. Sufficient obviously, for whoever believes in the existence of the Christian God must also believe in the existence and the value of his children: and necessary, for whoever does not believe in God will not believe in others either. Nor long believe even in himself alone.

CHAPTER VI

THE GRACE OF GOD
by Basil Mitchell

I

ONE of the essential differences between Christianity and any form of Humanism is that the Christian saint feels impelled to ascribe whatever good he does to the grace of God. 'By the grace of God I am what I am. . . . I laboured more abundantly than they all. Yet not I but the grace of God which was with me.' (1 Cor. xv. 10).

It is this simple and central affirmation that I want to discuss in this chapter.* For, although the concept of grace has been differently interpreted by Catholic and Protestant theologians, they agree in the belief that God enables men to do and to be what they otherwise could not. It is true that the developed Christian tradition goes beyond this simple statement to speak of various kinds and channels of grace, and this, too, may be thought to require justification, but the *primary* logical problem concerns the divine activity in grace, however exercised.

Belief in grace follows from belief in creation, for this implies that man, as a created being, is sustained by God's creative will, and, as a spiritual being, owes to God his freedom and power to do good; but although based on a theological foundation, it draws empirical support from the religious experience of individuals and communities. St Paul himself seems to have been aware of the grace of the God as an invasive power, as many saints have been. And this awareness of an 'interior accretion' (to use Marcel's phrase) is matched by the impression the saintly character often makes upon others. To take a contemporary example, J. H. Oldham, writing of Florence Allshorn, says 'Yet she was able to

---

* I shall, however, restrict myself to the question of evidence, and shall not attempt to deal with the traditional problem of reconciling the doctrine of grace with human freedom.

conquer and control her impatience and what impressed others was often the *supernatural* quality of her patience and understanding.' The recognition that someone is 'deeply religious' on the part of an acquaintance who does not share his beliefs is perhaps sometimes an incipient awareness of the same thing. It may be just a testimony to genuine conviction and a life sincerely lived in accordance with it; but it sometimes amounts to a sense of a quality which it is tempting to call 'saintliness'. Certainly the palpable *absence* of any such quality is often rightly made a reproach to believers.

Although it is the saints who are most aware of the grace of God and in whom it is seen most clearly, there are many who have an occasional fitful awareness of it. They are often not 'religious' people at all, and might not describe their experience in these terms. However, it is such experiences, whether they are only occasional or have become a strong and settled habit, which provide the empirical basis for the theological doctrine of the grace of God. This is not to identify grace with human experience of it or to deny that grace often works unrecognized. Nor is it to attach more importance to its detectable than to its secret workings. But if we are asked to point to the activity of God, we can only point to where it makes a detectable difference.

There are, then, these two types of 'religious experience' to which appeal is made, but how they justify the doctrine of grace, or how it explains them is far from clear. As soon as the attempt is made to get it clear we find ourselves in serious and notorious difficulties.

One natural response to this situation is to ask: in that case why *try* to get it clear? The case might be put like this: 'we know how to use religious expressions (like "Not I, but the grace of God") in their appropriate contexts. We don't in practice get into muddles then. Let us leave well alone.' This reaction is not confined to the simple and devout, but is shared by some sophisticated philosophers. It is only, they say, when we take these relatively simple, spontaneous utterances about God's helping us and guid-

ing us and try to fit them into a theoretical framework that we get
into trouble.

There is more than one answer to this protest. To begin with,
the utterances in question are spontaneous, no doubt, but they are
far from simple. They are the utterances of people in a religious
tradition (or under its influence) who tend to interpret what
they experience in terms of that tradition. These utterances are
theological from the start. Then, we shall *in fact* adopt some
device for co-ordinating our experiences – this being a deeply-
rooted instinct (the metaphysical instinct?). The choice is, in
effect, whether to do it reflectively or not. There are dangers both
ways. The pursuit of clarity can be an escape from the experience
itself, or, perhaps, a way of taming it into a superficial appearance
of docility and order. The refusal to reflect can become a surrender
to unexamined prejudices.

But the chief and most serious consideration is that we have
other ways of describing and assessing human experience and
behaviour, some of them simple and familiar enough, others
relatively new and complicated. It is when we try to adjust
religious ways of thinking to *these* that the difficulties start and
we can't prevent them starting by choosing to dwell in a state of
linguistic innocence. Although in the end we may well find that
the traditional language of devotion is the best way of saying
what we wish to say, there is no avoiding the challenge to explain
the logical features of this sort of language.

We have suggested that belief in grace is supported in two
ways. It forms part of the Christian Revelation, understood as a
body of truths communicated to us through the inspired writers
of the Old and New Testaments; and it is confirmed by the
religious experience of Christians and of mankind in general. A
provisional account of the relation between the two sorts of
justification might be this: it is not enough for the Bible to be
read; it has to be understood, and it cannot be understood unless
the reader has the necessary imagination and experience. In this
respect it is not unlike trying to understand, e.g. a Romantic poet.
You have to be able to recognize what your poet is talking about.

There has to be something in your experience to which he can appeal. But in helping you to interpret your experience he will at the same time deepen it. It is not a straightforward matter of seeing at once how the description fits. A man will not make much of Wordsworth if he has never had Wordsworthian moments; but it is reading Wordsworth that fixes and illuminates them. There is a similar reciprocal relationship between revelation and personal decision in the acceptance of Christian ethics. It looks on the face of it as if a *revealed* ethic must be a contradiction in terms, since morality to be genuine must be freely and responsibly adopted. If we accept God's law as binding upon us it must be because *we* judge God's will to be good. So it seems that the revealed morality has to be tested in the last resort by reference to an independent and autonomous moral standard. However, this is too simple a version of what happens. The convert starts by being attracted to some aspects of Christian morality and not to others, and at this stage the degree of his critical understanding depends upon this partial acceptance; but though, if he is to be sincere, he goes on testing what he is offered against his own moral insight, that insight is not entirely independent, but is constantly being deepened and extended by increasing Christian faith. It is in some such way as this that, in the present instance, the appeal to revelation and the appeal to religious experience have to be related. When men revolt against theology as an arid discipline drying up the wells of the spiritual life it is because they suspect, sometimes with reason, that its concepts have become cut off from the living experience which enables them to be understood.

The concept of grace has, then, to be understood in relation *both* to the experience of individuals and communities *and* to the traditional doctrine of the Church; on the one hand the sense of a power at work in oneself or in others; on the other, the theological interpretation of this as the work of grace.

To the reader who protests that he has no such experience the argument of this chapter has nothing to say; he offers no purchase to it. But even those who are prepared tentatively to recognize 'the facts' may reasonably wish to protest against the theological interpretation of them.

The protest might take this form:

(i) These experiences *can* be interpreted differently. Take, for example, the impression made by the saint. To be sure he does make an impression, but if we label this 'holy' or 'supernatural' are we committed to anything more than when, for example, we call a cataract 'awful' or 'tremendous'; or when we praise a poet or dramatist or a composer for producing a 'supernatural' effect? In all these cases we are making a kind of aesthetic judgment which carries with it no inference as to how the effect was produced.

As for the alleged 'experience of grace', this may well be compounded of two wholly natural elements: an experience, genuine enough, of an influx of power from subconscious layers of the mind; and an equally genuine, but wholly natural, humility about their resources and achievements which is characteristic of good men. It does not require us to postulate the operation of a divine spirit. Indeed it is hard to see how the saint's 'I could not have done it of myself' could possibly be verified. How is a man to tell how far his resources can be stretched?

(ii) Not only *can* these experiences be interpreted differently. There are compelling reasons of a logical kind why the theological account *must* be rejected, or, at least, drastically amended. For if we say that it was by God's grace that St Paul laboured more abundantly, we seem to be offering a kind of causal explanation, and in that case we ought to be able to defend our explanation by contrasting St Paul's case with others in which God's grace was known *not* to be at work. But this is just what Christian apologists cannot or will not do. They simply fall back on the general formula 'If good, then by grace'.

The difficulty lies in the absence of any empirical test. St Paul is claiming that his labours were abetted by the labour of God, that in all his doings God was active, but no evidence is offered of the kind that is normally available to check the assertion that A helped B.

This generates the suspicion that a religious assertion of this kind should not be taken as a statement of fact at all, but as something more like the expression of an attitude or an ascription of praise. This is the line most likely to be taken by the empiricist philosopher who is genuinely anxious to make sense rather than nonsense of the religious claim, but is impressed by its logical difficulties. On this view St Paul in ascribing his achievement to the grace of God is not putting forward any sort of *explanation* of them, but is simply refusing to take the credit for them and cutting off any movement of his readers to praise him. He is saying 'Don't praise me, praise God'. And in so doing he is, of course, praising God himself. '*Non nobis domine, sed tibi gloria.*'

In this way he reaches a position like that of Professor Toulmin, who argues* that the function of religious language is not (like that of scientific language) to predict our experiences, nor (like that of ethical language) to harmonize our purposes, but to reassure us in the face of the unknown and enable us to put heart into the discharge of our moral duties. From which, of course, it follows, as Professor Toulmin says, that 'theological arguments, and religious questions and answers are on quite a different footing, as a matter of logic, from scientific and ethical arguments, questions and answers.' A position of this kind is all the more attractive as it seems to agree with a great deal that religious people say about 'the language of faith'.

The point might be sharpened in this way. If it is a *fact* that the power of God enters into and guides the actions of men, then these divine operations must in principle be open to scientific test. The relevant science here is presumably psychology and we are bound, therefore, to ask: could psychology tell us whether in a given case the grace of God had been at work or whether it had not, or to what extent it had operated? If psychology could, in principle, tell us this, then the issue is an experimental one and the pious may, perhaps, be allowed the benefit of the doubt until it has been settled. But if it could not, even in principle, be settled, then it is not a question of fact at all.

* Stephen Toulmin, *The Place of Reason in Ethics*, p. 212 ff.

The issue has been stated crudely for the sake of emphasis, and no scientist would in fact put it this way. The case needs modifying. In particular our statement of it creates the impression that all the sciences would claim the same degree of accuracy and universality, and that this degree permits the complete confirmation or rejection of a hypothesis. In point of fact the psychologist would be far more modest than this. The most he would claim would be to establish statistical generalizations for which there is a greater or lesser amount of evidence. And he certainly would not think of claiming that he could as yet even in this way cover anything like the whole of human activity and experience.

However, these qualifications do not affect the main contention, which is that if statements about the divine activity are not even *in principle* amenable to scientific test, they are not to be regarded as statements of fact.

And it is, indeed, hard to see how they *could* be tested. The psychologist could scarcely take account of grace even 'in principle', because 'grace' is not a psychological concept, nor capable of becoming one. The psychologist is no more able to operate with concepts like 'grace' and 'sin' than the physiologist with 'will' or 'desire'. The most he could do would be to give an account in psychological terms of the same observable phenomena that the theologian interprets in terms of these concepts. For example, a sociologist might tackle the question of the efficacy of grace by endeavouring to establish significant correlations between religious belief and social behaviour (or something of the sort). This is often done in social surveys. It is possible to find for the purpose rough, but reasonably objective criteria for religious belief, such as the individual's testimony or church attendance. But whether the results indicated that 'religion' was an effective social force or not, it is clear that they could have no tendency to show that the good it effected was accomplished by the grace of God. Of course, the believer may have his own reasons for believing that this is the case, but they are not reasons open to this form of scientific test.

Along these lines, then, we reach the conclusion that the findings of psychology can neither confirm nor contradict those of the theologian. There is, in fact, no ground upon which they could meet – a friendly solution likely to commend itself to both parties.

But it begins to look less satisfactory when we recall how this enquiry started. The suggestion was that if religious utterances, like St Paul's, are to be understood as factual statements they must, as a matter of logic, be amenable to scientific test; and it is supposed that in the present case the relevant science would be psychology. If we now find that a saying like St. Paul's could not even in principle, be made amenable to psychological tests, must we not drop the claim that it is a statement of fact?

The argument up to this point has been a logical one, turning on an apparently clear-cut distinction between statements of fact and other uses of language. We are asked to interpret St Paul's confession either as a straightforward 'scientific' assertion or as something more like an expression of emotion or ascription of praise. The discussion concerns the logical character of statements about God's activity, and we are forced into it as soon as we raise questions about how such statements are to be justified.

Nevertheless, the enquiry, though inescapable, is apt to seem trivial; and sometimes actually is rather trivial, when logical acumen is exercised without much understanding of the workings of the religious mind. But even when this danger is avoided, the entire discussion makes an assumption which, some would say, is open to serious challenge. It is the assumption that theology is concerned with thinking and talking *about* God and His dealings with His creation. Many thinkers would now say that this betrays a fundamental misunderstanding of the theologian's task. We are told that we need to distinguish from the start between the I-Thou and the I-it relationship,* the one a relationship of personal encounter, the other of objective scientific investigation. Man's relationship with God is of the I-Thou kind. Hence it is a funda-

* This distinction was first elaborated by Martin Buber in '*I and Thou*' (English translation by R. Gregor Smith, 1937). It has since been developed by a number of Christian theologians.

mental error to suppose that it can be described in an order of language designed to express objective matters of fact. It is for Man to speak *to* God in prayer and worship, not to talk *about* Him in a mood of speculative enquiry.

This criticism points to a dimension of mystery of which the philosophic student of religion needs to be constantly reminded. However, our job is to recognize mysteries, not to make them, and there is some danger of making them here.

The personalist protest owes much of its rhetorical force and its power as a stimulus to two dichotomies, which are neither of them as sharp as they are made to seem. They are (i) between talking *to* God, and talking *about* Him; (ii) between the personal I-Thou relation of encounter and the objective I-it relation of scientific investigation.

(i) Normally when we talk to someone we are in a position to say something *about* him, to answer questions about his situation, character and behaviour. What we believe about all this will affect how we address him and what we say. We should expect something analogous to this in the case of encounter with God, otherwise the metaphor would seem to be entirely 'eroded'.* And we do in fact find that men pray to God as having certain properties. The Book of Common Prayer provides many familiar examples: 'Almighty God, unto whom all hearts are open, all desires known and from whom no secrets are hid', 'Maker of all things, judge of all men', 'Thou art the same Lord, whose property is always to have mercy'. Men pray to God as they have been taught to think of Him, and would pray differently if they thought of Him differently.

It is true that a man cannot talk about the mysteries of religion and at all understand what he is saying without a sense of creatureliness which is akin to humility and worship; and this is the beginning of an 'encounter' with God. But emphasis on the personal nature of his relationship must admit its cognitive side too.

* For this notion of 'eroding' an analogy see Antony Flew, 'Theology and Falsification' in *New Essays in Philosophical Theology*, p. 98. Cf. also Dr. Farrer in Chapter III, p. 96 ff.

(ii) The dichotomy between the relation of encounter between persons and that of objective scientific investigation looks deceptively clear-cut. But what is it precisely that differentiates them? We may start confidently by placing the lover and the poet at one extreme and the physicist and the mathematician at the other, but where are we to put the sociologist, the psycho-analyst or the historian? The sociologist in his field work and the psychoanalyst in his consulting room cannot avoid entering into and to a greater or lesser extent affecting the lives of their subjects; the historian can enter into no such relationship with his. Yet the historian's task may call for equal or greater powers of imaginative sympathy. The motive for all three may be simple desire for knowledge (I-it?) or some general concern for people as such (I-Thou?).

There is not one distinction here, but many, and to identify them leads us to greatly oversimplify the activities of scientists and to draw too sharp a line between them and other rational activities.

Thus the protest cannot be accepted as it stands. The metaphysical problem of how we are to understand the divine activity in grace is not to be circumvented by restricting religious language to the second person singular.

However this protest, with its accent on the personal, compels us to look again at the engagingly simple alternatives first presented to us: *either* scientific statement *or* expression of attitude. It becomes clear that it is not going to be as easy as it looked to characterize 'scientific' statements, so that they will fit neatly into this classification.

The distinction was introduced in the first place in order to explain the apparent failure of religious statements to fulfil the logical requirements for statements of fact. The suggestion was that they failed to pass this test *either* because they were primitive and unsuccessful attempts at science *or* because they represented a fundamentally different use of language, whose purpose was not to convey information but to express an attitude to life or a resolve to live it in a certain way. In the latter case no question of 'evidence' arises; or if the term is retained it is to be used in a Pickwickian sense.

The believer is thus offered immunity from criticism at the price of abandoning any claim to deal with objective truth. It is a price he is for the most part unwilling to pay. And, indeed, it must be confessed that a great deal of this kind of discussion strikes the ordinary Christian and, indeed, the ordinary unbeliever too, as being curiously artificial and unrealistic. The atheist is agreed with the theist as to what they disagree about and neither is content to have the philosopher disengage them neatly from the conflict.

The whole question is further confused by wider and narrower uses of the word 'science', which will affect our interpretation of the phrase used earlier 'amenable to scientific test'. Theologians are, perhaps, specially to blame here. Some in their anxiety to stress the status of their subject as an intellectual discipline claim that theology is a science. Others, in order to emphasize the element of personal commitment in religion, tend to restrict the term 'science' to those basic sciences which are capable of exact mathematical treatment. (There are similar and scarcely less emotionally charged disputes as to whether psycho-analysis, or social anthropology or even history is to be reckoned a science.)

The truth surely is that there is no clear-cut distinction to be drawn between the sciences and other disciplines, but that they shade off gradually into humane studies, which are not susceptible of precise formal treatment.* It is characteristic of these humaner disciplines that they demand the exercise of sensitive, trained judgment, which is open to check only by the judgment of others.

In the light of this it becomes clear that the demand for scientific test masks two quite different requirements. One is a *logical* requirement; that for a statement to count as an assertion (as distinct from, say, a command or a wish) it must be possible to conceive evidence which would tell against it. The criterion proposed is for factual statements rather than scientific ones (unless

* See J. R. Lucas, 'The Lesbian Rule', *Philosophy*, 1955, for a full discussion of reason in the humanities.

'scientific' is used in a very wide sense). The other is a *metaphysical* requirement; that all factual statements must 'in principle' be capable of being worked into a scientific system governed by universal laws. Of these, the first is an entirely legitimate requirement, which can be satisfied by all sorts of non-scientific statements. The second is a requirement we have no *a priori* ground for accepting and as yet very little empirical evidence for.

One might put this in another way and say that it is reasonable to ask for evidence for theological statements, but not reasonable to require in advance that the evidence supplied should conform to canons based on the natural sciences, still less on any particular science. Indeed one would expect the pattern of theological thinking to resemble that of the humane studies rather than of the sciences. But this does not, of course, imply that we are here outside the domain of objective truth and that no question of rational justification arises. It seems, however, to be the case that the sort of judgment needed in these studies grows out of wide human experience and depth of sympathy, and, in the case of theology, is not developed independently of the practice of worship and the attempt to live the Christian life. This is where the emphasis on 'the personal' is justified.

We may sum up the argument so far:

(1) The demand for 'scientific' test may amount either to (*a*) the *logical* requirement that for a statement to be regarded as factual some conceivable evidence must bear on its truth or falsehood; (*b*) the *metaphysical* requirement that any statement of fact should be capable of being worked into a tight scientific system.

(2) Theological statements cannot meet the second requirement because they involve concepts such as 'grace' which are not suitable for incorporation into such a system.

But (i) there is no *a priori* reason for accepting this requirement.

(ii) There is a strong presumption against it when we look at the sciences which deal with human behaviour. These shade off into the humanities, where no such requirement is made.

(3) The type of thinking used in theology is likely to resemble that found in the humanities.

If the argument thus far has any force, the most it can have done is to show that theologians cannot be expected to produce evidence of a scientific kind; and that this does not mean that they cannot produce evidence at all. This, perhaps, should have been obvious from the start. Nevertheless the point needs making, because a good deal of misplaced criticism and mistaken apologetics trades on neglect of it. Religion is attacked as being non-rational, and defended as being immune from rational criticism, in each case because it is not scientific.

II

If the doctrine of grace is not open to scientific test and yet, as has been argued, is not without factual content, it remains to show how it can meet the logician's legitimate demand. What evidence can be called in support of it? If, as has been admitted, it does not function like an ordinary causal explanation, how *does* it function?

It was asserted at the beginning of this essay that belief in God's grace follows from belief in Him as the creator of free persons. It is a necessary development from the Christian doctrine of God. Hence whatever evidences (if that word is at all appropriate) can be found to support that doctrine will go to support this too.* But it was also suggested that there was independent support for the doctrine of grace in the religious experience of individuals and communities; but not *entirely* independent, because that experience is interpreted in terms of a religious tradition, based in its turn on the inspired scriptures. The argument has a circular motion, but this is not vicious, because each revolution brings in new material.

It *might* have been the case that Christians were bound to

* Mr Stead has dealt at greater length with this question in Chapter IV.

believe in the grace of God as a consequence of the Christian Revelation as a whole, but that it was not given them to know, because they had no need to know, when and where it was at work. They could not then appeal to this sort of religious experience in part confirmation of the general Christian claim. That this appeal *is* often made suggests that the Church does sometimes and in some places claim to recognize the actual intervention of the Holy Spirit. We must now ask how we could ever be in a position to make such an assertion.

It was suggested at the beginning of this essay that there are two kinds of experience which invite interpretation in these terms, the impression of holiness made by the saint and the sense of a liberating power at work in oneself. The appeal to such things forms part of the familiar 'argument from religious experience'. It is an argument which is hard to state in a way which is at all convincing and hence is treated by philosophers and theologians with reserve. Yet such is the impact of the experiences themselves that it is never finally abandoned.

Too often it has been claimed that such experiences are cases of direct awareness of the divine activity, of an infallible intuition. But this is a mistake. We cannot claim for human judgment in this context an infallibility which it does not possess elsewhere. We may take for divine inspiration what in fact was not, and fail to recognize what was. 'Insights' however profound need testing and interpreting. Indeed the traditional attitude of the Church in such matters is one of extreme caution—'Prove the spirits, whether they be of God'.

But this does not, of course, mean, as some critics have supposed, that we can never be in a position to be reasonably sure — any more than the possibility of optical illusions entails that one cannot recognize a familiar object in a good light. And, although the individual may be wise to be tentative, there are some cases where there have been too many good judges for them all to have been mistaken.

The use of the word 'experience' is itself dangerous in that it invites the rejoinder 'I see. You are talking about a peculiar sort of *feeling*. But feelings of all sorts can be induced by a wide variety of causes. They are far from self-authenticating. Even if, for the sake of argument, your experience *is* God-sent, you cannot experience it *as* God-sent.' This line of argument is reminiscent of the sense-datum theory of perception and has the same invincibility about it. No matter how much we protest that the experience has 'felt depth' in it (that the sense-datum, to quote Professor Price's example, is bulgy) we are told that this is just a quality of the experience. It gives us no warrant for inferring that the experience is *caused* in a certain way, in this instance by God. To know *that* requires some means of correlating such experiences with the divine acts which are said to cause them. And it is clear that no such means are available.

There is more to be said about this, but for the present we must protest against this choice of alternatives: viz. that *either* (*a*) the feeling is self-authenticating, in the sense of being a case of infallible direct awareness (on the sense-datum model) *or* (*b*) the recognition of this experience as an experience of grace is a matter of inductive inference from effect to cause.

A move in a slightly more promising direction would be to construe the grace of God (as is sometimes done), on the model of the theoretical concepts of physics, as an unobservable force postulated to explain certain observable phenomena. The difficulty here, as our previous argument has suggested, is that we cannot make the grace of God the basis of exact predictions which can be experimentally checked; and this is an essential feature of the physicist's models.

These accounts have one feature in common. They start with something called 'the experience' and try in their different ways to trace it to a supernatural origin. They tend to represent the experience as a more or less simple 'slab' of feeling or sensation to be recognized and identified in the same sort of way (though, being a rare phenomenon, not so easily) as a smell or a headache. There are two difficulties about this. Even if we were to succeed in discovering a supernatural cause, it could be no more than a mere πλανωμένη αἰτία, definable simply as 'the cause of these experiences' and having no predictive or explanatory value. And any such attribution becomes extremely hazardous because whatever sensation we choose to fasten upon as the core of the experience could be reproduced in a variety of other ways, as by drinks or drugs.

It is only when we have confirmed that the experience is a genuinely religious experience that it can provide the premiss for our argument. The sensation, in fact, is only one element in the complex whole which is the religious experience. It must occur in an appropriate context and be accompanied by appropriate dispositions and behaviour. If the man was drunk or drugged at the time, it probably wasn't a religious experience (though it just conceivably might be; God *might* choose these means). If it followed prayer or other religious devotions and issued in conspicuous acts of charity, then it almost certainly was. And so on. But there are no hard and fast criteria specifiable in advance.

There is an analogy to this in the way in which we recognize familiar emotions. We tend to think of love as a simple feeling, which a man just knows whether he has or not and can recognize by, as it were, looking. But careful introspection might reveal that it was felt largely as a sensation in the solar plexus. It is not the character of the sensation that makes it love but the part it plays in a total response to a special situation. But if we try to specify these further features, we cannot do so except in the most general terms, for there are innumerable forms and manifestations of love.

We must look, then, for *genuine* religious experiences and this means that we have to learn to recognize them. We have, in fact, to master a conceptual apparatus which will make sense of the experiences in question and relate them significantly to each other and to further facts. It is part of the function of a religious tradition to provide us with such an apparatus, and part of the verification of a religious revelation lies in its capacity to do this. It is for this reason and not from sheer obscurantism that the theologian does not start, as empiricists would like him to do, with an unexplained 'raw' phenomenon and try to frame some hypothesis to explain it. He starts with the promise of the Holy Spirit and looks for signs of His activity.

Believing, as he does, that human life rests on the sustaining power of God and is designed for perfect conformity with his will, he sees all good as the product of grace. So, if asked to point to instances of grace, he will for his own part feel justified in pointing to *any* genuinely good works. But this will naturally persuade no one who is not already convinced. To satisfy his critic he needs signs less generously distributed, more strikingly and unambiguously expressive of a supernatural origin. Where shall he find them?

To begin with, he might appeal to the witness of the saints; that is, he might try to establish some correlation between the sincere attempt to do God's will and the resultant quality of living. The test is not easily applied. It is not easy to test sincerity or to allow for all the variables. Yet opponents of religion habitually apply this test and, for all its limitations, rightly. If what Christians believe is true there *ought* to be a detectable difference here.

But though the test is applied, people notoriously differ about the results. For what qualities are to be looked for? It will not do to say simply 'outstanding goodness' for it is just the criteria of goodness that are often in dispute. The Christian has his own criteria, and many virtues that men have admired and honoured are omitted from St Paul's list of the fruit of the Spirit. 'For the fruit of the spirit is love, joy, peace, long-suffering, goodness, faith, meekness, temperance' (Gal. v. 22–23). No one would have compiled this list before the Christian era. It has little in common with Aristotle's catalogue of moral virtues. St Paul has listed the pre-eminently Christian virtues.

And it has to be admitted that these virtues are not simply the result of a fresh evaluation made independently of fresh experience. They are the characteristic attitudes of men in whom the love of God and their neighbour has replaced the love of self. They are the fruit of a spiritual discipline whose end is not primarily moral. And they are valued among other reasons *because* they are believed to be the effect in human nature of the divine love. They are, in fact, the qualities that in their completeness go to make up 'holiness' or 'saintliness'.

So in the face of the legitimate demand for evidence for (or against) the grace of God, the believer points to saintliness, as being the perfection of human goodness, yet at the same time manifesting a more than human quality, a love for men grounded in the love of God, growing to fruition in the soil of religious practice.

The saint, by contrast with the man of conscientious moral goodness, is spontaneous. The good he does appears to be less the deliberate object of his endeavours than the natural expression of what he is. He is like a spring perpetually welling up from an unseen source. To call a man 'holy' is not to praise him or to prize him but to recognize and respond to something in him that commands respect rather than deserves it. However great his moral stature he is, as von Hügel was always insisting, concerned more with 'isness' than with 'oughtness'.

It is in this context that we must consider that immediate impression of the holy which was one of the two types of peculiarly religious experience to which we earlier appealed as providing empirical support for the doctrine of grace. This man, we feel, when confronted with the saint, is strikingly different from ourselves, yet is thereby not less human, but more so. The strength and graciousness of his personality is somehow incommensurate with what we know of their natural antecedents. We are constrained to report the impact he makes upon us in the passive voice – we are 'moved', 'impressed', 'inspired', 'disturbed'. We cannot ourselves remain apart and unaffected, for the impact involves something like a moral demand upon us. In theological terms it 'convicts of sin'.

All these considerations conspire to produce the thrilling sense of the supernatural which the saintly personality characteristically excites in those who confront it. The 'thrill' itself, if it could be isolated, would be a sensation of no great interest or significance, yet as an element in this total situation it has great persuasive power.

In this way we may hope to avoid the standing objection to any argument from religious experience, such as Otto's appeal to the sense of the numinous. The objection is this. If the sense of the numinous is a *sufficient* criterion of the divine presence, then we must admit that God appears under a number of highly ambiguous forms. Experiences of the numinous are widespread and are often associated with cults of little or no religious value. If, on the other hand, it is made a *necessary* criterion we shall be forced to deny that God is active in many instances where on general grounds we wish to assert it – in all the many cases of simple, inconspicuous goodness.

This dilemma tends to drive philosophers of religion into one or other of two extreme positions. Some are led to see religion as fundamentally the awareness of a numinous substratum, and to dismiss dogmatic differences between the historical religions as the product of so much sociological conditioning, whilst others in defence of orthodoxy flee from this conclusion into a firm denial that religious experience has any evidential value whatever.

Both these positions rest upon a misunderstanding of the role which such a criterion may be expected to play. The sense of 'the holy' is neither a necessary nor a sufficient criterion of the divine presence, but it is nevertheless highly *characteristic* of it. In the same way people who know one another very well may experience sometimes an almost mystical sense of the other's presence:

'Our souls, which to advance their state
Were gone out, hung twixt her and me.

And whilst our souls negotiate there
We like sepulchral statues lay;
All day the same our postures were,
And we said nothing, all the day.'

Such an experience, though perhaps only momentary in an exchange of glances and not protracted, as in Donne's 'Ecstasy', is recognizably characteristic of close personal relations. But it may, of course, be quite illusory, a product of the evening and the scene, and it is certainly rare and may be entirely absent from a relationship which is close and genuine. But where it is *not* illusory (and there are ways of telling) we are justified in taking it for what it purports to be, not a superficial and superfluous emotional thrill, but a moment of insight. And if we were ever seriously tempted to doubt whether other people were conscious beings like ourselves, then such experiences, though far from universal and sometimes illusory, might legitimately be called in evidence.*

About the other kind of religious experience – the sense of being helped or guided, a similar account must be given. In us who are not saints it is certainly elusive and often illusory. Even when we dare to believe it genuine, it is an altogether slighter thing than the wind which blows through the saints. Nevertheless, such as it is, it serves as a clue to what the grace of God might mean, since it bears sufficient resemblance to the experience of the saints, in whom its characteristic fruits are found in their fullness.

It will be noticed how very difficult it is to describe these 'experiences' except in question-begging terms. The religious vocabulary keeps obtruding itself. And the suspicion awakened at this point might well extend to the whole argument. Is it not *all* question-begging?

---

* A familiar philosophical parallel is afforded by Hume's proposed criterion for distinguishing between impressions and ideas, namely the greater 'force and vivacity' of the former. His critics have pointed out that as a criterion it is neither necessary nor sufficient; not necessary, for an impression may be relatively faint, as when one's attention is absorbed; not sufficient, because ideas may be relatively vivacious, as in dreams. Nevertheless Hume is justified in appealing to this difference in defence of his distinction if he can show that 'force and vivacity' is highly characteristic of impressions.

He cannot, of course, in this case make 'force and vivacity' the *sole* criterion, nor, in our case, can the presence of 'the numinous' be made the sole criterion of the activity of the Holy Spirit.

For consider. The theologian, when pressed to be empirical and show how detectable features of our experience support the doctrine of grace, begs leave to start at the other end, with the doctrine itself. He then argues that if you understand what grace is (in its full theological context) you can, if you look in the right direction, discern signs of it at work. But, as soon as the critic fastens on the evidence offered, he begins to qualify and select. Religious experience is evidence, but only *genuine* religious experience. This may be tested, in part, by good works. So good works are evidence, but only as the Christian measures goodness. And so on.

This looks very much like a policy of accepting a given type of evidence where it is favourable and rejecting it where it is discrepant; and justifying this special pleading (when challenged) by reference to more fundamental beliefs which will in turn be supported in a similar way.

Yet this procedure, which can be made to look so disreputable, is not peculiar to theological discussion. It is, in fact, inseparable from the process of learning to use and coming to understand a large number of our non-scientific concepts. If asked to say what constitutes a tragedy or a revolution, an act of bravery or a fit of jealousy, we cannot specify in advance, except in the most general terms, the criteria we shall adopt. Yet it needs judgment to assign these terms correctly and we can defend our judgment rationally by pointing out the features upon which in each particular case we rely.

Such a judgment is not made in isolation: it is framed in a whole context of beliefs, moral, aesthetic, historical, psychological, themselves drawing support from other particular judgments. If, *per impossibile*, we could go over *all* the cases with a dissentient we could not compel him to learn our concepts or to agree in our application of them. But we should not for this reason admit the charge, so freely made in the religious case, that we were arbitrarily reading off our conclusion from a set of fixed presuppositions.

It is natural for those whose conception of rationality has been

modelled upon the natural sciences to insist that a final stand be
made somewhere and the doctrine of grace be put to some
decisive test. But the challenge has to be refused, because we are
dealing, if the Christian claim is correct, with the expression in
human life of a Creative Spirit, who is a Person. That His activity
issues in discernible differences I have been at pains to argue, but
we cannot with confidence predict what these will be.

The appropriate comparison is with other types of creative
activity. It would not, for example, have been possible to predict
what Shakespeare would make of the original story of Macbeth
or Coleridge of *Purchas his Pilgrimage*. Nevertheless when confronted with the completed tragedy and 'The Ancient Mariner'
we recognize them to be characteristic of their authors. If challenged to defend our attribution we refer (among other things) to
observable features of these works. Suppose then a critic tries to
pin us down to a list of Shakespearean or Coleridgean features;
we may assent in general terms, but always with a proviso, which
allows us to discount features we have included in the list, or lay
weight on some we have omitted from it. The author may always
surprise us by new departures, unpredictable, yet recognisably
his. Indeed the genius of a creative writer is in proportion to his
capacity to achieve what could not have been predicted, while
convincing us of its inevitability. But this does not mean that *any
result whatsoever* will earn our subsequent acquiescence.

As with the author, so with his characters. Tolstoi convinces
us that we know his characters so well that we can foretell just
how they are going to act in an impending crisis, but in the event
he astonishes us by making them behave quite differently. We are
forced to admit our error. *This* is, after all, how they would have
acted.

Hardy, by contrast, makes his characters act quite as unpre-
dictably but often fails to convince us, because we are left feeling
that he has contrived the effect in the interest of his *weltanschauung*. They appear as puppets, not men. It is the same with
Sartre, whose people are as much the victims of their inner freedom as are Hardy's of his cosmic fate. This shows that our

inability in such cases to predict does not license us to claim *any* effect that is produced as confirming our judgment.

Thus far we have done two things: we have stated a case for the doctrine of grace, by claiming that it is open to empirical check, though not by scientific methods, and we have sought to defend this *way* of stating the case as being appropriate to an enquiry of this sort.

Suppose now the critic concedes, as I think he must, that an argument along these lines is legitimate, he may still object that, nevertheless, in this case it entirely fails to convince him. 'What you have said is all very well', he says, 'but it does not establish your claim that the so-called experience of grace or the recognition of holiness is an experience or recognition of the divine at work in the human. All it does is to suggest that "religious" experiences and "religious" geniuses occur. It may be conceded that criteria can be found for both of these (though, perhaps, none that are necessary and sufficient), and that there is no way of predicting scientifically how they will manifest themselves. But the same can be said of any form of human creative activity, as you yourself have argued. So you still lack any justification for going *beyond* these phenomena and claiming that they are expressions of grace; unless, of course, this is simply a religious way of saying that they are unique and irreducible. An artist may feel inspired; such a feeling is indeed highly characteristic of artistic activity. His work may impress others as inspired, too. And this *was* once ascribed to the Gods or the Muses, but no one makes this attribution nowadays, except figuratively. Why should the religious case be different?'

Now it is, of course, no part of our case to deny the possibility or propriety of natural explanations, so long as these are not held to be exclusive and exhaustive. But we have pointed to certain happenings (whether naturally explicable or not) as signs of God's activity and expressive of His nature. This means that the natural explanations, though legitimate, must in these cases be felt inadequate to exhaust their full significance.

The problem is, how to convince the *critic* of their inadequacy, how to induce, or revive, in him a sense of dissatisfaction with the 'flat' naturalistic account (since there is, in the nature of the case, no way of *coercing* him out of it).

In the present case language itself points a difference. If we have any use for the expression 'religious genius' we mean by it something significantly different from a saint, and a great part of the difference is due to our feeling that the saint is a God-centred man. It would not be so much false, as inappropriate and incongruous to call St Paul or St Augustine or St Vincent de Paul great men. We can talk about the giants of literature, but scarcely about the giants of religion. St Paul may have started life as a 'religious genius'; but he became a saint.

This is not to be taken as simply a verbal point. As such it would be clearly unfair. The objector need not maintain that the word 'saint' could be dropped and the expression 'religious genius' substituted without change of meaning. He is simply maintaining that to call a man a saint is to recognize in him certain fine, but wholly natural qualities of character. Yet to think of saintliness in this way would in effect be to understand it very differently from the way we* do and to make it something much more like what we mean by 'genius'. The concept of saintliness as we receive it from our common Christian tradition is closely bound up with the notion of God-dependence and cannot be detached from it without radical change of meaning. The qualities we select as our criteria of sanctity are decisively determined by this central relationship. That is why, when John Stuart Mill is called 'The Saint of Rationalism' it is so very hard to guess what positive qualities are being ascribed to him.

We cannot regard saintliness as a purely natural flowering of the human spirit without affirming that it contains as part of its essence the capacity to be fundamentally deluded. For the saint's life is characteristically centred upon God. A man can

* 'We' perhaps here means 'we who have been influenced by a Christian tradition and whose language has been shaped by it.' See Mr Foster's essay, Chapter IX, esp. p. 206 ff.

be a poet without caring a fig for poetic inspiration. He can scarcely be a saint without recognizing his dependence upon God.*

It might, of course, simply be a contingent fact that certain rare qualities of character were found to flourish in association with certain characteristic mythological beliefs. Yet, if this were so, it would be hard not to regard them as, in the last resort, splendid faults.

Here much will depend on the estimate we form of the mental balance of religious people and of the morbidity or otherwise of our own spiritual inclinations – judged by ordinary standards. Our argument has been that, if in certain people there appears a quality of life which is out of scale with its natural antecedents, and if such people move us in an unaccountably profound and yet not morbid fashion, and if we ourselves from time to time are aware, or seem to be aware, of an unsuspected power, informing but not distorting our natural faculties, then we may see in these things the grace of God perfecting nature. They impel us in the direction of the supernatural, although they do not and cannot provide us with an adequate conception of it. The doctrine of grace offers an interpretation of them which, within the context of the Christian Revelation as a whole, affords them the signifi- cance they ask for. This works both ways (as was suggested tentatively at the beginning). For someone who lacked any experience of these things could scarcely begin to give meaning to 'grace'. There would be nothing in his experience answering to the conception.

III

The doctrine of the grace of God, as we said at the outset, follows from belief in God the creator and sustainer. It cannot, then, be adequately explained or substantiated independently of

* This recognition may be more or less explicit; but it is, for the most part, quite explicit.

that belief. Yet it has been the argument of this chapter that this doctrine has its own relatively independent evidence which goes some way to support the whole system. Belief in the grace of God cannot be established by empirical evidence but, once accepted, it can be seen to have empirical application.

But there is danger of a certain unbalance in approaching the doctrine from the empirical end. Challenged to defend the factual character of statements about grace by pointing to cases where it makes a detectable difference, we have been led to emphasize its more remarkable and striking manifestations. And this may easily convey the impression that grace has to do only with abnormal, *spectacular* irruptions into the lives of the professedly religious. This is one more reason why the argument from religious experience has not appealed to many sensitively religious minds. But a more broadly theological approach teaches us that we cannot presume to limit the divine activity to those instances in which it may be discernible to us. Such instances may be clearly revelatory (must be, if our previous argument is to have any force) yet they are revelatory of the God, whose activity we believe on general grounds, to underlie even the most tentative and inarticulate movements of the human soul towards conformity with the pattern of Christ. They are like the phosphorescent crest of a wave which enables us to detect a sea whose boundaries we could not chart. Having made an entry for the concept of grace by tracing it as it breaks through more or less spectacularly into human experience, we are led to extend its application to all good works, whether characterized by the numinous or not, whether or not associated with religious belief. It is enough that they tend in the direction of that complete holiness, which is the 'fruit of the spirit'.

What secret workings of the human soul *do* tend in this direction, we are for the most part unable to say. We are rarely in a position to chart any man's spiritual history. Hence together with the conviction that in such conspicuous instances as the labours of St Paul the grace of God is clearly at work goes a marked hesitation to deny outright the activity of God even in the most unpromising events.*

One further disclaimer is needed. We have been concerned to deny the charge that religion has no dealings with rationality, to counter the old gibe that 'a theologian is one whose premisses are arbitrary, but whose methods optional'. But this must not obscure the fact that the place of reason in religion is chiefly to trace the boundaries of mystery. Our argument has sought pointers to the divine activity in grace. It has said little or nothing of the mystery which is its nature. Here we must fall back on metaphors†, which are apt to mislead if overpressed, and which generate intractable problems, if their incomplete and analogical character is not clearly recognized. It is not surprising if most of the metaphors of grace are drawn from personal relationships, for they alone do full justice to human freedom. Thus we talk of God's guiding, comforting, supporting, consoling, forgiving us. But we also have need of more crudely physical analogies, as of an 'influx' or 'infusion', by which we contrive to stress man's utter dependence. Perhaps of all these metaphors that of light gets nearest to what we want to say, from the grandeur of Milton's:

> So much the rather thou celestial light
> Shine inward and the mind through all her powers
> Irradiate.

to the more everyday 'The love of God shone through him'. This metaphor gives the needed suggestion of causal dependence as well as of revelation.

But it has been my task, not to elucidate such language, but to examine those features of our experience which impel us to learn it.

---

* Though the word 'grace' itself is, perhaps, limited by definition to God's activity in and through the human person, *in so far as it is expressive of His nature.*

† For a fuller discussion of the role of images or metaphors in theological language see Chapter II, p. 73 ff.

CHAPTER VII

RELIGION AND MORALS

by R. M. Hare

THIS paper is an attempt to indicate the bearing on the philosophy of religion of recent discussions in the field of moral philosophy.* I am still not at all certain what I want to say about this difficult subject; and I have been persuaded to publish the paper in the present volume by two considerations only. The first is that the type of view here tentatively put forward is attacked by some other contributors to the volume; and readers may therefore find it useful to have to hand a statement of the view which is being rebutted. The second is that, since I am at the moment not able to make much progress in this enquiry, others may be helped to do so by my setting out some considerations which seem to me important. They are to be warned, however, that much in this paper is undigested, and the last section, at least, positively indigestible.

The recent history of moral philosophy has been the history of the impact upon it of that philosophical movement which is usually referred to loosely as Logical Empiricism or Logical Positivism. From the point of view of moral philosophy the most challenging thing the Logical Empiricists did was this: they directed their attention to a certain type of language, namely to those sentences which express 'scientific propositions' and other statements of fact, in the narrow sense; and they examined the conditions under which we are prepared to allow that such sentences are meaningful. They claimed that the criterion which we employ is this: to know the meaning of such a sentence is to know what would have to be the case for the statement which it expresses to be called true, or false. There are various ways of formulating this criterion; but I will not here discuss their relative merits, nor whether the criterion *can* be formulated in a satisfactory way. It is enough to say that this criterion, when it was first

* It is adapted from a lecture given at the Royal Institute of Philosophy in February, 1954.

propounded, aroused much enthusiasm among empiricist philosophers. For here, they thought, was a way of eliminating from the pages of philosophy, once for all, those sentences (of which there are, it must be confessed, too many) that do not carry any weight of meaning. Philosophical books, it was said, are full of statements or so-called statements to which, when we examine them in the light of this criterion, we cannot assign any significance at all; we cannot think what would have to be the case for us to call them true, or false. Such books the empiricists, following Hume's prescription, were prepared to commit to the flames as containing nothing but sophistry and illusion.

The result of following this prescription was to sweep language too clean. At the time, the impact on both moral philosophy and the philosophy of religion was startling; for by this criterion it was thought that both moral statements and statements of religious belief could be shown to be only 'pseudo-propositions' and the sentences expressing them 'literally senseless'. But it later appeared that all that had been done was to isolate *one* kind of use we make of language, and to give a criterion of meaningfulness for statements made in this field. If we confine ourselves to what are ordinarily called statements of empirical fact, the criterion is enormously useful. Indeed, it might be said that the criterion provides us with a way of ascertaining, not whether what somebody says has meaning *of any sort*, but at least whether it has empirical meaning. For to call a statement an empirical one is perhaps to include it in the class of those statements of which we can say or show what would have to be the case in our own experience or somebody else's for us to call them true or false. What we have here, then, is not really a criterion of meaningfulness (a way of separating wheat from chaff) but a criterion of empiricality (a way, as we might say, of separating wheat from oats, or barley, or rice). Or, to use St Paul's metaphor, our language

is not one member, but many. If the foot shall say, Because I am not the hand, I am not of the body; is it therefore not of the body?

And if the ear shall say, Because I am not the eye, I am not of the body; is it therefore not of the body? If the whole body were an eye, where were the hearing? If the whole were hearing, where were the smelling? But now God hath set the members every one of them in the body, as it hath pleased Him. And if they were all one member, where were the body? But now they are many members, yet but one body.*

Anatomy and its related disciplines (physiology, pathology, etc.) are the study of the several parts of the body to see what they are like, how related to one another, what the function of each is, and how it can go wrong. The more these sciences have progressed, the less inclined people have become to despise or depreciate parts of the body whose use they do not yet know. It has often been discovered that some insignificant-looking piece of the body, to which nobody had paid any attention, is in fact so important that we could not live without it — that some small organ, which seemed to be only a part of a larger one, has in fact its own peculiar function, without which the whole body would perish.

Logic, as it is being studied in many of the most important philosophical schools at the present time, is the anatomy of language. Since among the functions of language are thought and communication, the physiology of language, which goes along with its anatomy, is the study of the different ways in which we think and the different sorts of things that we communicate to each other. The most important result of the challenge made by the Logical Empiricists has been to stimulate an intensive study of these various uses of language. We have been forced to recognize that there is a very large number of different things that we do with words, and that they all have a vital part to play in our thought and discourse. The logician who thinks that he can confine his attention to one of them and ignore the rest is not doing the whole of his job.

About some kinds of words quite a lot has been discovered;

* 1 Cor. xii. 14.

this applies, I think, to various kinds of words used in scientific discourse, and also to moral words. How much has been discovered about any kind of discourse has depended, first of all on the amount of time and interest philosophers have given to it; but more on the relative complexity and difficulty of the kind of discourse in question. Religious discourse has come off badly on both these counts. For in the first place few philosophers nowadays are interested enough in religious questions to make them their main study; not many are even sufficiently conversant with the use of religious language to succeed in such an enquiry. And secondly, religious language is, as I hope to make clear, a very difficult subject; there are a great many different kinds of things that we say, which are all part of religious language; and some of these things can be said or listened to with comprehension only by people whose experience of the religious life has gone much further than that of most of us modern philosophers. But, on the other hand, many of the logical problems raised are not such as can be dealt with by logical amateurs. For this reason some who know very well how to use religious language have not been able to give a very convincing *account* of its use, just as some gardeners can grow very good vegetables without being able to tell us clearly or even correctly how they do it.

The present essay is intended only as a first attempt to explore part of this field. I wish first of all to draw attention to some points of similarity between moral language and some sorts of religious language. At the very least it will, I hope, be agreed that all or nearly all religions have what may be called a moral aspect. By this I mean, not merely that the adherents of a particular religion have in fact usually adhered to a particular set of moral principles, but that the moral principles are linked in some intimate way with the religious belief. Thus we find religious teachers, as part of their religious teaching, uttering moral precepts. The most tangible way (if I may so put it) of distinguishing between different religions is to see how their adherents behave. What was it that happened to St Paul when he stopped being an ordinary Jew and became a Christian? There may be a more recondite answer to this question; but at any rate there is this obvious answer, that he stopped doing one sort of thing (persecuting Christians) and started doing another (converting new Christians). Thus one obvious thing that happened to him was that his ideas about what he ought to do (his principles of action, or, in a wide sense, his moral principles) changed radically. And this is also true of lesser converts. Part of what it means to stop being a drunkard or a cannibal and become, say, a Methodist, is that one stops thinking it right to consume gin or human flesh. That religion is very intimately linked with morals, so that one cannot be said to adhere to or accept a religion, unless one accepts and at least tries to act on its moral precepts, is implied by St James:

If any man thinketh himself to be religious, while he bridleth not his tongue but deceiveth his heart, this man's religion is vain. Pure religion and undefiled before our God and Father is this, to visit the fatherless and widows in their affliction, and to keep himself unspotted from the world.*

This may afford some comfort to the Christian empiricist; for the logical character and significance of moral judgments can by this time, I think, be stated in a way that would meet with fairly general acceptance among empiricists. To realize, therefore, that what religious people say in the course of their religious activities is in part moral is to realize that at any rate not all religious discourse is senseless. But this will be regarded, perhaps, as only a small contribution to the solution of the problem; for, it will be said, the *distinctive* character of religious discourse is not thereby illuminated. We may admit that part of this discourse consists of moral judgments; but not the central part. The moral judgments, as we may say, arise out of the religious belief; they do not constitute it. St Paul thought that he ought to stop persecuting Christians because he had changed his belief about a specifically

* St James, i, *sub. fin.*; cf. ii, 14 ff.

religious matter which was not itself a matter of how one ought to behave, but more like a matter of fact; he had come to believe that Jesus was the Christ, the Son of God.

I do not think that it is possible to sort out this question without a more thorough investigation of the way in which factual beliefs and principles of action are related to each other, and the way in which both are related to our actual conduct. There is a famous doctrine of Aristotle's which, I am convinced, offers the key to a great range of problems in this field, namely the theory of the practical syllogism.* Aristotle said, roughly, that when a man does anything, there are two things that lie behind what he does. He calls these two things the two premisses of the practical syllogism. The major premiss is some kind of precept or aim or prescription. The minor premiss is a statement of fact. The conclusion of the syllogism is an action. Thus, if I accept the principle that one ought always, if one has a streaming cold, to stay away from public places, and if I know that I have a streaming cold, I do stay away. Aristotle includes among major premisses of this sort of syllogism everything that can be called, in a phrase that Professor Braithwaite has used, 'springs of action'.† That is to say, he includes both desires, and purposes, and principles. Since what I wish to say can be said without discussing the important though troublesome distinctions between these different things, I shall adopt Professor Braithwaite's phrase. I shall also from time to time use the particular expression 'moral principles', although I should more correctly express what I have in mind if I used some more general and cumbrous expression such as 'principles

* For references see D. J. Allan, 'The Practical Syllogism', in *Autour D'Aristote: Receuil d'Etudes offert a Mgr. A. Mansion* (Louvain, 1955), p. 325.

† *Proceedings of the Aristotelian Society*, Supp. vol. xx (1946), p. 9.

Professor Braithwaite's Eddington Memorial Lecture on 'An Empiricist's View of the Nature of Religious Belief' (Cambridge University Press, 1955) was delivered too late for consideration in this paper. I have, however, benefited greatly from the study of his other published and unpublished writings on this subject. Few writers indeed can match his sincerity, courage, and understanding of the question.

governing conduct'. That is to say, I do not wish here to raise, any more than did Aristotle, the important and difficult question of what distinguishes moral principles from other principles of action.

I have said elsewhere that a man's moral principles are most reliably ascertained by seeing what he *does*.* This view has been strongly attacked; but I still hold it. For I think that if a man consistently breaks a moral principle which he professes, this inclines us to say that his professions are insincere. But it has also been commonly held that the way to find out about *any* of a man's beliefs, factual or otherwise, is to study what he does. And this must be true, provided that the word 'does' is given a sufficiently wide interpretation. For the only thing that we *can* study about a man is what he does. We cannot take his mind out and look at it (even if such an expression is meaningful); and, therefore, if we are to find out anything about his thoughts, we can do so only by studying his actions (including, of course, those actions which consist in his talking to us). I need not now raise the question whether the actions are merely *evidence* of the thoughts, or whether, as some have held, thinking *consists* in acting in a certain way. But at any rate it follows from what I have said that if believing something is a kind of thinking, we can only find out what a man believes by studying his actions; and likewise, if holding a moral principle, or desiring something, or having a certain purpose, are in a wide sense kinds of thinking, we can only find out about a man's principles or purposes or desires by studying his actions.

An example will help to illustrate the view which I am presenting, and some of its difficulties. If we see a visitor from another town, who has no other means of conveyance than the train, looking at the clock, which says 10.25, and going on talking unconcernedly, we may conclude either that he *believes* that the last train leaves after about 10.30 or that he does not *want* to get home to-night. The possibility of drawing *either* of these two conclusions presents us with a problem. If we assume that he

* *Language of Morals*, p. 1.

wants to get home to-night we can conclude from his behaviour
that he believes that there is a train after 10.30. If, on the other
hand, we assume that he believes that there is no train after 10.30,
we can conclude from his behaviour that he does not want to get
home to-night. What we cannot do is to draw both these conclusions at once without making any assumptions. In Aristotelian
terms, from the premisses 'Let me do whatever is necessary to get
home to-night' (major) and 'To get home to-night it is necessary
to catch a train at or before 10.30' (minor) there follows the
conclusion 'Let me catch a train at or before 10.30'; and this
conclusion would be expressed in action by catching the train.
So if the man does not catch the train we can conclude that he
does not accept one of the premisses, if we assume that he does
accept the other. In short, actions are evidence for springs of
action, if we assume beliefs; or for beliefs, if we assume springs
of action; but they cannot be evidence for both at the same time.
This, it may be noticed in passing, presents a very real, though
perhaps not insuperable, difficulty for those who wish to analyse
statements about *all* mental states, including both desires and
beliefs, in terms of statements about behaviour.

Let us now return to St Paul. He had always believed that he
ought to follow the Christ when He appeared. Thus, it might be
said, his conversion was not an alteration in his moral principles;
they did not change at all. What was altered was the minor
premiss – his factual belief. For whereas he had previously
believed that Jesus was a pretender, he now came to believe that
He was the Christ. This altered his actions, not through altering
his moral principles, but through altering his opinion about a
matter of fact.

Yet I find it very difficult to accept this view either. For when
a man says 'Jesus is Christ' or 'Jesus is Lord' is he stating a fact
(in the ordinary sense) at all? I think it would be agreed that of the
people who were familiar with Jesus in His earthly life, some were
ready to make this affirmation, and some were not. St Paul,
perhaps, knew in one sense all the facts about Jesus *before* his

conversion. He even knew, perhaps, that He cast out devils – but then non-Christian Jews had an explanation of this; He cast out devils, they said, by Beelzebub, the prince of the devils. Now what is the *factual* difference between casting out devils by Beelzebub, and casting them out by the finger of God? Or between either of these and curing mental disorders by suggestion (if that is the correct term)? The *fact* is that the symptoms of the disorder cease. It seems to me that one might, in one sense of the word 'fact', know all the facts about Jesus and still refuse to call Him 'Lord' or 'Christ'.

'But' it might be said, 'this leaves out what from St Paul's point of view was the most important fact of all, namely what actually happened to him upon the road to Damascus. Surely here was a new fact, and one which made him ready to acknowledge that Jesus was the Christ.' Yet someone else might say 'What happened to St Paul was that he had a very powerful emotional experience, accompanied by an illusion of someone talking to him, which shook him a great deal, so that he couldn't even see for a bit, and after which he changed his pattern of behaviour.' The same objector would, no doubt, say the same sort of thing about the other appearances of Jesus after His death. What, then, when we are dealing with 'supernatural' facts, is the difference between facts and illusions?

There is another possibility which might be suggested at this point. It might be said: 'If one person says "Jesus is Christ" and another denies this, they may not be differing about the facts; it may be that they have different attitudes to the facts. St Paul, when this thing happened to him, changed his whole way of life; another person, if the same thing happened to him, might have said "Sign of overstrain! I've been driving myself too hard, persecuting these Christians; I must take a holiday and then I'll feel better"'. According to this view St Peter, when he said 'Thou art the Christ', was not stating a fact; he was *doing* something, namely worshipping.

Now there is indeed such a thing as an attitude of worship; and it is plausible to say that to take up this attitude is part at any rate of what a person does when he is converted. It is therefore necessary to consider, in what can only be a superficial way, what is meant by 'worship'. The first thing to notice is that it is nearly always much easier to say of somebody *that* he is worshipping than to say *what* he is worshipping. 'The heathen in his blindness bows down to wood and stone'; but can we say that wood and stone, considered in themselves, are the real objects of his worship? We are not, for our present purposes, concerned with the answer to this old question, but with the logical character of the question itself. If we find a heathen bowing down to a piece of wood, and doing all the other things that would normally be called 'worshipping' it (suppose, for example, that he will not use the wood of that kind of tree for any profane purpose), then we can surely say that he is worshipping the piece of wood. If someone says 'He isn't really worshipping the piece of wood, but some invisible god whom he conceives of as resident in the piece of wood', then we may if we like agree with this; but I can think of cases in which this might well seem a distinction without a difference. We are reminded here of Professor Ryle's views about the mind.* Suppose that we ask 'What is the difference between, on the one hand, doing all the things that I habitually do to my wife, and on the other, doing all the same things and in addition thinking of her as a person?' It is not at all clear to me how one would answer such a question. It may be said 'If you can love something in the way that you love your wife, you must be thinking of it (her) as a person.' But this remark is two-edged. For it is intended to be an analytic statement; and therefore it would seem that on this view thinking of something as a person is an analytically necessary condition for being said to love it (him, her). But if so, then loving it (him, her) is an analytically sufficient condition for being said to think of it (him, her) as a person. And if this is applicable to worship as well as to love, then we may say that worshipping something is an analytically sufficient condition

* See *The Concept of Mind*, by G. Ryle, and comment by Mr Lucas on pp. 135, 138–45, of this volume.

for being said to think of it as a person. By this I mean, not that if we find someone worshipping something we are entitled to say that that thing *is* a person; but only that we are entitled in such a case to say that he *thinks* of it as a person. The further question remains, how we tell whether he is *right* to think of it as a person.

How then do I tell whether I am right to think of my wife as a person? I do not wish to answer this question at too great length. But if she does all the things which I expect persons to do, does not that show that I am right? And can we not say this of the piece of wood? Of course the piece of wood does not walk about or talk. But that is not what its worshipper expects. He expects only that worship of the piece of wood will be followed by a course of events favourable to him (rain at the right time, for example) whereas neglect of its worship will be followed by an opposite course of events.

Now if a person adopts an attitude of worship towards some object, and therefore thinks of it (or of something resident in it) as a person; and if everything which he expects to happen actually happens, shall we not say that he is right to worship it? Shall we not say that it is for him a proper object of worship? And if a proper object of worship, then a god; for only a god can be a proper object of worship (this statement is analytic). Moreover, on this interpretation the statement 'This piece of wood is a god' is falsifiable; for when the missionary comes and casts down the piece of wood, and the results which its worshippers expect do not follow, this is just the sort of thing that makes people say that it was false to call it a god, or, for short, that it was a false god. The more primitive a religion is, the more readily are its statements open to empirical falsification; religion has advanced from its more primitive to its less primitive forms partly by the empirical falsification of the claims of the more primitive forms, which then come to be known as superstitions. The less primitive a religion becomes, the less willing are its adherents to make predictions about what their god will do; in particular, they become less certain that he will act to what *they* conceive to be their advantage. Thus the prescriptive, attitudinal element in religious belief gains at the expense of the descriptive factual element.

If it be so, our God whom we serve is able to deliver us from the burning fiery furnace; and he will deliver us out of thine hand, O king. But if not, be it known unto thee, O king, that we will not serve thy gods, nor worship the golden image which thou hast set up.*

This process, as is well known, has caused certain empiricist philosophers to maintain that religious 'advances' have been made at the cost of making statements of religious faith less open to empirical falsification, and, therefore, by the empiricist criterion, less meaningful. A possible answer to this attack is that, first, as it is the purpose of this paper to show, the empirical component in the meaning of religious language is not the only one, nor even, perhaps, the most important; and secondly, that even advanced religions require of their adherents *some* empirical expectations.

Likewise, even in the most primitive forms of religion, what is being stated is not just empirical fact. For if, as I have implied, the meaning of the word 'god' (with a small 'g') is 'a proper object of worship', the word 'proper' in the *definiens* is a value-word. Here we come back to something rather like morals (for 'proper' as used here, though not a moral word, is, like moral words, prescriptive). According to this view, in calling something a god, we are saying, not merely that worshipping it will have certain results, but that it is *proper* to worship it; that is to say, we are at least in part prescribing the taking up of a certain attitude towards it. And whether we are to say that a person really believes in a certain god will depend on what attitude he takes up to the object which is said to be a god; that is, it will depend on what he *does*. Those who have followed recent discussions of the various elements of meaning possessed by value-words will recognize here familiar features. The word 'god' has both evaluative and descriptive meaning. In virtue of its descriptive meaning statements containing it may be said to be verifiable and falsifiable by those

* Daniel iii. 17.

who accept the same standards of evaluation as the speaker (and this does not necessarily involve accepting the *whole* of his religious beliefs). In virtue of its evaluative meaning we say that a person who does not behave in a certain way towards a certain object is not treating it as a god.

I return now for the last time to St Paul. It seems fairly clear that it will not do to try to find some one thing about St Paul which changed when he became a Christian. If we ask 'Was it his beliefs about matters of fact which changed, or his moral principles, or some other kind of value-principles, or his attitude to something or other, or something else?' then we are asking for trouble. Surely we must say that almost everything about St Paul changed; he became 'a new creature'. If this is true, we shall not find a single simple analysis of religious statements which solves all philosophical problems concerning them; for not only are there many kinds of utterances which religious people make in the course of their religion (this would be difficult enough); but almost all these kinds of utterances are, so to speak, in circuit with all the rest. A religious person may make what is *prima facie* a statement of fact – perhaps even a statement of quite ordinary empirical fact like 'If I do but touch His garment I shall be made whole' – and yet perhaps he would not have made this statement at all unless it were bound up with all sorts of other beliefs, dispositions, attitudes, and so on. This is, to my mind, the chief reason why religious discourse has always baffled philosophers – and, I am inclined to add, long may it continue to baffle them if they think that to understand it is a merely *philosophical* problem.

I wish, therefore, to conclude this paper by giving what is little more than a bare classification of some of the chief sorts of things that religious people say and do in the course of their religion, and which, taken together, constitute religious belief. I do not wish to claim that the list is either comprehensive or sufficiently finely distinguished. It will be noticed that the items group themselves into a triad rather like the thesis, antithesis and synthesis of an earlier philosophy. I started, it will be remembered, by considering the suggestion that moral judgments are the distinctive constituents of religious discourse. This view I rejected, and then considered in turn the claim of statements of religious belief to be called statements of fact in the ordinary sense; and this, too, appeared unsatisfactory. If we take religious language as a whole, it is too factual to be called specifically moral, and yet too closely bound up with our conduct to be called in the ordinary sense factual.

I therefore came back to a position which has affinities with both the preceding ones. Taking up an attitude of worship to an object considered as a person is not quite like adopting a purely factual belief; nor is it simply subscribing to certain principles of conduct; but it involves both these things. The person who worships is bound to govern his conduct (or let it be governed) in a certain way; and he is also bound to believe in the truth of certain factual statements (empirical ones about what has actually happened in the world, and what is likely to happen). As a first sketch of a synthesis, it is plausible to say that in so far as religious discourse seems to refer to supernatural facts, this is the result of the superimposition of the attitude of worship upon factual beliefs which are themselves not other than empirical; that, in fact, we have here a case like that of 'non-natural qualities' in ethics. When we say that a strawberry is good because it is sweet, and yet by calling it good mean to say something else of it than simply that it is sweet, we are tempted to think that by calling it good we are attributing to it some *quality*, somehow like sweetness yet of a different, 'non-natural' kind – a quality which cannot be tasted but only grasped by thought, and which is the consequence of the natural quality of sweetness. In truth, however, what we are doing is not attributing to the strawberry any other quality at all besides sweetness; but we are, as well as attributing to it that perfectly ordinary quality, *commending* it for having the quality. In the same way it might be that the *facts* that religious discourse deals with are perfectly ordinary empirical facts like what happens when you pray; but we are tempted to call them supernatural facts because our whole way of living is organized round them; they have for us value, relevance, importance, which they would not have if we were atheists. If this view were correct, then the belief that there are specifically religious, supernatural facts could be said to be the result of failing to distinguish in logic what cannot be distinguished in practice, namely, facts, and our attitudes to them.

Even this, however, will not do. For it implies that there *is* a clear distinction in logic between facts and our attitudes to them. But though it is most important to start by making this distinction, it is important to end, not by blurring it, as is often done, but by articulating the relations between these two kinds of thing.

People sometimes talk as if facts were somehow given us entirely independently of any dispositions of our own with regard to them. Kant saw that this is not so; but I will not attempt to formulate what I wish to say in his language. I can put the point briefly (at the cost of obscurity) by saying that any statement of fact which claims *objectivity* will be found on analysis to contain an element which is ineradicably *modal* (a reference to causal necessity); and that such modal statements are not analysable in purely descriptive terms, but have a prescriptive element. This element is not the same as, but it presents certain analogies with, the prescriptive element in moral judgments. From this it follows that without principles of some sort we do not get any facts; there is no distinction between fact and illusion for a person who does not take up a certain attitude to the world.

This is obviously not the place to expand these somewhat pregnant remarks. But fortunately, in a subject the full logical discussion of which is too complicated to be attempted until logical studies have advanced further, a great deal of light has been shed by recent discoveries and probable conjectures of physiologists. That physiology should shed light on a logical problem may seem impossible to a philosophical purist; but if the thinking which is expressed in language is done by, or involves the use of, the brain, it is to be expected that there will be certain formal analogies between the features of language which logicians study and the processes which physiologists find going on in the brain. In the same way, if a calculating-machine does mathematics there will be formal analogies between the expression in mathematical language of the calculations which it does and the physical operations of the parts of the machine.

It is therefore extremely significant that, in his recent Reith Lectures, Professor Young, speaking of the brain, said some things which must have a familiar ring to any philosopher who has read Kant.* This is all the more paradoxical in that Kant himself would have considered it outrageous that empirical discoveries about the brain should have any relevance to his doctrines. But to us it may appear that, since to talk we have to use our brains, the fact that a student of the brain echoes what has been said several centuries before by a student of metaphysics shows that the latter's studies were very firmly based, as they should be, in the facts of our use of words. At any rate it seems to me that Professor Young has paid to Kant the same sort of back-handed compliment as Kant paid to Swedenborg; the dreams of the metaphysician have been considerably elucidated by the dreams of the neuro-physiologist.

'We cannot speak', says Professor Young, 'as if there is a world around us of which our senses give us true information. In trying to speak about what the world is like we must remember all the time that what we see and what we say depends on what we have learned; we ourselves come into the process.' And elsewhere he says: 'The brain of each one of us does literally create his or her own world. To explain this we must answer the question: How does each brain set up its own characteristic rules? How do those regular patterns of activity in the cells of the brain . . . develop? This is the process that I call the establishment of certainty, and it is a process that we may consider as beginning in each human being at the moment when, as a newly born baby, his eyes open on to the world.' In his lectures Professor Young gives an account in some detail of how these rules, as he calls them, are formed in the brain (how, we might say, we learn to distinguish facts, or to

* *Doubt and Certainty in Science*, by J. Z. Young. See esp. pp. 61, 108.

understand the concept 'fact'). It is to be hoped that these new discoveries will finally and effectively remove from the repertory of philosophical theories that one which Professor Popper has called 'the bucket theory of the mind'* – the theory that facts drip into the mind like water into a bucket, where they accumulate and are called 'knowledge'. The lesson that is to be learnt from Professor Young, as from Kant, is that (as Kant might put it) nothing can become an object (or a fact) for us unless in our thinking we follow certain rules or principles – that the mind plays an active part in cognition, and that therefore the principles which govern its action are part-determinants of what we experience.†

Considerations like these make one very chary of working uncritically with a terminology which relies on an absolutely hard-and-fast distinction between principles or rules or dispositions on the one hand and facts on the other. For it would appear that until we have accepted rules for discriminating between facts and illusions, we cannot talk of facts at all, or for that matter of objects or entities in the sense of 'things really existing'. Now Christians believe that God created the world out of chaos, or out of nothing, in the sense of no *thing*. What I am now going to say I say very tentatively. Is it possible that this is our way of expressing the truth that without belief in a divine order – a belief expressed in other terms by means of worshipping assent to principles for discriminating between fact and illusion – there could be no belief in matters of fact or in real objects? Certainly it is salutary to recognize that *even* our belief in so-called hard facts rests in the end on a faith, a commitment, which is not in or to facts, but in that without which there would not be any facts. Plato, it will be remembered, said of the Idea of the Good, which was his name for God, that it was not itself a being, but the source or cause of being; the passage is worth quoting in full, and I will end with it:

* *The Open Society and its Enemies*, by K. R. Popper, Vol. II, pp. 201 ff.
† Cf. Kant, *Critique of Pure Reason*, § 14, 'Transition to the Transcendental Deduction of the Categories' (Kemp Smith's translation, pp. 125 ff.).

In the case of those things which we see by the light of the sun, the sun is the source, not merely of the possibility of our seeing them, but also of their very coming to be, their growth and their sustenance. But it is not itself a coming to be. And in the same way in the case of those things which we know by the light of the Idea of the Good, it is the source, not merely of the possibility of our knowing them, but also of their very being – for from it their being comes. Yet the Good itself is not a being, but rather lies even further off, on the yonder side of being, excelling it in majesty and power.*

* Plato, *Republic*, 509 b.

CHAPTER VIII

'WE' IN MODERN PHILOSOPHY*

by M. B. Foster

I

I WISH to discuss the significance of sentences in the first person plural as they occur in the writings of modern philosophers, especially of those who represent the philosophy of Analysis.

The following are examples of these sentences:

'The philosopher, as an analyst, is not directly concerned with the physical properties of things. He is concerned only with the way in which *we speak* about them.'†

'In ordinary language *we call* a person 'rational' if he is capable of learning from experience.'‡

'A full understanding of the logic of value-terms can only be achieved by continual and sensitive attention to the way *we use* them.'§

'The primary task of philosophy is to describe the *use* of words and expressions. . . . One part, albeit the root part, of this task is to give a logical account of the way in which *all of us employ* certain key expressions, like "know", "cause", "see" and others.'‖

'*We do not know* what to reply to "Do shadows exist?" in the way

* Both Professor G. E. Moore (in 'The Philosophy of Common Sense', *Contemporary British Philosophy*, second series (1925), pp. 202–7), and R. G. Collingwood (in *Essay on Metaphysics* (1940), Ch. XXXIV (Epilogue)) have called attention to the significance of 'we' when used by philosophers. I discovered both passages in the course of writing this chapter, having read both earlier and forgotten them. I cannot estimate how much acknowledgement I owe to them, nor how much they would be willing to accept.

† A. J. Ayer, *Language, Truth and Logic*, Ch. II. My italics.

‡ H. Feigl in 'Logical Empiricism', *Readings in Philosophical Analysis*, ed. Feigl and Sellars, p. 15. My italics.

§ R. M. Hare, *Language of Morals*, p. 126. My italics.

‖ Morris Weitz (expounding G. Ryle) in 'Oxford Philosophy,' *Philosophical Review*, 1953, p. 229. 'Use' author's italics; other italics mine.

we do to "are there shadows on the moon?" and the reason is plain. *We do not in fact use* the word "exist" in talk about shadows.'*

'Philosophers' arguments have frequently turned on references to what *we* do and do not say, or, more strongly, on what *we* can or cannot say.'†

The examples which I have chosen all come from contexts in linguistic philosophy. The philosophers who employ them are all engaged in the philosophical analysis of language (whether or not they would say that philosophy consists entirely in such analysis). A similar use of 'we' sentences can occur in other contexts, and I will quote some examples from non-linguistic philosophers later; but I wish at present to examine this use as it occurs in linguistic philosophy.

When a philosopher says, e.g. 'We do not use the word "exist" in talk about shadows,' what kind of sentence is this? It seems clear that it is not an empirical statement.‡ The philosopher is not reporting a usage which he has observed in himself and among his associates. The utterance seems more like those which Professor

* Weitz, *ibid.*, p. 226, quoting G. J. Warnock from *Proceedings of the Aristotelian Society*, 1951. My italics.

† G. Ryle, 'Ordinary Language' in *Philosophical Review*, 1953. My italics.

‡ Not an empirical statement. This fact may have been obscured, because it may be said that the sentence 'We do not use . . . etc.' is equivalent to a statement about the use of words in ordinary language, and a statement about the use of words in ordinary language looks like an empirical statement. But in spite of appearances, statements of the uses of words in ordinary language are not empirical statements (they are not statements of the ways in which words are *in fact* most commonly used.) Professor Ryle points this out in 'Ordinary Language,' *Philosophical Review*, 1953. Apart from specific avowals, the practice of analytic philosophers is sufficient testimony. They do not adopt empirical methods (statistical enquiry, mass-observation and the like) to establish the existence of the linguistic uses which they analyse. Bertrand Russell points this out with his customary pungency in an article on 'The Cult of Common Usage' in the *British Journal for the Philosophy of Science*, Feb., 1953. 'What in fact they believe in is not common usage, as determined by mass observation, statistics, medians, standard deviations, and the rest of the apparatus. What they believe in is the usage of persons who have their amount of education, neither more nor less – less is illiteracy, more is pedantry – so we are given to understand'.

Austin has taught us to call 'performatory'. In using the first person plural I am not merely describing a usage but am subscribing to it, or expressing my own adhesion to it. I am *owning* the usage, and this is an avowal rather than a statement. I am not merely stating that a certain group uses language in this way, but am ranking myself in that group as a member of it, and this ranking is not a description but an act. Sentences in the third person do not exhibit this performatory character.

The performatory element of these sentences is comparable to the evaluative element which Mr Hare discerns in all genuine moral judgments.* This element, on Hare's account of it, may be mixed in varying proportions with a descriptive element, and the descriptive element increases in proportion as the judgment loses vitality and becomes ossified. Thus 'You ought to do so and so' can degenerate until it is *hardly* more than the descriptive statement that so-and-so is required by the customary standards of a certain society. 'It is wrong to do so and so' can become *almost* equivalent to the factual report that I have certain psychological inhibitions in regard to it. But if this process is completed, so that the judgment becomes wholly factual, then it has lost the essential character of a value-judgment. The evaluative element involves something more than a description, namely the speaker's adhesion to the standard which he enunciates. 'The test, whether someone is using the judgment "I ought to do X" as a value-judgment or not is, 'Does he or does he not recognize that if he assents to the judgment he must also assent to the command "Let me do X"?'†

---

* *The Language of Morals*, Ch. 11.

† *Ibid.*, pp. 168–9. The same point could have been illustrated by reference to H. Reichenbach's theory of moral judgments (see *The Rise of Scientific Philosophy*, pp. 287–91). According to his theory moral obligation depends on a group-will. But to say objectively 'such-and-such an action is in accordance with the group-will' is not in itself a moral judgment. The judgment that 'he' (or 'I' or 'you') *should* do so-and-so in a moral sense means more than this. It has an ineliminable subjective element. It implies that I, the speaker, endorse the group-will. 'We use the phrase when we share the group-will: and only in this case is the phrase meant to express a moral obligation' (p. 291). This endorsing of a group-will is parallel to the *owning* of a linguistic usage.

Mutatis mutandis, I suggest that a corresponding element is present in sentences enunciating a linguistic usage in the first person. No doubt in these sentences also a descriptive element is present in varying proportions. It is a fact that the usage is prevalent among a certain human group which is capable of historical or sociological definition. But if the sentence became wholly descriptive, so that it could be adequately expressed in the third person instead of in the first*: if, in other words, it became a report upon linguistic usage of the kind which might be established by empirical (e.g. statistical) enquiry, then (like Hare's degenerate value-judgments), it would have lost an essential element.

Would it have lost thereby the element which makes it capable of serving as the datum (the analysandum) of logical analysis? In order for analysis to be philosophical is it necessary that it should begin with sentences in which meanings are not only reported, but are also *owned*? So that, e.g. it would not be of philosophical interest to establish that such and such a usage is, or has been, prevalent (a third-person utterance), i.e. that such and such forms of language have been used with such and such meanings; unless the speaker were able to add 'and this is what I mean by them myself' so that the 'they' sentence gave place to a 'we' sentence?

Analytical philosophers of course themselves realize that the linguistic uses which it is philosophically fruitful to analyse are not such as are capable of being established empirically. Professor Ryle has expressed this by distinguishing between the 'use' and the 'usage' of a word or expression.† 'A usage is a custom, practice, fashion or vogue. It can be local or widespread, obsolete or current, rural or urban, vulgar or academic.'‡ The discovery that a given linguistic usage is, or has been, prevalent is not of philo-

---

* Or rather: a sentence in the first person *can* be descriptive. I may give a report based on self-observation of my own use of words. But this is exceptional, and the 'we' sentences which I am discussing are of a different kind.

† 'Ordinary Language', *Philosophical Review*, 1953.

‡ *Ibid.*, p. 174.

sophical interest. 'Appeal to prevalence is philosophically pointless.'*

To this extent I can claim Ryle's support for the distinction which I am making. But I cannot do so for my suggestion as to what it is that qualifies a statement to be the subject of philosophical analysis. The philosopher, Ryle says, analyses the *use* of a word, not its usage. What is the 'use' of a word? It is, according to Ryle, what a person would need to learn in order to learn how to operate with the word. 'A way of operating with a razor-blade, a word, a traveller's cheque or a canoe-paddle is a *technique*, knack or method. Learning it is learning how to do the thing.'† The philosopher's task includes (*a*) the description of 'the mode of employment of an expression,' and (*b*) 'perhaps the extraction of the logical rules implicitly governing a concept, i.e. a way of operating with an expression.'‡

I am doubtful whether this is satisfactory. Certainly tools have a proper use, which is not necessarily the same as the use which they are most frequently put to. Corkscrews may be found in fact to be employed as paper-weights or as wedges to prevent the window from rattling. This does not alter the fact that their proper job is to draw corks. And to learn how to use a corkscrew correctly is quite a different thing from learning by empirical enquiry how corkscrews are in fact most commonly employed.

Certainly also we need to distinguish a proper use (or variety of proper uses, for there need not only be one) of linguistic expressions from the prevalent use or uses, and the learning of the proper use or uses from the investigation into what uses are prevalent. But the question is whether the proper use of linguistic expressions is fixed in the same way in which that of a tool is, and whether the coming to use it properly is a technical matter.

One standard of linguistic propriety is investigated by the philologist. This is what is set out in such books as Fowler's

---

* *Ibid.*, p. 177. Cf. 'Ordinary language *is* correct language'. N. Malcolm, 'Moore and Ordinary Language' in *The Philosophy of G. E. Moore*, p. 357.
† P. 175.
‡ P. 177.

Modern English Usage, and what a foreigner who wishes to learn English sets himself to learn. The use which such a foreigner seeks to master is the grammatical and idiomatic use, and he is not concerned to enquire whether or not this use is in fact prevalent among the largest sections of the population. He will go to the section which has the reputation of speaking English well, whether it is a minority or a majority.

But linguistic propriety in this sense is a matter of philology rather than of philosophy. In order to gain a starting-point for philosophical analysis we need a different criterion of proper use. What is this criterion? This is the crux.

Let us illustrate the problem by considering an ethical term such as 'right'. How does the beginner learn its proper use? The beginner will normally be a child, and he will learn, as children do, by imitation and by trial and error, the correct ways of using moral as well as other terms. We may say that the child is learning the use of language, and this is true: but in order to use moral language correctly, a moral as well as linguistic training is required. With a child, these two trainings take place side by side, and without clear separation one from another. But we can see how separate they are if we suppose a man who sets himself in adult years to acquire a correct use of an unfamiliar language. He will achieve linguistic mastery by the familiar methods of language-study – learning the grammar, taking lessons from language-masters, use of gramophone records, attendance at language-institutes, and conversation with anyone who knows the language. But in order to apply the moral terms of the language with propriety he will need also something quite different from this. He will need to be initiated into the basic moral attitudes by which the use of the language is determined.* What a man needs to learn in order to use words correctly in *this* sense (not purely linguistic facility) – this is what provides the basis of philosophical analysis.

I have illustrated the difference with moral terms, but it holds

* For this and what follows cf. H. A. Hodges 'Languages, Standpoints and Attitudes'. Especially Ch. III.

also of other terms. Think for example, of the terms 'reasonable' or 'real'.

The contexts in which they are properly to be applied are not determined solely by linguistic considerations. You cannot learn what is to be deemed reasonable behaviour and what unreasonable merely by taking language-lessons. By what lessons, then? Whatever it is that these other lessons teach, will be the starting-point of philosophy.

Propriety in the use of language, in the sense of propriety which is other than merely linguistic, is relative to the basic attitude which the speaker assumes. Imagine, for example, a Hindu, a Marxist and a scientific humanist, who have all acquired a mastery of the English language, but without surrendering their fundamental beliefs. Then they will agree in their standards of linguistic correctitude, but will differ in the other standards which determine propriety in the use of moral and other terms.*

Among different possible standards of propriety how is the proper standard to be selected? Granted that there is an accepted standard of linguistic propriety ('standard English usage') can this determine not only linguistic, but also (so to speak) moral and metaphysical correctitude in the use of language? Perhaps we must admit that, to a certain point, it can even do this. Languages have been informed by the basic attitudes of those who have used them, and so the mere use of a language may have a powerful effect in inducing a congruous attitude. (Thus a German writer who fled from Hitler's Germany to America — or his publisher – writes of his efforts to master the English language, 'that wonderful exercise in reason and sanity'†). But though this is true, it does not answer our question. We may say of an attitude that it is congruous to the genius of a given language, our own or another, but this is in itself no more than an historical statement, and it does not mark this attitude out from others which may be congruous to other languages.

* The difference is vividly illustrated by Mr T. D. Weldon, *Vocabulary of Politics*, pp. 42–3.

† Frederic Lilge, *The Abuse of Learning*, Dust Cover.

How, then, is the *use* (in the philosophically important sense) of a word decided? If I am right, there is not an external standard which the thinker can first recognize and then adopt. On the contrary, the adoption is primary. The correct use, that is the philosophically important use, for him is that which he can adopt. The act of adoption, making his statement more than an historical one, is the source from which philosophical analysis can flow.

Hence the importance of the 'we' sentences. They are the expressions of this act of adoption. Let us consider these sentences a little further.

An older logic would have assumed that we can discover the proper meaning of a word by analysing the concept. Modern analysis discards this assumption. Words do not mean but people mean things by words.* 'To mean' thus becomes an active, personal verb, no longer an impersonal one. It is possible to repeat forms of words without meaning them, or only half-meaning them. When this happens, thought lacks authenticity (if I may borrow a word from the Existentialists). The starting-point of philosophy is there when I have the courage (as Ayer had) to discard what is unauthentic, and to restate only that which I can commit myself to meaning in good faith, thereby *revalidating* it. Such a commitment is expressed in a linguistic 'we' sentence. The philosophical activity of analysing which then succeeds is not discontinuous from the initial act of affirmation. It makes clearer what the initial affirmation involved; indeed it will be only after the analysis that the speaker fully realizes what it was that he was affirming.

If this is true, it gives a somewhat different appearance to disagreements between philosophers (especially to disagreements between contemporary philosophers and those of previous ages) from that which is often assumed. A common assumption is that the meaning of the expression to be analysed is fixed independently of the analysis, and identically for all philosophers. The philo-

* Thus Mr Nowell-Smith questions the assumption 'that we can ask what a certain word means, instead of asking "What does so and so mean by it?"' (*Ethics*, p. 62).

sophical differences have to be held to arise wholly from the
process of the analysis, and to be due to logical errors committed
by one of the parties. Hence the difference of theory is ascribed to
a technical defect in the earlier philosopher, which has now been
exposed and corrected. Thus, for example, Plato's 'theory of
Ideas' is ascribed to a logical naiveté on his part, which caused him
to construe general words as though they were proper names.
Descartes is said to have based his metaphysics of mind upon a
'category mistake', which deluded him into thinking that the
word 'mind' must stand for a thing, and that in consequence, since
it was clearly not a material thing, it must be a non-material
thing.*

But if what I have said is right, we shall not be able to adopt
this attitude towards the philosophers of the past. Even if we
regard them as having been themselves engaged unconsciously in
the analysis of linguistic use (I think it legitimate up to a certain
point to think of them like this), we shall not be able to attribute
all the divergences of their results to faults of analysis unless we
assume that we have independent knowledge of their analysandum. But this, it seems clear, we have not got. On the contrary,
the result of their analysis is part of the evidence which reveals to
us what their analysandum was.†

This does not commit us to an historical relativism, as though
we could only say different philosophies are the outcome of
different 'absolute presuppositions',‡ and must renounce all

* G. Ryle, *Concept of Mind*, Ch. I.
† I think this notion is borrowed ultimately from Professor É. Gilson:
I owe it proximately to Dr E. L. Mascall. Professor H. H. Price suggests that
the traditional proofs of the existence of God ought to be regarded not as
proofs, in the sense that they 'would follow logically from premisses which
every reasonable man is bound to accept', but rather 'as analyses or clarifi-
cations of propositions which religious persons antecedently believe' (*Some
Aspects of the Conflict between Science and Religion*, Eddington Memorial
Lecture, 1953, p. 18). In a somewhat similar manner linguistic analysis
clarifies a meaning which the analyst owns.
‡ R. G. Collingwood's term. See his *Essay on Metaphysics*, Pt. I. I think
that Collingwood's position *is* one of historical relativism.

criticism of them in the light of our own. But the criticism will take a different form. It will require us to reveal our own presuppositions and to confront the others with them, committing ourselves in witness. We shall not be able to confine ourselves to refutation from the vantage-point of a technical superiority.*

II

The linguistic philosopher commits himself in his selection of those expressions of which he is prepared to say 'we' use them. It may be instructive to compare his 'we' sentences with first-personal utterances occurring in other, non-linguistic philosophies.

It is characteristic of G. E. Moore to use 'we' sentences in stating the views of Common Sense about the nature of the Universe. I will quote examples at some length from his lectures recently published (but originally delivered in 1910–11) on 'Some Main Problems of Philosophy'.

'There are, it seems to me, certain views about the nature of the Universe which are held nowadays by almost everybody. They are so universally held that they may, I think, fairly be called the views of Common Sense. . . . I wish therefore to begin by describing what I take to be the most important view of Common Sense: things which *we* all commonly assume to be true about the Universe, and which *we* are sure that we know to be true about it.'†

Moore then sketches the generally accepted modern picture of the universe – physical, biological and human, and concludes: "All this *we now believe* about the material universe: it is surely Common Sense to believe it all." '‡

The Common Sense picture of the Universe is shown to exclude some beliefs which have previously been held – animism,

---

* See Hodges, *op. cit.*   † *Op. cit.*, p. 2. My italics.
‡ P. 3. My italics.

and the belief in disembodied acts of consciousness.* It is later found to be incompatible with the philosophical theory of Idealism in regard to material objects, and is Moore's ground, as is well known, for rejecting that theory. 'It seems to me that these views' [Idealist views, namely] 'are utterly different from what *we all commonly believe*, when *we believe* in the existence of material objects. . . . *We believe – we all cannot help believing*, even though we may hold philosophical views to the contrary – that this something which exists now or existed a moment ago, is not merely a something which may or may not have shape or be situated in space . . .' [but that it really has the characteristics of a material object].†

These statements of Moore, which I have italicized, are instructive because they form a link between two things which I wish to bring into comparison with one another.

(*a*) They seem clearly akin to the 'we' sentences of linguistic philosophers. Moore's characteristic appeal to Common Sense can pass by imperceptible gradations into an appeal to linguistic use. Consider, for example, the following sentences from the same book.

'A doubt arises with regard to those very words which we set out to consider – the word sense-perception itself, and the words which express the different forms of sense-perception – the words to see, to hear, to feel, to smell, to taste, etc., *when* these words are applied to a material object. What relations did, in fact, hold between us and the envelope, the *material* envelope, when we all saw it? Was it any one of those four?' [*sc.* four relations previously distinguished by the author] 'or was it some other, different from any of those? In other words, what kind of relation is expressed by such words as perceive, observe, see, feel, *when* these are used to express some relation between us, and a *material object* or *the space occupied* by a material object?'‡

(*b*) Secondly, they are like credal affirmations.

* Pp. 7–8.   † P. 115. My italics.
‡ P. 82. Author's italics.

'We believe, we all cannot help believing, even though we may hold philosophical views to the contrary – that this something which exists now or existed a moment ago, is not merely a something which may or may not have shape or be situated in space – something with regard to which we cannot possibly tell whether it has shape or not. We believe quite definitely that the sense data which we now see are *signs* of the present or immediately past existence of something, which certainly has a cylindrical shape. . . . I, for instance, claim to *know* that there does exist now, or did a moment ago, not only these sense-data which I am directly apprehending – seeing and feeling – but also something else which I am not directly apprehending. And I claim to know . . . I claim to know. . . . And moreover I claim to know. . . . It is, I think, plainly things like these that we all of us believe, when we believe in the existence of material objects.'*

Using Moore as a middle term, can we not see the credal element, the affirmation of faith, which is involved in the linguistic 'we' sentences? If we find the comparison hard to accept, is it partly because we need to modify preconceptions about the kind of thing that an affirmation of faith is?

Let us turn from the person to the number of these sentences. They are in the plural. Analysis starts from the affirmation of what *we* mean, not of what *I* mean. What difference does this make?

To state what *I* mean by a word is to give notice of the sense in which I have resolved to use it. The word is then a technical term and its meaning is for me to decide. I can, of course, systematize my decision, and determine what consequences shall follow from the word in the use which I have given it. But each step here depends upon my decision. This is not analysis in the ordinary sense; I am not here unravelling a meaning which was latent in my affirmation unknown to myself.

* Pp. 115–6. Author's italics. Compare these sentences with the sentence 'We do not now believe that [Jesus Christ] was the son of God', which is quoted on p. 212 below.

This means that the 'we' sentences which are analysed in philosophy are not prescriptive; they must possess some indicative content. Yet we have seen that they are not indicatives of empirical fact, so that they seem to escape a descriptive-prescriptive dichotomy.

What *we* mean by a word is not something to be determined solely by my decision. What I decide in this case is to place myself in the ranks of those who mean in this way. What is the boundary of these ranks? Who are 'we'? When we say that *we* mean so-and-so by such-and-such a word, do we mean 'We English'? or 'We analytical philosophers'? or 'We Western Europeans'? or 'We Twentieth Century men'? or 'We men'?

Different answers to this question are suggested by the philosophers who have broached this problem.

Collingwood, in the passage which I have mentioned,* cites from modern philosophers a list of examples similar to those which I have collected at the beginning of this chapter,† underlining the 'we', and asking whom it includes. 'All these writers, it will be seen, attach themselves to some group or society of persons to whom they refer as "we". . . . What is this group or society?'‡

Collingwood then proceeds to answer his own question. He finds the common bond of this group in the fact that they all assume a certain definition – he calls it the Kantian definition – of the term 'cause' (the whole question arises in the course of a discussion of the meaning of 'cause'), and he asserts that 'we' means the group of people associated by this bond. 'What is this group or society? It is the group or society of persons who accept the Kantian definition of the term 'cause'. They are not, and do not include, contemporary natural scientists. . . . They are a group of neo-Kantians whose reverence for the master has induced them to accept not indeed all his doctrines but this particular doctrine.'§

It is not necessary to raise the question whether or not Colling-

---

* P. 194 sup., footnote *.

  † Except that his examples are confined to philosophers' statements about *causation*.

  ‡ *Op. cit.*, p. 340.

  § Pp. 340–1.

wood is right in his discernment of a common element in the philosophers whom he groups together, nor whether or not 'neo-Kantians' is an appropriate name for them. Let us grant for the sake of the argument that he is right in these points. Where I think he is wrong is in the denotation which he ascribes to the 'we' in the sentences which he quotes. He supposes that when a 'neo-Kantian' philosopher uses a 'we' sentence, he *means* by 'we' the 'group or society of persons who accept the Kantian definition of the word "cause".' I do not quite know who Collingwood thought of as being included in this group. If he meant the group of 'neo-Kantian' philosophers, it seems that he is wrong. 'We' in the mouth of a 'neo-Kantian' philosopher never means merely 'we neo-Kantian philosophers', but claims community with the usage of a wider group.

Or rather: not never. There could be a usage in which it would mean 'we neo-Kantians', but this would be a special use. This would be its use in the context of a sort of party manifesto, to proclaim a linguistic policy. Such policy could then no doubt be specified into any amount of detail, but this specification would not be philosophical analysis.*

* A. G. N. Flew has a passage which illustrates a similar point. He is questioning the assumptions that 'our moral convictions', sometimes assumed to be the basis of ethical theory, are either (i) in agreement, or (ii) unchanging. He comments: 'Both are false. Though in both cases, of course, it depends a lot upon whom 'our' is referring to. But with the former assumption, even taking British professional philosophers as the us-group, it is difficult to believe that debate about the ethics of contraception, abortion, homosexuality and suicide, would not reveal differences both in the weight given to different admitted *prima facie* obligations, and even perhaps what were admitted as obligations at all.' ('The Justification of Punishment', *Philosophy*, Oct. 1954, p. 298.)

But if the us-groups were really confined to British professional philosophers, the assertion of their convictions could not give a starting-point for philosophical ethics. It would be the proclamation of a moral programme or code.

Philosophical ethics seems to require that the philosopher should be able to *appeal to* a set of moral convictions, which he can at the same time endorse by his adhesion. This means that the 'we' must apply more widely than to a philosophical group.

The 'we' to whose usage the analytical philosopher appeals does not denote merely the group of like-minded philosophers, but a wider group. What wider group? The group of English-speaking people? Of modern Europeans? Of Twentieth Century men? There seems to be some truth in each of these suggestions; and yet it seems impossible to suppose that he is referring to any of these groups *considered as an empirically delimited group*. If he were doing so, he would be making an empirical statement about the linguistic usage of certain historically determinable groups of men, and we have already seen that this is not the kind of statement from which philosophical analysis starts.

It seems in some cases that the reference of the 'we' cannot stop short of the whole of mankind. This conclusion is expressed or implicit in the passages in which Moore treats this subject.

'No philosopher has ever been able to hold such views' [e.g. views inconsistent with common sense belief in the existence of other human beings] 'consistently. One way in which they have betrayed this inconsistency is by alluding to the existence of other philosophers. Another way is by alluding to the existence of the human race, and in particular by using 'we' in the sense in which I have already constantly used it, in which any philosopher who asserts that 'we' do so and so, e.g. that 'we' sometimes believe propositions that are not true, is asserting not only that he himself has done the thing in question, but that *very many other human beings who have had bodies and lived upon the earth* have done the same.'*

'If there is any "we", and if we know that there is, this must be so' [i.e. it must be the case that we *know* some things, and know that we must have had evidence for them, and yet not know now what the evidence was]; 'for that there is a "we" is one of the things in question. And I do know that there is a "we", *that is to say, that many other human beings*, with human bodies, have lived upon the earth, it seems to me that I do know for certain.'†

* 'The Philosophy of Common Sense' in *Contemporary British Philosophy*, second series, pp.202–3. Author's italics.

† *Ibid.*, p. 206. 'Know', author's italics. Other italics mine.

Moore says in a passage preceding the one last quoted that to make propositions about 'us' implies 'making propositions about *human knowledge* in general'.* Mr G. C. J. Midgley seems to be restating this in linguistic terms when he maintains in a recent and most interesting paper that 'ordinary language' is 'our' language, and that ' "our" language is *the language of mankind*'.† Not that there is a language of mankind. There are only particular languages, English, French, Hebrew, Chinese. But linguistic expressions are fitted for philosophical analysis in so far as they are not peculiar to a language but are inter-translatable. This seems to be something like what Ryle means when he says that the *philosophical* enquiry is not into the *word* but into the *use* which is made of it, and illustrates by saying that the *use* which is made of the word 'cause' is the same as that made of 'Ursache'.‡ This identity of use is what makes the words inter-translatable.§ If 'we' sentences affirm our membership of a company it looks as though the 'we' sentences from which logical analysis springs are those in which we affirm our membership of the human race, i.e. in which 'we' means 'we men'.

But if 'we' refers to the whole of mankind or to the human race, neither can this be taken as an empirical concept, for the reasons already given. Thus, when Moore says that to make propositions about 'us' implies 'making propositions about human knowledge in general', these propositions are not to be thought of as the laws of an empirical anthropology. If they had been this, Moore would not have been in a position to make them, for he does not use the resources of empirical investigation.

---

* *Ibid.*, p. 205. Author's italics.

† Contribution to Symposium on 'Linguistic Rules and Language Habits' in *Proceedings of the Aristotelian Society*, Supplementary Volume, 1955, p. 209. My italics. What is said about 'we' sentences on pp. 195 and 197 of Midgley's paper, and about 'ordinary language' on pp. 207–212, is very relevant to the subject of this chapter.

‡ *Philosophical Review*, 1953, pp. 171–2.

§ Does it follow that language, in so far as it is not translatable, (e.g. poetic language) is not capable of logical analysis; and that philosophy, in so far as it is not translatable (e.g. Heidegger's) is not philosophy?

Of course, there may be sentences in which 'we' applies to a smaller group. 'We dress for dinner at week-ends during term,' need include no more than myself and the fellow-members of my college.* But linguistic sentences ('We mean so-and-so by so-and-so') would not qualify for *philosophical* analysis if they were restricted to a local use.

'We', then, in the mouth of a modern philosopher, seems to mean 'we men'. The kind of philosopher he is will depend upon what he believes a man to be. Thus 'we' for Kant meant 'we rational beings, who are bound by our human condition to a physical nature'. To say 'we' in Kant's sense is to affirm ourselves to be members of the intelligible world. But when Moore speaks of 'human beings with human bodies' who 'have lived upon the earth', this expresses a different conception of what man is. 'We' now commits me to membership of a differently conceived society, and involves me in a different affirmation of my own being. Is not this new anthropological affirmation really what is basic to Moore's philosophy? Other philosophers had gone on talking the language of a spiritual anthropology which no longer resonated with what they or their hearers were prepared to affirm existentially. Moore refused to say what he could not authentically affirm.†

'We' sentences of the type which is under consideration affirm an anthropology, but not a descriptive anthropology, they do not express my adhesion to an anthropological theory. Nor do they exactly express a decision of policy. It is not that I am giving notice of my intention *in future* to be such and such or to do so and so. Or so far as they can be said to express such a decision, this must be thought of as a decision to be what I am. In the

* It is perhaps worth pointing out that these sentences in which 'we' applies to a smaller group are not usually descriptive sentences either. 'We dress for dinner' is not necessarily falsified if someone replies 'But Jones doesn't'. The rejoinder might be, 'Oh, *Jones*', with the implication that when it is a case of affirming a standard Jones doesn't count. (Though if exceptions were sufficiently numerous, I should be obliged to withdraw the assertion.)

† Cf. his repudiation of belief in immortality and in the divine creation of the world in his *Philosophy of Common Sense*.

previous paragraph I used the word 'existential' to describe such affirmations. I am tempted to use another word and to call them 'theological'.

It is worth while to distinguish two forms which a humanist anthropology has taken. To recognize myself as man may mean (i) the affirmation that I share in manhood by exhibiting a certain universal character (human nature), or (ii) an affirmation of my solidarity with mankind conceived not now as an abstract class-concept, but as a race fulfilling its destiny in history.

(i) Humanism of the former sort was characteristic of the great British Empiricists of the seventeenth and eighteenth centuries.* They thought of man as exhibiting human nature, this being a timeless and universal character.

(ii) But the nineteenth century began to think of man as belonging to the human race, which is an historical entity.† To affirm myself as man in this sense seems to be characteristically modern, and this affirmation seems to be involved in some analytical philosophy.

It is revealed by the use of tensed verbs in place of the timeless present, as in the following examples:

'All this we *now* believe about the material universe. It is surely common sense to believe it all' (Moore).‡

'Ordinary languages and calculi like logic, geometry and arithmetic are devices which *we have invented*' (T. D. Weldon).§

'There was a real Jesus Christ who preached to the Jews and

---

* It is noteworthy how the adjective 'human' recurs in the titles of the principal works of Locke, Berkeley and Hume. (*Essay on the Human Understanding, Principles of Human Knowledge, A Treatise of Human Nature.*) Contrast the titles of Descartes' philosophical works (*Rules for the Direction of the Mind, Discourse on the Method of Rightly conducting* the Reason, *Meditations on First Philosophy, The Principles of Philosophy, The Search after Truth, The Passions of the Soul*) and of Kant's *Critiques.*

† J. S. Mill thinks of man like this. See e.g. his *Utilitarianism*, pp. 13–18, 21–23 (*Everyman* edition).

‡ Quoted above, p. 203. My italics.

§ *Vocabulary of Politics*, p. 191. My italics.

was crucified; but *we do not now believe* that he was the son of God and of a virgin, or that he rose from the dead.'*

There is a similar implication in the use of the phrase 'We now know', in cases where the context makes clear that what is referred to is an increase of human knowledge (e.g. that the earth goes round the sun).†

But although 'we' sentences of the latter type are about mankind as an historical entity, they are not simply historical, any more than sentences of the former kind are empirical. The following passage may illustrate this point:

H. Reichenbach is speaking of the supersession of Euclidean geometry and of Newtonian physics which has formed part of the experience of our age. He writes:

'Such experience has made us wise enough to anticipate the breaking down of any system. It has not discouraged us though. The new physics has shown that we can have knowledge outside the frame of the Kantian principles, that the human mind is not a rigid system of categories into which it packs all experience, but that the principles of knowledge change with its content and can be adapted to a much more complicated world than that of Newtonian mechanics. We hope that in any future situation our minds will be flexible enough to supply methods of logical organization that can cope with the given observational material. That is a hope, not a belief for which we pretend to have a philosophical proof. We can do without certainty.'‡

The 'we' who are not discouraged, who can have knowledge outside the frame of the Kantian principles, who can do without

* From a broadcast talk. My italics, I think.

† This example incidentally may illustrate again a point made previously. The 'we' in this sentence must mean mankind as a whole. Surely not, you may say: does it not mean a specified class of men, such as 'educated modern Western men'? No, for in that case the 'now' would be incorrect. The 'now' implies that the we who now know are *the same* as those who previously did not know.

‡ *Rise of Scientific Philosophy*, p. 49.

certainty, are surely mankind; yet what kind of statements are these which are being made?

Such assertions as these are logically homogeneous with theological statements; I mean by this that they can contradict theological statements and be contradicted by them. Two further passages from Reichenbach will illustrate this:

'As we have discovered that . . . the feeling of obligation cannot be transformed into a source of the validity of ethics, let us forget about the appeal to obligation. Let us throw away the crutches we needed for walking, let us stand on our own feet and trust our volitions, not because they are secondary ones but because they are our own volitions. Only a distorted morality can argue that our will is bad if it is not the response to a command from another source.'*

What is asserted here is surely logically homogeneous with the doctrine of Original Sin, which is confessedly theological.

Again:

'Speculative philosophy strove to establish moral directives in the same way that it constructed absolute knowledge. Reason was considered the giver of the moral law as well as of the cognitive law; ethical rules were to be discovered by an act of vision, analogous to the vision revealing the ultimate rules of the cosmos. Scientific philosophy has abandoned completely the plan of advancing moral rules. It regards moral aims as products of acts of volition, not of cognition; only the relations between aims, or between aims and means, are accessible to cognitive knowledge. The fundamental ethical rules are not justifiable through knowledge, but are adhered to because human beings want these rules and want other persons to follow the same rules. Volition is not derivable from cognition. Human will is its own progenitor and its own judge.'†

* *Ibid.*, pp. 291–2.
† *Ibid.*, p. 304.

Compare statements in the Bible that human will is judged by Jesus Christ.*

Mr. P. F. Strawson writes: 'What makes predicates incompatible? . . . I want to answer . . . it is we, the makers of language, who make predicates incompatible. . . . It is we who decide where the boundaries are to be drawn.'† This 'we' can refer only to mankind, and to mankind as an historical body. But it is not an historical statement.‡ Logically, does it not belong to the same realm as the statement in Genesis ii., that Adam gave names to the living creatures? ('Adam' means man).

Contemporary British philosophy is often described as Empiricist, and its representatives regard themselves as heirs of the classical tradition of British Empiricism. From this point of view it is natural to think of the opposition between this philosophy and the philosophy of the Continent (Descartes, Spinoza, Kant and his Idealist successors) as being that between a metaphysical (the latter) and an unmetaphysical philosophy. I do not deny truth to this contrast, but I have suggested a different one. I have suggested that the Empiricists (the moderns as well as their Seventeenth and Eighteenth Century predecessors) are based on an affirmation of humanism which is not empirical. From this point of view, the contrast between British and Continentals will be that they affirm different anthropologies. To what I have read was Plotinus' question, 'Who are we?', the latter answer, 'We are mind (or spirit, or mind linked with matter, or spirit linked with nature)',

---

* Cf. perhaps especially John v. 27: the Father has given the Son authority to execute judgment 'because he is the Son of man.'

† *Introduction to Logical Theory*, p. 5.

‡ Perhaps it could properly be called 'meta-historical'; not in the sense which this term would have in the mouth of an analytical philosopher, but in the sense which it bears in the following passage: 'Genesis . . . speaks of the Eternal which cannot be grasped in human experience, it is 'metahistorical'; but while it is beyond history, it never suppresses history. The historical figures of the patriarchs are not to be identified with folklore or mythology'. Suzanne de Dietrich, *Discovering the Bible*, p. 46.

the former answer, 'We are men'.* I wish to pursue this contrast a little more at length.

Descartes began not with a 'we' sentence but with an 'I' sentence. 'I thence concluded that I was a substance, whose whole essence or nature consists only in thinking.'† This is of course no more an empirical statement than are the 'we' sentences hitherto considered. It, like them, is an existential affirmation, but a different one. Descartes is not affirming himself to be a man, nor claiming solidarity with mankind, but is affirming himself to be mind or spirit, naturally immortal, and claiming solidarity with the timeless and infinite substance of mind as such.‡

Kant's philosophy was still spiritual and not human. In his ethics he insists that we are subject to the moral law not *qua* human but *qua* rational; this means *qua* spiritual. The capacity of determining his will by the moral law gives man 'dignity (or prerogative) . . . above all the mere things of nature'.§ Our 'will as intelligence' which gives us this capacity is 'our proper self',||

---

* 'Men are not machines, not even ghost-ridden machines. They are men – a tautology which is sometimes worth remembering.' Ryle, *The Concept of Mind*, p. 88.

† *Discourse on Method*, Pt. IV., *Everyman* Edition, p. 27. Contrast Moore's statement 'I am a human being' (*The Main Problems of Philosophy*, p. 195).

‡ What in the world can this mean? we naturally say. Those phrases have become meaningless to us because we have lost the faith of which they are the expression. Hence we are tempted to interpret Descartes as though he must have meant something different. It seems to me, for example, that Ryle is wrong in supposing that the 'privacy' of the individual mind is part of what Descartes affirms. Descartes is worried about the relation of 'mind' to 'body', because he began by affirming himself to be a mind distinct from a body. But he is not (so far as I know) worried about the relation of his mind to other minds, because he had not affirmed its individuality as something separate from mind in general.

§ *Foundation of the Metaphysic of Morals*, Paton's translation *The Moral Law*, p. 105.

|| 'The law interests us because it is valid for us as men in virtue of having sprung from our will as intelligence and so from our proper self.' *Ibid.*, p. 129.

(whereas man 'as a human being . . . is merely an appearance of himself').* In affirming ourselves as spirits, we affirm our membership of a spiritual world. 'When we think of ourselves as free, we transfer ourselves into the intelligible world as members.'† The concept of an intelligible world is that of 'the totality of rational beings as ends in themselves'.‡ Kant speaks elsewhere of a *corpus mysticum* of the rational beings in the sensible world, 'in so far as the free will of each being is, under moral laws, in complete systematic unity with itself and with the freedom of every other.'§

The basis of Kant's ethics is thus that I should recognize myself as spirit and affirm my membership of a spiritual world. When we turn to Mill, we find that this spiritualism has given place to humanism. I am to recognize myself as man, and to affirm my solidarity with mankind – mankind being now conceived not as an abstract class-concept but as a race fulfilling its destiny in history.‖

In his epistemology Kant's metaphysics takes a different form. The self knowing nature affirms itself as spirit distinct from nature and giving laws to it: but it is not thought of here as affirming its membership in a society of spirits. Instead it affirms its solidarity with 'consciousness as such'; this is like Descartes' identification of himself with 'mind' or 'mental substance'. Hence it would not be surprising, though I have not confirmed this by inspection, if in Kant's epistemology and in the epistomologies bearing a Kantian impress which held the academical field for so long after his death, 'we' sentences are not prominent or characteristic. What is spoken of is 'the mind'.

---

* 'In [the intelligible world] reason alone, and indeed pure reason independent of sensibility, is the source of law; and . . . since he is there his proper self only as intelligence (while as a human being he is merely an appearance of himself), these laws apply to him immediately and categorically.' *Ibid.*, p. 125.

† *Ibid.*, p. 121.

‡ *Ibid.*, p. 126.

§ *Critique of Pure Reason*, A. 808, B 836. Kemp Smith's translation, pp. 637–8.

‖ See reference given p. 211 sup.

An early document of the philosophy of Analysis, a paper of 1922 by C. I. Lewis, entitled 'The Pragmatic Conception of the a Priori',* illustrates the transition from the Kantian to the humanist basis.

Lewis maintains the thesis that 'the *a priori* represents an attitude in some sense freely taken, a stipulation of the mind itself, and a stipulation which might be taken in some other way if it suited our bent or need'.† He maintains this against anticipated resistance from 'those who would conceive the *a priori* in terms of an absolute mind or an absolutely universal human nature'.‡ The point which Lewis is making is that we must think of the categories through which we perceive things as being chosen, not necessitated. This is a departure from what we have come to regard as the traditional 'metaphysical' language; but notice that what it substitutes is not more positive or empirical than what it rejects. The acts of free choice attributed to mind are not datable acts performed by individual minds. They are more like the acts of decision which the social contract theorists postulated as the origin of the state; or like the decisions which Professor Toulmin postulates as the origin of everyday language.§ These are not decisions which anyone can be supposed ever to have actually *taken*, or the taking of which could be verified by empirical evidence in the ordinary sense.

A consequence of the alteration is that one must think of the chosen categories as being subject to variation, not as fixed once for all by the nature of mind. The conceptions and principles with which we are concerned 'have altered in human history'.‖ (We

---

* Reprinted in *Readings in Philosophical Analysis*, ed. Feigl and Sellars, pp. 286–94.

† *Op. cit.*, p. 286.

‡ P. 292.

§ 'If the decisions on which our physical theories rest are easy to forget, those which have gone to the making of every-day speech are yet more easily forgotten.' S. E. Toulmin, *The Philosophy of Science*, p. 129. Cf. Weldon, quoted p. 211 sup.

‖ P. 293.

should think, for example, of the displacement of Newtonian ways of looking at nature by Einsteinian ones.) Yet it is not simply empirical proof or disproof which has caused the substitution. Rather, they 'represent the uncompelled initiative of human thought,' without which no 'growth of science, nor any science at all, would be conceivable'. *Logical* laws have a permanence in human thought which is relatively greater than that of physical principles, but this is a difference only of degree.

'The difference between such conceptions as are, for example, concerned in the decision of relativity *versus* absolute space and time, and those more permanent attitudes such as are vested in the Laws of Logic, there is only a difference of degree. The dividing line between the *a priori* and the *a posteriori* is that between principles and definitive concepts which *can* be maintained in the face of all experience and those genuinely empirical generalizations which *might* be proven flatly false. The thought which both rationalism and empiricism have missed is that there are principles, representing the initiative of mind, which impose upon experience no limitations whatever, but that such conceptions are still subject to alteration on pragmatic grounds when the expanding boundaries of experience reveal their infelicity as intellectual instruments.'*

The transition which we are witnessing in these passages is that from a timeless deduction to a temporal story, and from a spiritualist metaphysics to humanism.† The categories of thought are not eternal, but are subject to change, the changes take place in history, and this history is human history.

We are witnessing the disappearance of metaphysics and its replacement by – what? It is not true that nothing has stepped into

* P. 293.

† Perhaps the latter transition is not quite complete in Lewis's article, for he has lingering references to 'the mind', as being the subject which adopts successive attitudes.

the place which metaphysics has vacated. What has stepped in is what I have called by the vague name of 'humanism'. This is not an empirical matter, as we have seen. The choices and stipulations with which it is concerned are not datable acts of individual human beings. To call it a humanist *metaphysics* would stress the fact that the old metaphysics has been replaced by something which is, so to speak, on the same level as itself, but it would be misleading, because we do not use the name 'metaphysics' to describe the kind of thing which it is.

In some ways 'humanist myth' would be a better description, since it indicates both its temporal character and the fact that it is not susceptible of empirical verification or falsification in the ordinary sense. But myth is unsuitable, too, because it suggests something unrelated to history, whereas humanism supplies a key for the understanding of history (it is metahistory, in the sense illustrated above, p. 214, note ‡).

Besides 'myth' suggests something which is poetical in character and not to be taken seriously, whereas humanism tells a history which we recognize and adopt as our own. Hence the characteristic 'we' appears in Lewis's article.

'The law of excluded middle formulates our decision that whatever is not designated by a certain term shall be designated by its negative. It declares our purpose to make, for every term, a complete dichotomy of experience, instead – as we might choose – of classifying on the basis of a tripartite division into opposites (as black and white) and the middle ground between the two. Our rejection of such tripartite division represents only our penchant for simplicity.'*

We have seen that these assertions are logically homogeneous with theological assertions. There would be something to be said for calling them themselves theological, and describing what they express as a theological anthropology: though it would be a

* P. 287.

paradoxical use, since it would involve us in speaking of a theology without God.*

* Some words which two recent editors have written (though it seems in defence of a somewhat different use of the word) are precisely apt for the justification of this use. 'We realize that many will be startled to find the word "theology" so used that: the expression "theistic theologian" is not tautological; and the expression "atheist theologian" is not self-contradictory. But unless this unusual usage of ours is adopted we have to accept the paradox that those who reach opposite conclusions about certain questions must be regarded as having thereby shown themselves to have been engaged in different disciplines: the paradox that whereas St Thomas's presentation of the *quinque viae* is a piece of (Natural or Philosophical) Theology, Hume's *Dialogues concerning Natural Religion* must belong to some other and nameless discipline.' Flew and MacIntyre, *New Essays in Philosophical Theology*, Preface, p. x.

INDEX OF PROPER NAMES